INTERNATIONAL TRADE

Second Edition

INTERNATIONAL TRADE
Theory and
Empirical Evidence

H. ROBERT HELLER
University of Hawaii, Honolulu

Prentice-Hall, Inc., Englewood Cliffs, New Jersey

Library of Congress Cataloging in Publication Data

HELLER, HEINZ ROBERT.
 International Trade.

 Includes bibliographies.
 1. Commerce. I. Title.
HF1411.H38 1973   382   72-3912
ISBN   0-13-473918-3

10   9   8   7   6   5   4

Printed in the United States of America

PRENTICE-HALL INTERNATIONAL, INC., *London*
PRENTICE-HALL OF AUSTRALIA, PTY. LTD., *Sydney*
PRENTICE-HALL OF CANADA, LTD., *Toronto*
PRENTICE-HALL OF INDIA PRIVATE LTD., *New Delhi*
PRENTICE-HALL OF JAPAN, INC., *Tokyo*

To OMA

Contents

List of Symbols Used

Preface

1   Theory and Methodology
of International Trade   1

Methodology of Economics, 1
Reasons for a Special Theory of International Trade, 3
Assumptions of the Theory of International Trade, 5
The Importance of International Trade, 7

2   The Basis of Trade   14

Partial and General Equilibrium, 14
Countries and Individuals, 15
Market Supply, 15
Market Demand, 16
Equilibrium, 17
Excess Supply and Demand and Foreign Trade, 18
A Small Country in World Trade, 19
A Large Country in World Trade, 20
Empirical Evidence, 21

vii

3 The Theory
   of Comparative Costs   29

The Aggregate Production Possibility Curve, 29
The Real Cost Theory, 34
Limits to the International Terms of Trade, 37
Equilibrium Conditions for the International Terms of Trade, 38
The Opportunity Cost Theory, 39
Effects of Country Size, 40
Effects of Increasing Costs, 42
Effects of Decreasing Costs, 44
Empirical Evidence, 46

4 Production
   and International Trade   50

The Effects of Returns to Scale, 51
The Effects of Factor Intensities, 58
The Effects of Factor Endowments, 63
Different Factor Intensities and Endowments:
   The Heckscher-Ohlin Theory, 64
Empirical Evidence, 66

5 Consumption
   and International Trade   72

Community Indifference Curves, 72
Direction of Trade, 79
Determination of International Prices, 80
Demand Reversals, 82
The Offer Curve, 83
Offer Curves and International Price Determination, 85
Empirical Evidence, 86

6 Equilibrium
   in International Trade   89

Consumption, Production, and International Trade, 89
The International Trade Offer Curve, 90
The Terms of Trade, 100
The Constant Cost Case, 108
Multi-Country and Multi-Commodity Cases, 112
Empirical Evidence, 116

7   Effects of International Trade
    on the Factors of Production   119

Definition of a Factor of Production, 119
Factor Price Changes Caused by Trade, 120
Factor Price Equalization, 125
Factor Quantity Changes Caused by Trade, 133
Empirical Evidence, 138

8   Economic Growth
    and International Trade   141

The Small Country and Economic Growth, 141
Factor Quantity Changes, 146
Technological Progress, 153
The Large Country and Economic Growth, 158
Empirical Evidence, 160

9   Tariffs
    and International Trade   163

Arguments for Protection, 163
Effects of a Tariff, 164
The Terms of Trade, 167
The Optimum Tariff, 170
The Effective Protective Tariff Rate, 175
Empirical Evidence, 179

10 Economic Unions
    and International Trade   183

Effects of a Customs Union, 184
Equilibrium Prices and Quantities, 188
General Equilibrium Analysis, 190
Other Gains From Union Formation, 193
Empirical Evidence, 194

11 Welfare Aspects
    of International Trade   197

World Welfare, 197
The Welfare of a Country, 200
The Welfare of an Economic Group, 207
The Utility Possibility Curve, 212

Appendix

The Closed Economy:
A Review of Some Basic Concepts   217

Production, 217
Consumption, 227
Equilibrium, 229
The Terms of Trade, 231

Index   233

List of Symbols Used

C	Consumption
CIC	Community Indifference Curve
D	Domestic
EX	Exports
I	Indifference Curve or Isoquant
IM	Imports
K	Capital
L	Labor
O	Origin
OC	Offer Curve
P	Production
TI	Trade Indifference Curve
TOC	Trade Offer Curve
TOT	Terms of Trade
ϵ	Elasticity

Superscripts

A	Person A
B	Person B
F	France
G	Germany
U	Union
UK	United Kingdom
US	United States
W	World

Subscripts

C	Cloth
i	Any Real Number
T	Tariff
W	Wheat

Preface

My purpose in writing this book is to assemble the minimum framework required for an understanding of international trade problems. *International trade* is defined narrowly as the set of problems that arises from and in connection with the exchange of physical commodities between nations. International monetary and financial problems are not treated in this volume. Several books are available to supplement this volume if the whole field of international economics is to be covered.

The approach is geometric throughout. No use of mathematics is required. More than in most other fields of economics has the graphical approach been utilized in international trade. The book tries to put many of the different concepts, which are scattered throughout the literature, into one concise framework. In a sense the book constitutes a tool kit for the student of international trade without which he might find it difficult to comprehend much of the literature. All unnecessary detail is left aside and attention is concentrated on the systematic development of the analytical framework.

This revision incorporates some of the recent developments in international economics. Literally no page has been left unchanged. Chapter 1 has been expanded to include empirical material on the importance of international trade. Chapter 2 is an entirely new chapter, dealing with the partial equilibrium analysis of international trade. The treatment is novel in that it places emphasis on the role of individual economic units in the world trade network. The next four chapters develop the general equilibrium model of international commodity trade. Chapter 3 presents the traditional comparative cost theory, Chapter 4 investigates the role of production functions and factor endowments, Chapter 5 deals with consumption, and in Chapter 6 the complete general equilibrium model is assembled. The following two chapters concentrate on the factors of production: Chapter 7 is concerned with the effects of trade on the factors of production, and Chapter 8 with the effects of technological progress and factor endowment changes on trade patterns. Chapter 9 deals with the theory of tariffs, with special emphasis on the effective protective tariff rate. Chapter 10 analyzes customs unions. Chapter 11 (formerly Chapter 8) investigates the welfare implications of international trade. World welfare, the welfare of a country, and the welfare of individual economic groups are analyzed. A new section on utility possibility curves has been added.

I am indebted for many helpful suggestions for improvement to Professors Kimura (Kansai University) and Murakami (Kobe University), who translated the book into Japanese, A. S. Trujillo, who translated it into Spanish, and Roland and Ekkehart Stiller (University of Hawaii), who translated it into German. Professor Sweeney (Texas A&M) commented in detail on the entire revision of the manuscript. Also, I am grateful to the numerous users of the first edition who were kind enough to make suggestions for improvement: Professors R. Balbach (California State College, San Fernando), Richard Baltz (Millsaps College), R. S. Elliott (UCLA), Thomas Glenn (Franklin and Marshall College), Wilhelm Hesse (Universität Göttingen), Richard Lipsey (Queen's University, Ontario), J. Moreh (The Queen's University of Belfast), Seiji Naya (University of Hawaii), Maseo Oda (Kansai University), K. Richards (University College of Wales), Pascal Salin (Centre Universitaire Dauphine, Paris), W. J. B. Smits (Free University, Amsterdam), and Yeong-Her Yeh (University of Hawaii). William Allen (Texas A&M), Peter Clark (M.I.T.), Duncan MacRae (Urban Institute, Washington, D.C.), and Birgitta Swedenborg (Industriens Utrednings Institut, Stockholm) contributed greatly to the first edition. Professor J. Black (University of Exeter) and Dipl. Volkswirt Eva Scharrer (Universität Kiel) made numerous suggestions for the reprinting of the second edition.

H.R.H.
Honolulu, Hawaii

INTERNATIONAL TRADE

1

Theory and Methodology of International Trade

In this introductory chapter we will explore some of the problems of methodology that arise in conjunction with the study of causes and effects of international trade. To do this we must first familiarize ourselves with the type of approach or methodology that we will use in attacking the specific problems raised in subsequent chapters. We will also show in this chapter the relationship of international economic problems to those of general economic theory. The final section will be concerned with problems encountered in connection with empirical verification.

METHODOLOGY OF ECONOMICS

Economists are concerned with the problems arising from the allocation of scarce resources within and among different economic units. Among all the different problems, we can distinguish two broad groupings: problems of positive economics and problems of normative economics.

Positive Economics

Positive economics is concerned with what is. It is concerned with the way the economic system functions and the effects of changes in some variables on other magnitudes. Essentially three steps are involved in constructing a useful positive-economic theory: (1) the development of a framework for analysis, (2) the construction of various hypotheses, and (3) the empirical testing of the hypothesis.

1

1. *The Framework for Analysis.*   The analytical framework consists basically of a set of concepts and definitions that help us state precisely and unambiguously what we shall infer, deduce, predict, or observe. The usefulness of the framework adopted can be judged by the efficiency with which it fulfills this objective.

Although the analytic framework has to be specific, it must also provide latitude for expansion and development of the theory if this should become necessary. The better the definitions are adapted to the purpose of the analysis, the easier will be the task of analysis itself.

2. *Construction of Hypotheses.*   The second task is to make analytically useful abstractions from reality. The world as we observe it is much too complex to allow us to draw directly meaningful conclusions about causal relationships. There are many phenomena that have little or no bearing on the issue at hand. The purpose of constructing hypotheses is to achieve order among the multitude of observable phenomena and to eliminate less important factors while focusing attention on important causal links. This is done through a process of abstraction and the formulation of hypotheses about the workings of the economic system.

The set of concepts and hypotheses is often referred to as an economic model. There are two ways in which economic models can be employed usefully: in analysis and in forecasting.

In analysis the model helps us to check the consistency of the various assumptions made. The effects of a change in the definitions and assumptions can be studied in detail, enabling us to isolate a few key variables that are crucial as far as the logical structure of the model is concerned. These key variables may then be studied more intensively. In this way we may increase our knowledge of the functioning of the economic system. To the extent that new insights are revealed by this process, we may reformulate our initial model in the light of the experiences gained in order to make the model more realistic and useful.

The second function of an economic model is to allow us to make predictions as to the probable effects of changes in some economic variable. The national policy maker uses models to predict the effects of contemplated changes in economic policy; the businessman uses economic models to ascertain the likely effects of exogenous changes on his firm as well as to predict the advisability of changing the parameters under his own control. A good economic model with a high predictive accuracy is a valuable tool to the economist studying these policy problems.

3. *Empirical Verification.*   Of course the validity of the predictions that follow from a particular economic model must be subjected to empirical testing. It is possible to construct an infinite number of logically consistent

models that may yield conflicting results. Only the empirical verification of the different economic predictions that the alternative models may yield will allow us to decide which model is the most accurate and useful one. The ultimate goal is to gain more insight into the functioning of the economic system, and empirical testing helps us to separate the useful economic models from the irrelevant ones.

Normative Economics

In contrast to positive economics, which is concerned with what is, normative economics is concerned with what ought to be. Normative economics, by definition, requires value judgments. Normative economics is involved both with the selection of rules to judge welfare changes and with the evaluation of the welfare changes themselves. Once a yardstick with which to assess the economic consequences of different economic policies is found, the task of determining the most desirable or beneficial course of action is made considerably easier. Often we are not in a position to devise a yardstick that is acceptable to everyone concerned. Under these conditions the application of different value systems may yield different results regarding the desirability of certain economic actions. Unfortunately these differences cannot be settled by resorting to empirical testing procedures, since a value system that is logically consistent cannot be found superior or inferior to other logically consistent value systems by empirical methods.

REASONS FOR A SPECIAL THEORY OF INTERNATIONAL TRADE

International trade theory can be regarded as an extension of general economic theory to the special problems encountered in trade between nations. Although the emphasis has traditionally been on trade between countries, the theory can also be applied to problems of trade between other economic units: trade between individuals like Robinson Crusoe and Friday poses theoretical problems similar to those between cities during the Middle Ages or in the time of the Hanseatic League. Today we may be interested in trade between different economic regions within one country; for example, between California and the rest of the United States. Much of international trade theory finds a fruitful application here. Trade theory can be applied to all the problem areas mentioned, but there are still several reasons to continue referring to the theory as international trade theory rather than as general trade theory.

First of all, there are several *economic* reasons for concentrating our attention on nations as the basic economic units. As a general rule a vast difference exists in the degree of mobility of resources between countries as opposed to within countries. Human beings, the factor of production labor, are often restricted in their freedom of movement between countries, although they are free to select their residence within countries. Immigration laws, different licensing requirements for professional people, citizenship requirements for government employees, and other obstacles inhibit the free flow of labor between countries. Similarly financial transactions within countries are usually unrestrained, but international capital flows are often prohibited or severely limited by governmental authorities.

Another important resource, land, is severely restricted as far as its international mobility in concerned. The physical transfer of land between countries is possible only if nations change the size of their territory by war, purchase of territories, or land grants to and from other nations. Even the acquisition of title of ownership by foreigners is severely restricted in many nations that have laws that either exclude or severely limit foreigners from owning real estate.

Also we will find that economic units located within the same country are subject to the same rates of taxation, raise funds in the same capital markets, and use much of the same economic infrastructure, such as communication, transportation, and information facilities. Thus the whole economic environment of individual economic units is much more homogeneous within a country than it is between economic units located in different countries.

Secondly, although the *sociopolitical* environment often differs greatly between nations, it tends to be more uniform within countries. Households and business firms in the same country operate within the same legal framework, are subject to the same social institutions, and are ruled by the same government. Similar habits and business customs prevail within the national boundaries, making it easier for businessmen to deal with other economic units even if they are geographically far removed. All these conditions hold only rarely, and then imperfectly, with reference to trade between different nations. Generally it is much easier and more convenient for a San Diego firm to arrange a business deal with a New York firm than to turn to a geographically much closer firm in Tijuana, Mexico.

There is a third, though much less important, reason for looking at international trade problems apart from other economic problems: for a considerable time there has been a *specialization of economists* in the international trade field. As a result we find that international trade theory has developed its own body of literature, often employing methods that differ from those used in other branches of economics. For instance, international trade theory relies greatly on general equilibrium analysis and does not restrict itself to the problems of partial equilibrium that characterize much of traditional price theory. Much of international trade theory deals with models incorporating several commodities, several factors of production, and several countries simultaneously. The greater complexity of the analysis has led to the development of special techniques for dealing with these problems. One consequence of this specialization within economics is that international trade theory has tended to either antedate or lag behind the developments in general economic theory. International trade specialists, for example, held to the labor theory of value for a much longer time than did economists in most other fields. On the other hand, much of modern welfare economics was first elaborated within the framework of international trade theory.

ASSUMPTIONS OF THE THEORY OF INTERNATIONAL TRADE

International trade theory has to deal with a greater number of variables at any given time than do most other fields of economics. In order to keep the theories manageable and compact, certain simplifying assumptions are usually made in the first stage of the analysis. All these assumptions can be removed, one by one, but only at the cost of increasing the complexity of the models. At this point it may be useful to make explicit the more important assumptions that we will make in the beginning of our analysis. Several of these assumptions will be dropped as we progress to more complicated and comprehensive models of trade, but others will be maintained throughout the book.

The first of the major simplifying assumptions is that all the real variables of the economic system are determined independently of the monetary system. This assumption is often referred to as the *neutrality of money*. Basically, this means that the real and monetary variables of the system are determined independently of each other. The real sector is concerned with questions of *relative prices*, for example, how many packages of cigarettes can be exchanged for one loaf of bread or how many hours of work will earn one pizza. All that concerns us here are rates of exchange between different commodities or factors of production (or their respective services). We deal with a pure barter economy in which monetary magnitudes have no influence on relative prices. The only function that money performs is to set the *absolute* price level. It is easy to see that in this system it is immaterial whether all monetary magnitudes within the economy are doubled, tripled, or halved; relative prices will not be influenced, and nobody will be either better or worse off. At times some countries have changed their monetary unit with precisely this result. France did so in 1960, when one hundred old francs were declared to be the same as one New Franc. All prices were reduced to one-hundredth of their previous level; so were all wages, assets, and liabilities. Nothing really changed except that the decimal place in all financial statements was moved two digits to the left. As a matter of fact, the old franc notes continued to circulate along with the new ones for a long period of time.

A second important assumption is that *all prices are truly flexible,* and that they are determined under conditions of perfect competition. In other words there are no economic, legal, political, or other considerations that might impede the free interplay of the forces of supply and demand in the determination of prices for any items. Thus we postulate the absence of minimum wage laws, maximum rents, fixed prices for certain commodities, and other restraints to price flexibility, as well as the nonexistence of monopolistic imperfections. Also flexible exchange rates are assumed.

On the production side we will assume initially that the total *amount of factors of production is fixed* for any one country. Thus we ignore the effects that changes in factor prices might have on the quantities that are effectively available. Increases in the wage rate, therefore, will not lead to increases in the labor force participation rate or in the number of hours worked. Higher land rents will not lead to irrigation and reclamation of previously unused land. And the total amount of capital resources of the economy is assumed to be fixed. This assumption implies that the supply curves for all factors of production are vertical straight lines; that is, that they are completely inelastic.

Closely associated with the assumption of fixed domestic factor supplies is the assumption of *international immobility of factors*. Although factors are assumed to be perfectly mobile within countries, moving in response to the highest reward offered, we postulate that they are completely immobile between countries. The arguments in favor of this assumption have already been presented and need not be repeated here.

We will assume also that the *technology* available to the producers of the same product within one country is the same. The production functions within each country are therefore identical. No patents or privileged information will restrict the use of any techniques of production to a group of business firms. On the other hand, production functions may or may not be different in various countries.

On the demand side of our analysis *tastes* are assumed to be given. In other words the indifference maps showing the preference patterns of the consumers are given and invariant, so that no changes in taste will occur as a result of the sudden availability of certain internationally traded goods.

In the same vein we assume that *income distribution* patterns are given and known. A shift in income distribution patterns in conjunction with dissimilar taste patterns of the different economic groups affected by the change in income distribution can give rise to many problems relevant to international trade.

As is common in most of the literature on international trade, we will assume throughout that there are no barriers to trade in the form of costs of *transportation, information*, and *communication.* All these costs would impose additional burdens on the traders, which would in most cases lead to a reduction in the volume of international trade. As a matter of fact, any one of these costs may be so great as to cause trade to cease completely.

Finally it should be noted that, owing to our assumptions of flexible prices and neutrality of money, the full utilization of all productive resources, within the economy is always assured. All factors of production available at the current prices and wage rates will be employed in the productive process. Prices and wages will adjust to equate the quantities supplied and demanded in different markets. Excess supplies or shortages of commodities do not occur.

THE IMPORTANCE OF INTERNATIONAL TRADE

International trade plays an increasingly important role in our economic life. The volume of world trade has increased during the last three decades not only in absolute volume and value but also in importance relative to GNP or other indicators of economic performance. World trade doubled approximately every decade since 1938. In that year total world exports amounted to \$24.1 billion. In spite of the disruptive influence of World War II, total exports grew to \$53.7 billion in 1948. In 1958 trade amounted to \$95.4 billion, and a decade later world exports had again more than doubled to \$212.8 billion. By 1970 world exports totaled \$279.0 billion. (See Figure 1–1 and Table 1–1.) Most of this trade, \$208.0 billion, was carried on between

TABLE 1–1

WORLD EXPORTS (FOB)
(IN MILLIONS OF U.S. DOLLARS)

	1948	*1950*	*1955*	*1960*	*1965*	*1970*	*1971*
World total	53,300	55,200	83,220	112,600	164,700	279,000	329,700
Indust. countries	32,610	33,240	54,750	78,770	118,320	208,020	236,190
United States	12,666	10,282	15,558	20,584	27,400	43,227	48,475
United Kingdom	6,657	6,356	8,605	10,611	13,710	19,351	24,000
Industrial Europe	9,700	12,700	23,810	37,690	60,220	109,249	127,180
Japan	258	820	2,011	4,055	8,452	19,333	19,722
Other Asia	4,830	5,720	6,040	6,900	9,330	14,000	21,300
Latin America	5,830	5,950	7,340	7,950	10,410	14,300	16,500
Africa	2,540	2,610	4,000	4,720	7,040	11,800	11,900

Industrial Europe *includes Austria, Belgium, Denmark, France, Germany, Italy, Luxembourg, Netherlands, Norway, Sweden, and Switzerland.* Industrial countries *include in addition Canada, Japan, United Kingdom, and United States.*
Source: IMF, International Financial Statistics, 1971 *and* 1972.

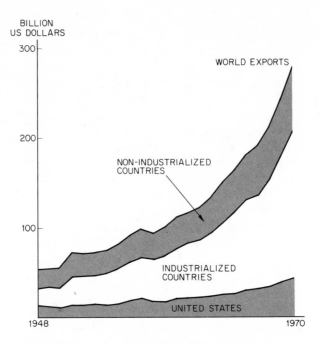

FIGURE 1-1   The Development of World Exports

the industrialized countries of the world, with the United States accounting for 15 percent and the European Common Market countries for 32 percent of the total.

In relative terms the role of international trade differs greatly from country to country. In some relatively small countries, like Belgium, Iceland, Ireland, Jordan, and Panama, imports account for more than one-third of all expenditures. On the other hand in the United States the foreign trade sector amounted to only approximately 5 percent of total GNP in 1970. But these figures may be seriously misleading in an overall assessment of the importance of international trade, as they do not reveal that even in an economy as large as the American, several commodities are not produced domestically at all and the entire country has to rely on imports to obtain these goods, which may be considered vitally important. For instance the United States relies entirely on imports for its supplies of bananas, copra, coffee, carpet wools, silk, tea, and crude rubber. Similarly exports play an important role in many American industries, with exports amounting to a substantial proportion of the total production of some industries. (See Table 1–2.)

Also the distribution of trading partners varies widely from country to country. Table 1–3 gives the export-import matrix for the entire world. The columns show the exports by the country or country group listed at the top to

TABLE 1–2

THE ROLE OF WORLD TRADE IN SELECTED U.S. INDUSTRIES, 1967

Imports as Percentage of New Supply		Exports as Percentage of Output	
Agriculture		*Agriculture*	
Bananas	100	Cotton	41
Copra	100	Grains	26
Coffee	100	Tobacco	37
Carpet wools	100		
Silk	100	*Minerals*	
Tea	100	Molybdenum	38
Crude rubber	100	Coal	19
		Sulfur	32
Minerals			
Iron ore	35	*Manufactures*	
Lead and zinc ore	27	Dried foods	13
Bauxite and aluminum ore	89	Milled rice	58
Manganese ore	96	Pulp mill products	28
Uranium ore	7	Synthetic rubber	17
Sulfur	16	Medicines	36
		Steam engines and turbines	10
Manufactures		Construction machinery	29
Canned seafood	20	Machine tools	12
Sugar	22	Textile machinery	19
Wines and brandy	19	Pumps and compressors	17
Liquor (exc. brandy)	28	Electronic computing equipment	11
Textiles	50	Calculating and accounting machines	28
Chinaware	34	Office machines	23
Pottery products	22	Sewing machines	25
Motorcycles	36	Aircraft	13
Clocks and watches	17	Locomotives	18

Source: Bureau of the Census, *Statistical Abstract of the United States*, 1970.

the countries listed on the left margin. Note that whenever country groups are listed, the terms along the diagonal refer to the trade between the countries of that group. All data refer to exports and import figures (f.o.b.) for the year 1970 and are expressed in millions of U.S. dollars.

To help us visualize the data presented in the world trade matrix the trade pattern of one country, the United States, is presented in Figure 1–2.

In this book we will be mainly concerned with four questions associated with international trade (1) What determines the *direction of trade*? Here we are interested in why a country tends to export one commodity rather than another. We analyze the factors determining the structure of trade. (2) Intimately connected with the direction of trade is the question of the physical

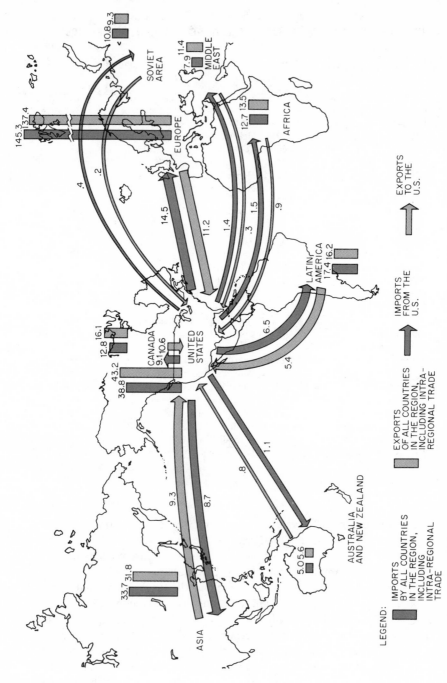

FIGURE 1–2   The United States and World Trade, 1970 (Source: Table 1–3. All data are in billions of U.S. dollars.)

10

TABLE 1–3

THE WORLD TRADE MATRIX, 1970 (MILLIONS OF U.S. DOLLARS, FOB)

Exports from ⟍ To	United States	Canada	Europe	Middle East	Africa	Latin America	Australia, New Zealand	Asia	Soviet Area	Imports of Region Listed on Left
United States	—	10,575	11,161	322	948	5,405	821	9,381	226	38,839
Canada	9,084	—	1,764	87	135	655	176	815	92	12,808
Europe	14,479	3,045	93,086	6,047	9,806	5,543	1,653	5,736	5,990	145,385
Middle East	1,437	95	3,926	665	106	68	103	990	596	7,986
Africa	1,477	174	8,144	341	796	94	150	1,198	349	12,723
Latin America	6,534	630	5,338	288	218	2,947	72	1,231	120	17,378
Australia, New Zealand	1,120	235	1,915	211	60	21	363	1,028	65	5,018
Asia	8,675	1,092	5,340	2,785	1,155	1,157	1,982	9,643	1,870	33,699
Soviet Area	354	330	6,782	646	297	323	275	1,749	?	10,756
Exports of Region Listed on Top	43,160	16,176	137,456	11,392	13,521	16,213	5,595	31,771	9,308	284,592

The entries along the diagonal show intraregional trade where applicable. Soviet intraregional trade is excluded. Also excluded are certain small islands that could not be easily classified.

Source: Derived from IMF and IBRD, Direction of Trade, Annual 1966–70, Washington, D.C.

volume of international trade and the *prices* at which the commodities are traded. Clearly, countries will not only be interested in knowing whether they should be exporting bananas or radios, but they will also want to know in what quantity these commodities can be exported and what prices their products will command in the world markets. (3) The effects of *trade restrictions* are also of interest. The imposition of tariffs and other restrictive devices will change many of the crucial variables, as will the formation of customs unions or common markets. (4) Finally we will be concerned with the effect of free trade and restricted trade on the *economic welfare* of the countries under consideration. This is doubtlessly significant, since one of the most important economic goals is to make all persons as well off as they can possibly be without making anyone else worse off. The first three problem areas mentioned are problems of positive economics, but the fourth problem belongs in the sphere of normative economics.

In each chapter we will also present some pertinent empirical evidence to the theoretical problems discussed. It should be pointed out, however, that much of the empirical data presented are subject to severe criticism. Some of the problems associated with the empirical data are discussed at the end of Chapter 2. Especially when we wish to make inferences with respect to the appropriate policy measures that a country should adopt in a particular situation, it is necessary to use empirical estimates that are up to date and to take the particular policy problems that the country faces at that time into consideration. Generalizations from sketchy empirical data are hazardous at best and very likely seriously misleading.

SUGGESTED FURTHER READINGS

BAER, DON V. T., and DANIEL ORR, "Logic and Expediency in Economic Theorizing," *Journal of Political Economics* (April 1967), pp. 188–96.

BAUMOL, WILLIAM J., *Business Behavior, Value and Growth*, 2nd ed., Chap. I. New York: Harcourt, Brace, & World, Inc., 1967.

CAVES, RICHARD, *Trade and Economic Structure*, Chap. I. Cambridge: Harvard University Press, 1960.

FRIEDMAN, MILTON, "The Methodology of Positive Economics," in *Essays in Positive Economics*. Chicago: University of Chicago Press, 1953.

HABERLER, GOTTFRIED, *The Theory of International Trade*, Introduction, Chap. IX. London: William Hodge & Company, Limited, 1936.

NAGEL, ERNEST, "Assumptions in Economic Theory," *American Economic Review* (May 1963), pp 211–19.

VANEK, JAROSLAV, *International Trade: Theory and Economic Policy*, Chaps. I, XI. Homewood, Ill.: Richard D. Irwin, Inc., 1962.

VINER, JACOB, "A Note on the Scope and Method of the Theory of International Trade," in *Studies in the Theory of International Trade*, pp. 594–601. New York: Harper and Brothers Publishers.

2

The Basis of Trade

PARTIAL AND GENERAL EQUILIBRIUM

Economists use two approaches in analyzing various problems: the partial equilibrium approach and the general equilibrium approach. The fundamental difference between the two approaches lies in the assumptions that are made about the interrelationship between the variables studied and the rest of the economy. If we analyze just a few variables in isolation and assume that all other variables remain constant or have no significant effect on the problem at hand, we are using a partial equilibrium approach. This approach may be compared to the laboratory experiments of the natural scientist, where the experimenter attempts to investigate the relationship between just a few variables, while holding all others constant. In economics, of course, it is generally not possible to duplicate the laboratory approach of the natural scientist, but this should not deter us from using the same partial equilibrium approach in situations where feedback effects are either absent or of such magnitude that they can be neglected without invalidating the results. If these assumptions are not fulfilled, a general equilibrium approach is called for. In general equilibrium all variables are analyzed and their interactions are studied. As a consequence the general equilibrium models tend to be more complex than the partial equilibrium models. In this chapter we will look at international trade from a partial equilibrium viewpoint, leaving the general equilibrium approach for the following chapter and, indeed, much of the entire book.

COUNTRIES AND INDIVIDUALS

In the elementary theory of international trade we typically view countries as economic units. We say, for instance, that the United States exported $42.6 billion of commodities to other countries in 1970 while importing $39.9 billion. But it really was not the United States that did the exporting and importing, but individual firms and households located in the United States that bought and sold goods from foreign economic units. To establish the microeconomic foundations of international trade theory, we will start our analysis by showing how we can aggregate the individual economic decisions taken by households and firms within a country. The aggregate manifestations of the individual decisions will then be analyzed as if they were the collective decision arrived at by all the residents of the country. This latter form of presenting the decisions taken by individuals will save much time and energy by allowing us to avoid needless repetition.

MARKET SUPPLY

We will assume that all industries are perfectly competitive. In order to qualify as a perfectly competitive industry four basic conditions must be fulfilled: (1) there must be many small firms in the industry, (2) entry into and exit from the industry must be easy, (3) the product sold by the various firms must be homogeneous, and (4) the individual firms engage in independent decision making. Under these conditions the price is determined in the market place and all individual firms can sell all they want to sell at the going market price. The firms are price takers and output adjusters.

In Figure 2–1a we show a supply curve for one firm (let us say a wheat producing farm), which is based on the firm's marginal cost curve. The supply curve shows the quantities of wheat that this individual farm is willing to supply at various market prices. If we assume that the number of firms in the industry remains fixed for the time being—a short run situation— we can now aggregate the individual supply curves to obtain the aggregate supply curve for the wheat industry in the whole country. For instance, if the U.S. wheat industry consists of one hundred thousand identical farms, then the market supply curve for wheat in the United States will be as shown in Figure 2–1b.

Of course the market supply curve of Figure 2–1b is only the short run supply curve for wheat. If we were to select a sufficiently long period of analysis so that new firms can enter and/or leave the industry, we have to adjust the supply curve to take account of the new number of firms in the industry. In general the long run supply curve, which allows for the number of firms

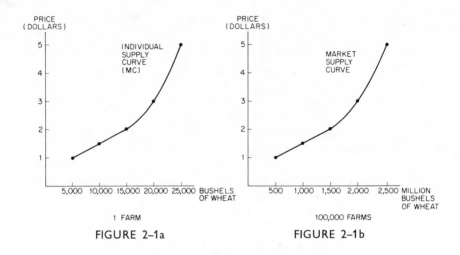

FIGURE 2–1a   FIGURE 2–1b

to vary, is more elastic than the short run supply curve, which assumes that the number of firms is constant. The exact shape of the long run supply curve depends on a number of factors, including the length of the time horizon under consideration, the mobility of resources used in the production process of that industry, the reaction of input prices to changes in the demand for these inputs, and the like. In our subsequent analysis we will assume that we are dealing with a short run situation, and that the market supply curve can be obtained simply by aggregating the individual supply curves of all the firms in the industry.

MARKET DEMAND

In a similar way we are able to derive the market demand curve for wheat for all persons in the United States. Let us assume that the country is composed of 100 million identical consumers each of whom has a demand curve for wheat as shown in Figure 2–2a. This demand curve is based on the consumer's indifference map and shows the quantity of wheat that he is willing to purchase at various market prices. The demand curve is assumed to slope downward to the right, showing that the consumer is willing to purchase a larger quantity in response to a lower market price.

Again we are able to sum all the quantities demanded by the individual consumers at each and every price and derive the market demand curve for all 100 million residents of the country. Such a market demand curve is shown in Figure 2–2b.

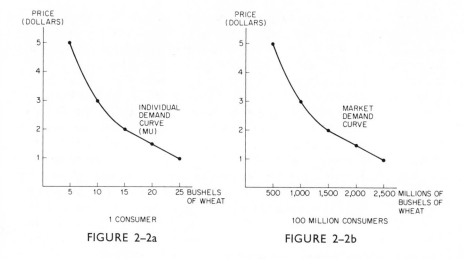

FIGURE 2–2a   FIGURE 2–2b

EQUILIBRIUM

As is well known, the intersection of the supply and demand curves in a competitive market determines the market price and the quantity that will be traded. Figure 2–3a shows the market supply and demand curves previously developed. The market supply and demand curves intersect at a price of two dollars. Only at this price is the quantity of wheat that farmers are willing to sell equal to the quantity that consumers wish to purchase. At prices above

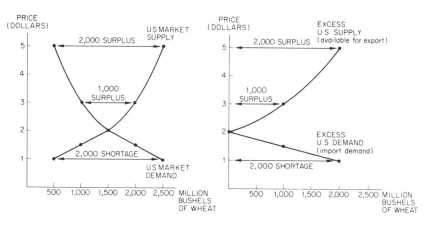

FIGURE 2–3a   FIGURE 2–3b

two dollars, the quantity supplied exceeds the quantity demanded; there exists a surplus or an excess supply. Conversely, at prices below two dollars the quantity demanded exceeds the quantity supplied; there is a shortage or an excess demand for the product. Only at a price of two dollars is the market cleared. If a surplus develops there is a tendency for the price to fall, just as there is a tendency for the price to rise in the face of a shortage. If there is no surplus or shortage the price will remain unchanged; the price has reached its equilibrium level—in our example two dollars. If the residents of the United States, the country of our hypothetical example, do not trade with foreign economic units, the two dollar price will be the price that prevails in the U.S. wheat market. In a new figure we may show the surpluses and shortages that would exist at various prices in the U.S. market. These are the excess supply and excess demand curves of Figure 2–3b. In Figure 2–3b we simply plot the horizontal difference between the market supply and demand curves of Figure 2–3a. If the quantity supplied exceeds the quantity demanded, we find that there is an excess supply; if the quantity demanded exceeds the quantity supplied, an excess demand situation prevails.

EXCESS SUPPLY AND DEMAND
AND FOREIGN TRADE

If we introduce the possibility of foreign trade into our hypothetical example, the excess supply curve shows the quantities that would be available for export at the various prices, and the excess demand curve depicts the amount that domestic economic units would want to import at the various prices. At the domestic market equilibrium price of two dollars neither exports nor imports are likely to result, because the country's domestic producers offer the same quantity for sale as is demanded by domestic consumers. Hence there exists no incentive for either group to engage in international trade.

The two dollar domestic equilibrium price also represents the change-over for the U.S. from a wheat-exporting nation to a wheat-importing nation. Only at prices above two dollars will the United States be a net exporter of wheat, while at prices below two dollars the United States will become a net importer of wheat.

Next we will have to determine the direction and volume of wheat trade in which American economic units wish to engage. To answer this question we must say something about the relative size of the country in world trade: we may assume that the United States is a relatively small participant in the world wheat market or we may assume that the United States plays a substantial role in the world market for wheat.

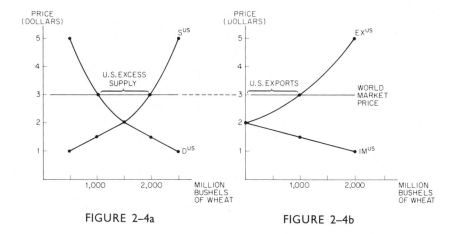

FIGURE 2–4a   FIGURE 2–4b

A SMALL COUNTRY IN WORLD TRADE

Let us start by analyzing the first case: the United States as a relatively small trader in wheat. Let us note that the term *relatively small trader* refers not to the absolute volume of trade in general, but only to trade in wheat. And then we say nothing about the absolute volume of trade, but merely something about the U.S. share of the world wheat market. By assuming that the United States is a relatively small country in the world wheat market we essentially say that the world market price is given as far as U.S. producers and consumers are concerned. The actions of all U.S. producers or consumers have no influence on the world wheat price. All Americans will be price takers in the wheat market.

Under this small-country assumption of a given world market price for wheat at which Americans are free to trade, we can easily determine the direction and volume of international trade. If, for instance, the world market price for wheat is three dollars, as shown in Figure 2–4, the United States will be a net exporter of wheat. American producers are willing to sell 2,000 million bushels of wheat at that price, but American consumers are willing to purchase only 1,000 million bushels—resulting in a domestic excess supply of 1,000 million bushels, which may be exported at the world market price.

Because producers can sell their crop to foreigners, the price of wheat in the United States will also adjust to the world market price of three dollars. Of course, all this rests on the so-far-unwritten assumption that there are no costs of transportation, information, or transaction that have to be met and that both buyers and sellers are able to transact at the stated market price.

A LARGE COUNTRY IN WORLD TRADE

Let us turn to the second assumption, namely that the United States plays a substantial role in the world wheat market. If this condition is fulfilled, the actions of American producers and consumers of wheat will have an influence on the world market price of wheat, although no unit takes account of this in its decisions. For simplicity let us assume that the rest of the world consists of one country only: the United Kingdom.

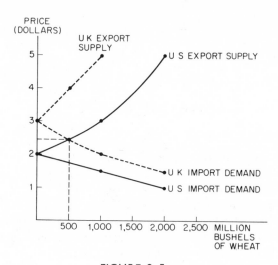

FIGURE 2–5

We are able to derive excess supply and demand curves for wheat in the United Kingdom in a fashion similar to that for the United States. In Figure 2–5 we reproduce the U.S. export supply and import demand curves for wheat from Figure 2–4b. In addition we show the hypothetical export supply and import demand curves for the United Kingdom. We note that at prices above three dollars the United Kingdom will be a net exporter of wheat, while at prices below three dollars it will be a net importer of the commodity. Immediately we are able to delineate the feasible price range within which trade between the two countries is possible. At prices above three dollars both the United States and the United Kingdom want to export wheat. Clearly, if only those two countries exist, there will be nobody to sell the wheat to. There will be an excess supply of wheat on the world market, and prices will fall. The reverse is true in the price range below two dollars. Now both countries wish to be net importers of wheat, and there are no suppliers who are willing to satisfy the existing excess demand.

Only between the prices that would prevail in each of the two countries in autarky, that is $2.00 for the United States and $3.00 for the United Kingdom, trade between the two countries is possible. The exact price and volume of trade taking place is determined by the shape of the export supply and import demand curves of the two countries. In our example, the U.S. export supply curve intersects the U.K. import demand curve at a price of $2.50 per bushel of wheat, resulting in a trade volume of 500 million bushels between the two countries. Let us note that this represents just the international trade taking place in the wheat market. In addition there are the trades between domestic producers and consumers of wheat that take place in the domestic sector of both economies. All these trades will take place at the new world market price of wheat of $2.50. At that price the total world wheat market is cleared, and no excess supplies or demands exist for the world as a whole.

Just as we looked at the wheat market in our hypothetical example, we may extend our analysis to cover all markets, thereby establishing prices and trade volumes for all commodities. But let us be forewarned that this approach is likely to be somewhat misleading because the basic assumption made in the partial equilibrium approach is not fulfilled: other things do not remain constant. As the price in the wheat market changes, the market for substitute and complementary commodities will be affected. Demand curves for these commodities will shift. Also wheat may be an input into various production processes and as the wheat price changes, production costs of those commodities change, causing supply curves to shift. Partial equilibrium analysis does not take account of these feedback effects, and therefore gives—as the name implies—only a partial picture.

EMPIRICAL EVIDENCE

Problems of Estimation

Clearly an important mission of economists is to provide empirical estimates for the supply and demand functions discussed so far. There are a few problems of empirical estimation that should be called to our attention because many of the empirical estimates available may be criticized on these grounds. Because the problems of estimation are many and severe, not too much confidence should be placed into most of the estimates. This is not a book on econometrics, and only some of the most rudimentary problems of empirical estimation can be discussed here. The reader is referred to the bibliography at the end of this chapter for sources that discuss the problems more thoroughly.

1. *Length of Time Period.* As is well known, the estimates of supply and demand elasticities depend crucially on the time horizon under consideration.

In the very short run when no additional quantities can be produced, or when consumers or users of inputs have not time to adjust their consumption and/or production patterns, supply and demand curves are highly inelastic. On the other hand in the very long run when industries may expand their production by the addition of new firms and consumers, and/or buyers of inputs can adjust fully to the price changes, both supply and demand curves are likely to be more elastic. Ceteris paribus, the longer the time horizon under consideration, the greater the elasticity of the respective supply and demand curves.

2. *Simultaneous Shifts of Supply and Demand Curves.* Let us assume that we are trying to use time-series data to estimate import demand or export supply functions. In free markets observed price and quantity pairs always refer to the intersection of a supply and a demand curve that exists at that moment in time. If the supply and demand functions stay constant over time, no time-series data are generated that allow us to estimate supply or demand curves. Instead we have only one price/quantity pair; that is, one point and not a curve. Therefore a precondition for time-series estimation is that some of the curves must have shifted over time. If we are trying to estimate a demand curve, our assumption must be that the demand curve remained constant over time, while the supply curve shifted about—thereby generating the various observed price/quantity pairs. The ideal case is illustrated in Figure 2–6a, which shows a stationary demand curve and a series of supply curves—S_1, S_2, S_3, S_4—that prevailed during four successive time periods. Under these circumstances we can properly identify the true demand curve from the data at hand.

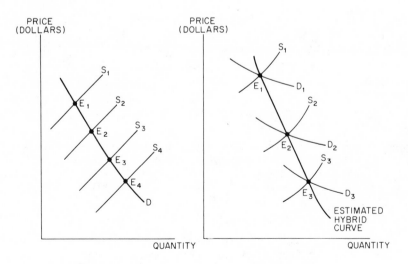

FIGURE 2–6a   FIGURE 2–6b

However, in many instances both the supply and demand curve will shift about. Figure 2–6b illustrates this case. If the demand curve shifts from D_1 to D_2 to D_3 as the supply curve moves from S_1 to S_2 to S_3, the actually observed price/quantity pairs E_1, E_2, and E_3 are not points that are located on the same demand curve. If we were to try to estimate a demand curve from these observations, we would in fact estimate neither a pure demand nor a pure supply curve, but a cross between the two. Depending on the relative magnitude of the shifts of the two curves, the resulting hybrid may have a positive or negative slope.

3. *Errors of Measurement.* When using the standard regression techniques to estimate supply or demand curves, we typically assume that all errors of measurement and observation occur in either the price or the quantity variable. In fact, both variables are likely to contain errors. If this is true, the standard assumption is violated, and the estimated demand or supply curves will be biased.

4. *Aggregate Elasticities.* Many of the empirical estimates refer to broad commodity groups rather than narrowly defined commodity groups. If commodities of different elasticity are included in the grouping, the aggregate elasticity measure tends to have a bias towards zero, because the greatest price fluctuations are likely to be observed in the commodities characterized by an inelastic response. Commodities with inelastic supply and demand curves are likely to be given too high a weight in the calculation of the aggregate price indices upon which the elasticity calculations are based.

5. *Time Path of Adjustment.* Adjustment to price changes is not instantaneous. It may take several months or even years before all economic units have fully adjusted to the price change. In the meantime, however, we may record several price/quantity pairs that do not lie on the true demand curve. For instance let us assume that in Figure 2–7 the price drops from P_A to P_B. If we observe the interim price/quantity pairs 1 through 6, the estimated demand curve will be more elastic than the true demand curve. Different time paths of adjustment will produce different biases in our estimates.

There are several other highly technical problems associated with empirical estimates of supply and demand elasticities, none of which can be discussed here. The interested reader is referred to the bibliography at the end of the chapter.

The Estimates

We will not attempt to give a comprehensive survey of all the empirical estimates that have been made. Instead we will limit ourselves to data from

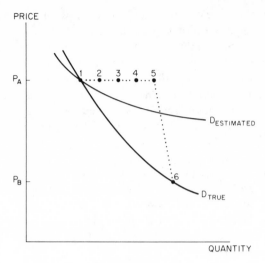

FIGURE 2–7

a study by Houthakker and Magee,[1] whose results are generally in agreement with previous studies by other authors. However, the Houthakker and Magee study yields comparable data for a wide variety of countries and commodity classes and represents one of the most recent contributions to a growing literature.

Houthakker and Magee provide us with three different sets of income and price elasticities for both imports and exports: (1) total imports and exports by country, (2) United States imports and exports to and from various countries, and (3) United States imports and exports by commodity group. The estimates for the first two groups are based on annual data from 1951 to 1966, and the third category of estimates is based on quarterly observations for the 1947 to 1966 period. The calculated elasticities are presented in Tables 2–1, 2–2, and 2–3.

A few observations regarding these estimates are in order. As countries grow the income elasticities show us the effects of this growth (assuming constant relative prices) on exports and imports and therewith on the trade balance. Those countries for which the income elasticity of the demand for imports greatly exceeds the income elasticity of the demand for exports will find that the trade account is likely to show deficits if no other adjustments are made and growth rates at home and abroad are approximately equal. Two countries for which this is true during the time period studied (1947–66)

[1] Hendrik S. Houthakker and Stephen P. Magee, "Income and Price Elasticities in World Trade," *Review of Economics and Statistics*, May 1969.

TABLE 2–1

INCOME AND PRICE ELASTICITIES FOR TOTAL EXPORTS AND IMPORTS OF COUNTRIES (ANNUAL DATA, 1951–66)

Imports			Exports	
Income Elasticity	Price Elasticity	Country	Income Elasticity	Price Elasticity
1.68	−1.03	United States	.99	−1.51
1.20	−1.46	Canada	1.41	− .59
1.45	− .21*	United Kingdom	1.00	−1.24
1.23	− .72	Japan	3.55	− .80
1.85	− .24*	Germany	2.08	−1.25
2.19	− .13*	Italy	2.68	−1.12
1.89	.23*	Netherlands	1.88	− .82*
1.66	.17*	France	1.53	−2.27
1.94	−1.02	Belgium-Luxembourg	1.87	.42*
.91	− .52*	South Africa	.88	−2.41
1.42	− .79*	Sweden	1.75	.67*
.90	.83*	Australia	1.16	− .17*
2.05	− .84*	Switzerland	1.47	− .58
1.31	−1.66	Denmark	1.69	− .56*
1.40	− .78	Norway	1.59	.20*

*These coefficients not significant at the 95 percent level. Data corrected for autocorrelation have been used where provided.
Source: Hendrik S. Houthakker and Stephen P. Magee, "Income and Price Elasticities in World Trade," Review of Economics and Statistics, May 1969, pp. 111–25.

are the United States and the United Kingdom with import and export income elasticities of 1.68 and .99 for the U.S. and 1.45 and 1.00 for the U.K. We might therefore expect that these two countries face a deteriorating trade balance if they grow at the same rate as the rest of the world and have the same rates of inflation.

Conversely, countries for which the income elasticity of the demand for exports exceeds the one of the demand for imports are likely to experience trade surpluses—assuming again equal growth and inflation rates. The most prominent case here is Japan, which has an export elasticity of 3.55 and an import elasticity of 1.23. This means that Japan is likely to run a trade surplus or is able to grow or inflate at a rate almost three times as high as the rest of the world without encountering balance of payments problems.

Similar observations may be made regarding United States trade with individual *countries* as shown in Table 2–2. Again the discrepancies between the income elasticities of the U.S. demand for imports from these countries

TABLE 2–2

INCOME AND PRICE ELASTICITIES FOR TOTAL UNITED STATES
TRADE WITH SELECTED COUNTRIES
(ANNUAL DATA, 1951–66)

U.S. Imports			U.S. Exports	
Income Elasticity	Price Elasticity	Country	Income Elasticity	Price Elasticity
1.94	.49*	Canada	1.13	−1.45*
2.39	−4.25	United Kingdom	2.58	−1.69
3.52	−4.96	Japan	2.10	− .41*
2.84	−8.48	Germany	1.21	−2.39
2.05	−3.82	Italy	2.40	−2.04
.75	−2.47	Netherlands	1.92	− .35*
1.87	−4.58	France	2.33	−3.14
1.38	−2.08	Belgium-Luxembourg	2.24	−2.38
1.82	−3.10*	South Africa	1.05	−2.68*
2.25	−2.49	Sweden	1.52	.73*
2.93	−4.69	Australia	2.68	−8.10
1.73	− .04*	Switzerland	1.59	−2.01
2.28	−6.05	Denmark	2.12	− .47*
1.48	−1.82	Norway	1.63	−2.26

* These coefficients not significant at the 95 percent level. Data corrected for autocorrelation have been used where provided.

Source: Hendrik S. Houthakker and Stephen P. Magee, "Income and Price Elasticities in World Trade," Review of Economics and Statistics, May 1969, pp. 111–25.

and their demand for U.S. exports points at likely future trade deficits and surpluses. According to our data the U.S. is particularly likely to run into deficits vis-à-vis Japan and Germany.

Looking at the individual *commodity* groupings of Table 2–3, we find that the highest income elasticity is found to be 2.63 for the U.S. demand for finished manufactures. We might consequently expect a strong increase in imports in that category in future years.

Turning our attention to *price* elasticities we again are able to isolate certain sensitive areas. Many of the price elasticities calculated were not significant at the 95 percent level and are presented with asterisks in the tables. The higher the elasticity, the greater the expected effects on quantity exported or imported in response to price changes due to inflation, exchange rate changes, and the like. A unitary price elasticity indicates that the value of exports or imports will not change due to price changes, because quantity changes will compensate exactly for any price changes that may occur. The export price elasticities of several countries, notably the United States,

TABLE 2–3

INCOME AND PRICE ELASTICITIES FOR SELECTED UNITED STATES
IMPORTS AND EXPORTS
(QUARTERLY DATA, 1947–66)

U.S. Imports			U.S. Exports	
Income Elasticity	Price Elasticity	Commodity Group	Income Elasticity	Price Elasticity
.61	−.18	Crude materials		− .31*
.30	−.21	Crude foodstuffs	.97	
1.28	−1.40	Manufactured foods	.86	−1.91
1.11	−1.83	Semimanufactures	.90	
2.63	−4.05	Finished manufactures	1.17	−1.22

* This coefficient not significant at the 95 percent level. Data corrected for autocorrelation have been used where provided.

Source: Hendrik S. Houthakker and Stephen P. Magee, "Income and Price Elasticities in World Trade," Review of Economics and Statistics, May 1969, pp. 111–25.

France, and South Africa are relatively high, indicating that price increases in the countries are likely to lead to a sharp deterioration of exports. Japan is characterized by a relatively low price elasticity for both her exports and imports.

It is interesting to note that the price elasticity for U.S. exports and imports to individual countries is markedly higher than the global price elasticity. This may be due to the possibility of substitution between various countries of origin, therefore making trade between individual countries more price sensitive.

In the commodity group table let us point out the high price elasticity of the U.S. demand for imports. It shows a great willingness of American consumers of finished manufactured products to substitute foreign for domestic commodities in response to relative price changes. However, in view of the presence of tariffs, quotas, and other distorting barriers to trade all these inferences should be taken with a great degree of caution.

SUGGESTED FURTHER READINGS

CHENG, HANG SHENG, "Statistical Estimates of Elasticities and Propensities in International Trade," *IMF Staff Papers* (April 1959).

HOUTHAKKER, HENDRIK S., and STEPHEN P. MAGEE, "Income and Price Elasticities in World Trade," *Review of Economics and Statistics* (May 1969).

LEAMER, EDWARD E., and ROBERT M. STERN, *Quantitative International Economics*, Chap. II. Boston: Allyn and Bacon, Inc., 1970.

ORCUTT, GUY H., "Measurement of Price Elasticities in International Trade," *Review of Economics and Statistics* (May 1950). Reprinted in AEA *Readings in International Economics*, eds. Richard Caves and Harry G. Johnson. Homewood, Ill.: Richard D. Irwin, Inc., 1968.

RHOMBERG, RUDOLF R., and LORETTE BOISSONNEAULT, "Effects of Income and Price Changes on the U.S. Balance of Payments," *IMF Staff Papers* (March 1964).

3

The Theory
of Comparative Costs

International trade theory as a special field of economic inquiry was first systematically developed by a group of economists now referred to as the "classical" economists. Although no one of these economists is likely to have held all the views later attributed to this school, Adam Smith, David Ricardo, John Stuart Mill, and Frank Taussig can nevertheless be considered as exponents of the classical doctrine. The international trade theory that they developed not only constitutes the beginning of international trade theory as such but also serves as a simple starting point for our inquiry into the causes and effects of international trade. Only after we have mastered their simple model will it be possible to tackle the more complex and, it is hoped, more realistic models.

The classical economists focused their attention primarily on the *gains from trade* in order to show that free international trade would benefit the trading countries. Implicit in their writings is also a theory of the *structure of trade*. Here the determinants of the direction of trade will occupy our attention first.

THE AGGREGATE PRODUCTION
POSSIBILITY CURVE

We can observe specialization in production, or division of labor, on different levels of the economic system: individual persons specialize in different occupations, firms specialize in certain products. The same is true for economic regions and for countries. The specialized economic units may then want to exchange or trade some of their products.

In most of the remainder of the book we will treat countries as economic units. However, it is appropriate to first consider the problem of aggregating individual production possibility curves into aggregate production possibility curves for entire countries.

The production possibility curve shows the maximum combinations of any two commodities or groups of commodities that may be produced with our given resources and technological knowledge. The Appendix offers a convenient review of the basic properties of production possibility curves.

production poss. curve

Now we are faced with the problem of having to aggregate the individual production possibility curves. The production possibility curve of a country is nothing but the sum of the production possibility curves of all the individual production units located within the country. To say that a country produces on a certain point of its production possibility curve really means that all the individual economic units within the country produce commodities that sum up to the country totals.

The Increasing Cost Case

In Figures 3–1 and 3–2 we show hypothetical production possibility curves for two individual economic production units: Mr. Alpha and Mr. Beta. Both Alpha and Beta produce cloth and wheat with their given amount of resources and technical knowledge. The production possibility curves for the two persons are concave as viewed from the origin, indicating that increasing costs of production prevail.

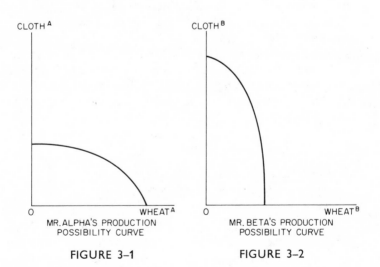

MR. ALPHA'S PRODUCTION
POSSIBILITY CURVE

MR. BETA'S PRODUCTION
POSSIBILITY CURVE

FIGURE 3–1

FIGURE 3–2

Our task is to determine the maximum cloth/wheat combinations that Alpha and Beta together are able to produce. That is, we wish to derive the aggregate production possibility curve for the two production units. In Figure 3–3 we show the production possibility curve for Mr. Alpha in its customary position. However, Mr. Beta's production possibility curve is shown upside down and sides reversed. Wheat production by Beta is measured from right to left and cloth production in the downward direction. The production possibility curves of Alpha and Beta are placed tangent to each other, and production is assumed to take place at point P on the

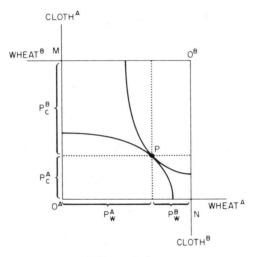

FIGURE 3–3

respective production possibility curves. Hence, Mr. Alpha will produce P_C^A of cloth and P_W^A of wheat, and Mr. Beta's production amounts to P_C^B of cloth and P_W^B of wheat. Total cloth production is equal to $O^A M$ ($= NO^B$), and total wheat production equals $O^A N$ ($= MO^B$). Hence, aggregate production of both commodities as measured from the origin O^A is given by point O^B, the origin of Mr. Beta's production possibility curve. Notice that for the quantity of wheat $O^A N$ this procedure maximizes the quantity of cloth produced.

We may repeat the procedure outlined above and derive the locus of all cloth/wheat combinations that are attainable by Alpha and Beta together. This aggregate production possibility curve is derived in Figure 3–4, where we slide Mr. Beta's production possibility curve along Mr. Alpha's production possibility curve in such a way that the two curves are always tangent to each other (points A, B, C, and D) while holding the coordinates parallel to each other. Beta's origin will trace out the new aggregate production possibility curve A'B'C'D'. This process may be repeated for any number of production units and the aggregate production possibility curve for a whole nation can be derived.

Let us note briefly that at point A in Figure 3–4 both production units are completely specialized in the production of cloth, with total cloth production amounting to OA'. Conversely, at point D we have complete

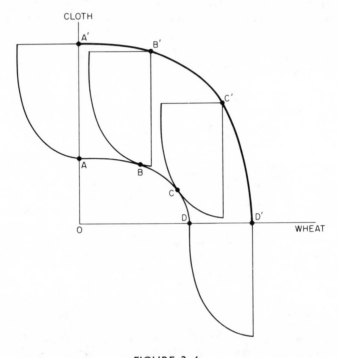

FIGURE 3–4

specialization of both Alpha and Beta in wheat production, with total wheat output at OD'. At in between points like B and C neither production unit is completely specialized; both produce some of each commodity.

The Constant Cost Case

Turning to the constant cost case we show the linear production possibility curves for Mr. Alpha and Mr. Beta in Figures 3–5 and 3–6. Following the same procedure as in the increasing cost case we slide Mr. Beta's production possibility curve along the one for Mr. Alpha as illustrated in Figure 3–7. But note that instead of tangencies we now obtain corner

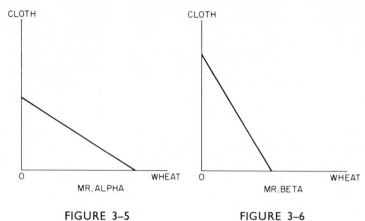

FIGURE 3–5   FIGURE 3–6

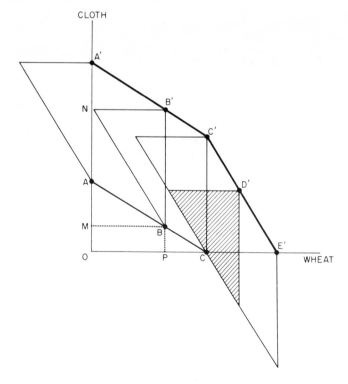

FIGURE 3–7

solutions for every possible position. At A both Alpha and Beta are completely specialized in cloth, producing a total of OA'. At B Mr. Beta is completely specialized in cloth, producing BB' of it. Mr. Alpha, however, continues to produce both commodities: OM of cloth and OP of wheat. Aggregate production amounts to ON of cloth and OP of wheat and is indicated by point B'. The aggregate production possibility curve is shown by the line A'B'C'D'E' and consists of two linear segments: A'C' and C'E'.

Again we are able to continue the aggregation process for many individuals. If all individuals experience constant yet different costs, the resulting aggregate production possibility curve many eventually resemble the increasing cost production possibility curve, because the linear segments will become relatively smaller and smaller. Only if all the individual production units have production possibility curves of equal slopes—indicating identical cost conditions—will the aggregate production possibility curve be a straight line showing constant cost conditions for the entire country. In this limiting case we cannot say anything about the pattern of specialization of the individual economic units. But in all other cases at most one of the producers will not be completely specialized in the production of one of the two commodities.

THE REAL COST THEORY

Ricardo is generally credited with having been the first economist to recognize the importance of differences in *relative* or, as he called it, *comparative costs* as the basis for international trade. His model of international trade contains several simplifying assumptions. In addition to the assumptions already mentioned in Chapter 1, Ricardo assumes the validity of the *labor theory of value*, which holds that there is one productive factor of importance as far as the value of a commodity is concerned: labor. Commodities that require different amounts of labor for their production will have different values, where the value of the commodity is directly proportional to the amount of labor required for its production. The output per unit of labor input is assumed to be constant over all relevant ranges of the production function.

Other factors of production, such as land and capital equipment, are assumed to be either (1) of no significance, (2) so evenly spread over all labor inputs that they always work in a fixed proportion with labor, or (3) merely representing stored-up labor. This latter assumption is particularly relevant to capital goods, because labor has originally been used in the production of these goods, and thus determines their value.

More sophisticated versions of the labor theory of value recognize the idea of different levels of irksomeness or disutility associated with the performance of different types of labor. In this case all labor units must first

TABLE 3–1

	Possible Physical Output of Cloth _or_ Wheat	
	Cloth	Wheat
United Kingdom	100	50
United States	200	150

be transformed into standard units—simple unskilled labor, for example— and then the value of the commodities produced will again conform to the amount of standardized labor units embodied in them.

It may be helpful at this juncture to introduce a simple numerical example of Ricardo's theory of comparative costs. Let us assume that there are two countries in this world, the United Kingdom and the United States, that they produce only two commodities, cloth and wheat, and that both have constant opportunity costs. If both countries use all the factors of production available to them, each might be able to produce either the quantity of cloth or the quantity of wheat (expressed in some appropriate unit) shown in Table 3–1.

The data in Table 3–1 show the production possibility schedule of the two countries. The same information is shown graphically in the production possibility curves of Figures 3–8 and 3–9.

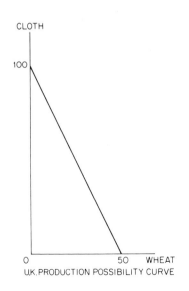

CLOTH

100

O   50   WHEAT
U.K. PRODUCTION POSSIBILITY CURVE

CLOTH

200

150   WHEAT
U.S. PRODUCTION POSSIBILITY CURVE

FIGURE 3–8   FIGURE 3–9

If the two countries do *not* trade with each other, we will find that cloth and wheat exchange in the two countries in the following ratios:

U.K.   1 Cloth = .50 Wheat
U.S.   1 Cloth = .75 Wheat

The physical exchange ratios that will be established accurately reflect the relative amounts of labor used up in the production of cloth and wheat in the two countries. British workers are able to produce exactly twice as much cloth as wheat; thus each unit of wheat actually produced embodies twice the amount of labor embodied in a unit of cloth, and each unit of wheat will therefore be twice as valuable as a unit of cloth.

We note that the United Kingdom can produce absolutely less of both commodities than the United States. Yet the United Kingdom has a *comparative* advantage in the production of cloth. For each additional unit of cloth produced the United Kingdom has to give up only .50 units of wheat, although the United States has to give up .75 units. Relatively speaking the amount of wheat that the United Kingdom has to give up for each additional unit of cloth is less than it is for the United States, resulting in a steeper production possibility curve for the United Kingdom than for the United States.

If we now introduce the possibility of international trade between the United Kingdom and the United States, the British will soon realize that they can exchange one unit of cloth in the United States for .75 units of wheat, but they will be able to obtain only .50 units of wheat in the domestic market for the same unit of cloth. The British cloth manufacturer who obtains his wheat in the United States rather than at home is therefore able to obtain .25 units of wheat more per unit of cloth exchanged. As a consequence it will be to Britain's advantage to import wheat from the United States in exchange for cloth.

The reverse argument applies to the United States, where wheat farmers can exchange one unit of wheat against one and a third units of cloth, while they could obtain two units of cloth in Britain. Naturally they will tend to import their cloth from the United Kingdom in exchange for wheat.

The result of our analysis so far is that the United Kingdom will tend to export cloth and import wheat, while the United States will tend to export wheat and import cloth. The *direction* of international trade is in this way determined. We can restate our findings as follows:

A country will tend to export the commodity whose relative cost (to the other commodity) or comparative cost of production is lower than it is in the other country.

Note, too, that if there are no differences in relative costs of production, that is, a situation of identical comparative costs, then there will be no incentive for trade. Graphically this is expressed by parallel production possibility curves.

No international trade will occur if there are no differences in relative production costs between countries.

LIMITS TO THE INTERNATIONAL TERMS OF TRADE

Having solved the problem of the direction of international trade, we now direct our attention to the problem of the determination of the physical exchange ratio and the relative prices of the commodities traded. We will restrict our analysis at this point to the determinants of the upper and lower limits of these ratios. A full analysis of the precise determination will be postponed until we have incorporated demand patterns into our analysis. However, cost considerations alone will allow us to make some inferences about the magnitude of the international exchange ratios.

Before free trade starts we have one distinct domestic exchange ratio of cloth against wheat for each of the two countries. After the opening up of trade relations these two different exchange ratios will be replaced by a single exchange ratio, namely the world market exchange ratio. This world market exchange ratio is generally referred to as the *terms of trade*.

We note now that the United Kingdom will not be interested in exporting cloth if it does not bring *at least* .50 units of wheat for each unit of cloth. This is the domestic pretrade exchange ratio, and any smaller quantity of wheat offered by the United States will be refused because British farmers themselves are able to produce .50 units of wheat with the same amount of resources as required for one unit of cloth production. At any exchange ratio that is better than .50 units of wheat for a unit of cloth, British producers will be only too happy to export cloth. In the previous section we found that the United Kingdom will tend to export cloth in exchange for wheat, and now we have some additional information on the *minimum* exchange ratio of wheat for cloth at which this exchange will take place.

On the other hand United States farmers will not be willing to trade internationally if they have to give up more than .75 units of wheat for each unit of cloth, that is, more than the amount that they would have to pay in the domestic market. This will set a *maximum* for the wheat/cloth exchange ratio, because it gives the maximum quantity of wheat that they are willing to exchange against a unit of cloth.

In this way we have determined the lower and upper limits of the wheat/ cloth exchange ratio. If the world terms of trade should for any reason fall outside these limits, *both* countries will want to export the same commodity and import the other commodity—a situation that cannot be realized in our two-country world. If, let us say, the exchange ratio were initially established at one cloth for one wheat unit, both countries would want to import wheat because they would get more wheat than they themselves could conceivably produce if they were to cut back their cloth production by one unit and devote these resources to wheat production. Yet, as there is no country willing to export wheat in a one-to-one ratio for cloth, their import desires will be frustrated.

The international exchange ratio of the commodities traded will have to lie between the limits established by the pretrade domestic exchange ratios.

EQUILIBRIUM CONDITIONS FOR THE INTERNATIONAL TERMS OF TRADE

Having determined the upper and lower bounds of the region into which the international terms of trade must fall, we are left with the question of the precise determination of the terms of trade. Like any other competitive exchange ratio the international terms of trade are determined by supply and demand for the products in world markets. Up to this point we have discussed only the influence of production, or supply conditions, on international trade and exchange ratios. The role of demand patterns in this context is considered in Chapter 5, and consequently the answer to the question of the precise determination of the international terms of trade will have to be postponed until Chapter 6, when all our tools of analysis are assembled.

There is, however, no reason why we cannot discuss the *equilibrium conditions* that will have to be fulfilled if the international terms of trade are to be stable. With any given set of terms of trade the United States will be willing to export a certain quantity of one commodity in exchange for a given quantity of the other commodity. The same will hold true for the United Kingdom. It is evident that the markets will be cleared only if the quantities that one country wishes to export and the quantities that the other country wishes to import are equal for every commodity. Only then will there be no further tendency for the international terms of trade to change. We can state this condition formally:

(3–1) $IM_i^{US} = EX_i^{UK}$ (where i stands for a particular commodity)

and

(3–2) $EX_j^{US} = IM_j^{UK}$

If this condition is not fulfilled, then the quantities that countries want to export and import do not exactly match, and there will be either surpluses or deficits in the international markets. If there is an excess supply of a commodity in the world markets, then exporters will eventually be willing to offer a large quantity of this commodity in exchange for other commodities. Thus the terms of trade will adjust themselves until the quantities supplied and demanded match exactly. This is the equilibrium condition for the terms of trade. To repeat: although we do not yet know *how* the equilibrium exchange ratio is determined in world markets, we are able to state the conditions that have to be satisfied if the exchange ratio is to be in equilibrium.

The international commodity exchange ratios (terms of trade) will be in equilibrium if the quantities of all commodities that countries wish to export are equal to the quantities of all commodities that countries wish to import at these exchange ratios.

THE OPPORTUNITY COST THEORY

In the previous section we examined the classical theory of the structure of trade as formulated by Ricardo and refined by Taussig and others. One of the fundamental premises of this theory is the labor theory of value. This restrictive assumption of the classical theory can be discarded in favor of a more general framework without otherwise changing the basic argument. This more modern approach was first formulated by Gottfried Haberler[1] and is customarily referred to as the *opportunity cost theory* of international trade. His basic contention is that the relative prices of different commodities are determined by cost differentials, where costs do not refer to the amounts of labor required to produce a commodity but to the alternative production that has to be foregone to allow for the production of the commodity in question. In case several alternatives have to be foregone the highest valued alternative determines the opportunity cost of the commodity in question. The value of each commodity can therefore be reckoned in terms of opportunity costs reflecting foregone production of other commodities.

This formulation means that the quantities of resources employed in the production of a commodity do not enter into consideration at all, because attention is focused solely on the choice between final products. We are not concerned with how many factors or how much of each factor is required to produce a commodity but rather with the other products that could have been produced with these factors.

The opportunity cost theory represents an improvement over the real cost theory in two respects: (1) by dropping the assumption of a single factor of production as the basis of our theory and starting with a given set of resources that may contain any number of factors, we make our assumptions

---

[1] Gottfried Haberler, *The Theory of International Trade* (London: William Hodge & Company, Limited, 1936).

more realistic; and (2) because we are able to derive the same results from a less restrictive set of assumptions, we make our theory more elegant.

The conclusions derived from the labor theory of value hold just as before, and there is no need to restate them here. The only thing we have to remember is that it is not the physical factor cost that determines the value of a commodity but the opportunities of production of other commodities that have to be foregone in order to produce the particular commodity in question. These opportunity costs will be reflected in the exchange ratios that will prevail between the different commodities.

EFFECTS OF COUNTRY SIZE

Countries may be relatively large or small as far as international trade is concerned. By large or small we do not mean size in absolute terms but in terms relative to the market with which we are concerned. For instance, although Switzerland is a small country by almost any standard, its watch industry plays a large role in the world market for watches. Hence when we talk about watches we will consider Switzerland a large country because the sum total of all the Swiss watchmakers' actions will have an effect on world prices.

Large Countries

If we consider two countries of approximately equal size in the relevant markets, both of them will have a certain influence on the final equilibrium price to be established. As a result the final market exchange ratio between the two commodities is likely to lie somewhere in between the domestic pretrade exchange ratios. Such a situation is shown in Figure 3–10. Here we show the production possibility curves for the United States and the United Kingdom, with the U.K. having a comparative advantage in cloth and the U.S. in wheat. Constant cost conditions prevail, and the U.K. specializes completely in the production of cloth and the U.S. in the production of wheat. The relevant production points are labelled P^{UK} and P^{US} in Figure 3–10.

Let us say that the final equilibrium exchange ratio is two units of cloth for one unit of wheat (indicated by the slope of the dashed lines in Figure 3–10). If the United Kingdom wishes to consume at point C^{UK}, she will import twenty-five units of wheat in exchange for fifty units of cloth. At the same time the United States exports twenty-five units of cloth against fifty units of wheat, reaching consumption point C^{US}. *Both* countries are completely specialized and export the commodity in which they enjoy a comparative advantage.

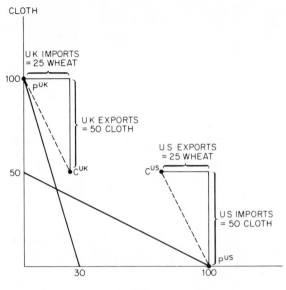

FIGURE 3–10

Large Countries and Small Countries

If countries are of unequal size, it is entirely possible that even complete specialization on the part of the smaller country in one of the commodities—cloth, for example—will not suffice to satisfy the total world demand for cloth. As a result we find that the larger country will continue producing both commodities. It will be importing some cloth from the small country but will produce a certain amount of cloth domestically in order to satisfy the home demand for this commodity.

In this case the international terms of trade will coincide with the domestic pretrade exchange ratio of the country that continues to produce both commodities after trade is opened. The small country is able to buy or sell any quantities at the exchange ratio prevailing in the large country. The small country is a price taker. Such a situation is shown in Figure 3–11. The United Kingdom (the smaller country of our example) produces at point P^{UK}, specializing completely in the production of cloth. She trades part of her cloth production against wheat imports from the United States, allowing her to consume the commodity combination indicated by C^{UK}. The United States wants to consume at point C^{US}. To achieve this consumption pattern, she imports IM_C^{US} from the United Kingdom and supplements this with D_C^{US} produced domestically. The United States thus produces a commodity combination shown by point P^{US}.

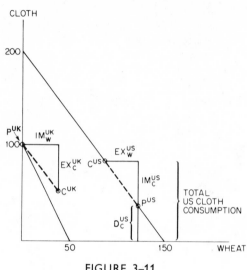

FIGURE 3–11

The key to much of the understanding of the production patterns that develop in countries of unequal size is found in the fact that the pretrade domestic terms of trade set the limits for the international terms of trade. If after one country has specialized completely in one commodity there is still some excess demand for this commodity, the international terms of trade can no longer change, because the limit to the terms of trade set by the domestic pretrade price ratios has already been reached. Any additional demand that remains at these prices must be satisfied by production under the cost conditions prevailing in the country not yet completely specialized. Therefore the international terms of trade must necessarily coincide with the slope of the production possibility curve of the country producing both commodities.

If the trading countries are of unequal size and constant costs prevail, international trade will lead to the complete specialization of at least one country. If one country continues to produce both commodities, the international exchange ratio will coincide with the domestic exchange ratio of that country. The small country acts as a price taker in world markets.

EFFECTS OF INCREASING COSTS

The analysis so far has been concerned with the special case of constant costs. In the real world we find that such idealized conditions hold only rarely. It is therefore appropriate to extend our analysis to cover both the increasing and decreasing cost cases. Nonlinear production possibility curves may be caused by a variety of different factors. Among the more important are: (1) different returns to scale and (2) the existence of factors of production that are specialized in the production of one commodity.

Returns to scale refer to the relationship between inputs and outputs as the scale (or level) of the production process is changed. If a doubling of all inputs leads to a doubling of the outputs, returns to scale are said to be constant; if a doubling of all inputs leads to more than a doubling of all outputs, returns are said to be increasing; and if a doubling of all inputs leads to less than a doubling of the outputs, returns to scale are decreasing. These differences can be caused by factors both inside or outside the firm itself.

Many factors of production are specialized in the production of certain commodities. Such factors are referred to as being product specific. Clearly any one of these product-specific factors is of relatively less use in the production of other commodities, and we can conclude that the existence of different factor intensities can be responsible for increasing costs in production. The precise way in which different returns to scale and different factor intensities shape the production possibility curve will be investigated further in Chapter 4.

Increasing costs of production give rise to a production possibility curve that is concave, viewed from the origin. A country producing any arbitrary combination of commodities described by a point on the production possibility curve will find that as she expands the production of one commodity, the cost of producing this commodity will increase. Figures 3–12 and 3–13 show the production possibility curves of the United Kingdom and the United States. Before trade opens up the countries produce all commodities

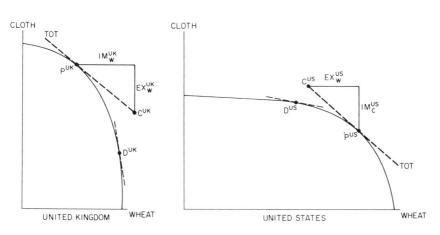

FIGURE 3–12   FIGURE 3–13

consumed domestically. Possible domestic production and consumption patterns are shown by points D^{UK} and D^{US}. The domestic exchange ratios between cloth and wheat are given by the slopes of the tangents to the production possibility curves at points D^{UK} and D^{US} respectively. After trade opens up the new international terms of trade will have to lie between the limits established by the domestic exchange ratios. Accordingly the United Kingdom will tend to produce more cloth (move to production point P^{UK}), while the United States will increase her wheat output (move to production point P^{US}). The United Kingdom will then export some of her cloth in exchange for wheat, moving to consumption point C^{UK}, while the United States will export wheat and import cloth, reaching consumption point C^{US}.

Both countries will specialize, but they will probably *not specialize completely*. This is due to the fact that as the country increases the output of the commodity in which she specializes, her costs of producing this commodity will increase. If costs increase so sharply that the country loses her comparative cost advantage vis-à-vis the other country before complete specialization has taken place, both countries will continue to produce both commodities. If a country reaches the end point of the production possibility curve before the new terms of trade are reached, specialization is naturally complete. We will continue to speak of specialization taking place in the commodity in which the country has a comparative cost advantage, and say that the country will *tend* to export the commodity in which she specializes. Specialization and exchange will again allow the countries concerned to achieve a commodity bundle for consumption that could not have been attained under conditions of autarky.

Countries experiencing increasing cost of production will specialize in the production of the commodity in which they enjoy a comparative advantage. The specialization need not be complete.

EFFECTS OF DECREASING COSTS

Decreasing costs of production[2] find expression in a production possibility curve that is convex to the origin. Under these conditions there is a multitude of possible outcomes, and we have to restrict our attention to the more important ones.

Figure 3-14 shows the production possibility curve of a country that produces under conditions of decreasing cost. Before specialization the

[2] Note that the economies of scale cannot be due to economies that are internal to the production unit. The existence of internal economies of scale would lead to a breakdown of perfect competition, and monopolistic pricing patterns would evolve that would invalidate some of our results.

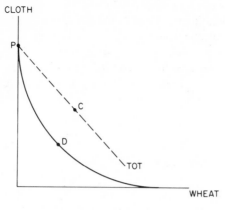

FIGURE 3–14

country can produce any commodity combination located on the production possibility curve, such as D. But given the possibility of international exchange, the country will specialize in one commodity, say, cloth, produce at point P on the production possibility curve, and exchange some cloth at the international terms of trade TOT for wheat. Thus she is able to reach consumption point C outside her production possibility curve, which could not have been attained without the possibility of international exchange.[3]

Once specialization in one of the commodities is under way the country can produce this commodity under conditions of continuously decreasing costs. The decreasing costs per unit will allow this country to outbid the other country to an ever-increasing degree. Thus once specialization has started, it is likely to continue until it is complete. Initially specialization in a particular commodity by a country may have been due to historical accident, but once the process has started there is no point of return. This may help to explain the high degree of specialization that we often find in the production of different commodities, where a product becomes associated with the name of the country or region that specializes in its production.

There still exists the possibility that even under these conditions we find one country continuing to produce both commodities. This would be the case if one country, even after complete specialization, were unable to satisfy the total world demand for the commodity in question. The other country

[3] Under certain conditions it may be advantageous for a country to specialize completely, even if there is no opportunity for international trade. This will be the case if there is a very strong domestic preference for one of the commodities. This could also occur under conditions of increasing or constant costs of production, though the chances for its occurrence are greater under decreasing cost conditions.

would then have to continue producing some of the desired commodity herself and would thus not be able to take full advantage of the decreasing cost afforded by complete specialization. This case is very similar to the one we encountered when dealing with the effects of differences in country size on specialization patterns under conditions of constant cost.

Countries that experience decreasing cost of production will tend to specialize in production. The specialization will be complete in at least one country but need not be complete in all countries.

EMPIRICAL EVIDENCE

Several economists have attempted to test the validity of the elementary form of the comparative cost theory. The most notable attempts were made by G. D. A. MacDougall,[4] Robert Stern,[5] and Bela Balassa.[6] All three investigators worked with data for the United States and the United Kingdom. MacDougall used 1937, Stern 1950 and 1959, and Balassa 1950 data.

All three investigations try to test the validity of the labor theory of value as the main determinant of international trade. According to this theory, differences in the productivity of labor will result in differences in the cost of production of various commodities, which in turn will affect the pretrade prices for these commodities. If a country has relatively low prices for a commodity, it will tend to export this commodity.

One of the major problems of testing this hypothesis is that we cannot observe the *pretrade prices* that would prevail under conditions of autarky. In the world in which we live countries do trade with each other, and product prices are already equalized (except for differences due to tariffs, transport costs, and the like). Because of this difficulty we will test directly the hypothesis that the country that has a relatively high productivity of labor in the production of a commodity will tend to export this commodity.

A second problem arises in connection with the tariffs and transport costs that exist in the real world. Especially in 1937, the date of the original study by MacDougall, United States and United Kingdom tariffs were generally high enough to wipe out any comparative cost differences that might have existed. As a result we find that the two countries traded relatively little with each other. For this reason the studies concentrate attention on the export performance of the two countries in *third markets*. In these countries

---

[4] G. D. A. MacDougall, "British and American Exports: A Study Suggested by the Theory of Comparative Costs," *Economic Journal*, December 1951.

[5] Robert Stern, "British and American Productivity and Comparative Costs in International Trade," *Oxford Economic Papers*, October 1962.

[6] Bela Balassa, "An Empirical Demonstration of Classical Comparative Cost Theory," *Review of Economics and Statistics*, August 1963.

the products of both the United States and the United Kingdom have to overcome the same tariff walls and are faced with often similar transport costs.

Third, a problem arises in the availability of export performance data. For some industries we have *quantity* of export data, although for others only *value* of export data are available. No great difficulties are to be expected from this handicap, because value of exports is nothing but quantity times price of the exported commodity. As both countries are able to obtain the

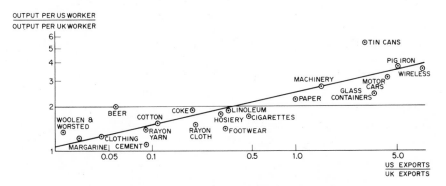

Source: Adapted from G. D. A. MacDougall, "British and American Exports: A Study Suggested by the Theory of Comparative Costs," *Economic Journal*, December 1951, p. 703.

FIGURE 3–15

same price in the world market, the two indices should yield the same results.

The theory would predict that the country whose productivity of labor is higher than that of the other country in the production of a certain commodity would capture the whole export market for this commodity. The actual results of MacDougall are shown in Figure 3–15, where the productivity of labor ratio is shown on the vertical axis and the export ratio on the horizontal axis. (Both are log scales.) We find that there is an approximately linear relationship between the productivity and export ratios. This shows that in those commodities where the United States labor productivity is the highest (relative to the United Kingdom), the United States will capture the largest share of the export markets. As the relative advantage of the United States falls, the export market share falls, too. We find that the process is continuous in the sense that no one country succeeds in capturing the whole export market as a result of a small comparative cost advantage. This is due to several causes: (1) The products shown here are not homogeneous within commodity classes. There are quality and design differences among all the automobile types lumped together in the commodity classification *cars*. Thus product differentiation is one reason no country can capture the whole export market. (2) There are imperfectly competitive markets in the real world. Oligopolistic or monopolistic industries tend to price their products differently than perfectly competitive industries, and these industries are often able to maintain certain markets because of their special pricing techniques. Both reasons mentioned will lead to a continuous distribution of the industries, where high productivity of labor is strongly correlated with a superior export performance.

We need to explain here why the line showing productivity of labor/ export performance relationship indicates that the labor productivity in the United States must be more than twice the British labor productivity for the former to capture the greater share of the export market. To begin, in 1937 wages in the United States were about twice the level of British wages. An American worker would have to be twice as productive as his British colleague if the product were to have the same production costs. This accounts for most of the difference. In addition there is the question of indirect labor. Indirect labor is the labor spent not in the direct production process of manufacturing the commodity but in transporting, distributing, and servicing it. It is argued that the amount of such indirect labor, which is not reflected in the productivity data shown here, is greater for the United States than for the United Kingdom. Finally there is the question of Commonwealth preference, the practice of member countries of the British Commonwealth of Nations granting preferential treatment to commodities produced by member countries. This practice also would tend to discriminate against the United States, requiring her to have a much higher labor productivity than Great Britain before she could capture the greater share of the export market.

The studies by Stern and Balassa for the postwar period confirm and amplify the conclusion reached in the pioneer effort by MacDougall. They found that other factors, such as capital costs per unit of output and the like, did not influence the export performance of the countries to any significant extent. Their results confirmed MacDougall's findings of a high correlation between productivity of labor and export shares.

However, the work of Jagdish Bhagwati[7] casts some doubt on the seemingly convincing studies cited. Using a somewhat more sophisticated technique Bhagwati finds that linear regressions of export price ratios (United States/United Kingdom) on labor productivity ratios yield no significant regression coefficients. Similarly regressions of unit labor costs on export price ratios for the same two countries yield no significant results.

The strong positive results of MacDougall, Balassa, and Stern regarding the usefulness of the classical theory of comparative costs should therefore be regarded with caution until more conclusive evidence becomes available.

---

[7] Jagdish Bhagwati, "The Pure Theory of International Trade: A Survey," *Economic Journal*, March 1964.

SUGGESTED FURTHER READINGS

BALASSA, BELA, "An Empirical Demonstration of Classical Comparative Cost Theory," *Review of Economics and Statistics* (August 1963).

BHAGWATI, JAGDISH, "The Pure Theory of International Trade: A Survey," *Economic Journal* (March 1964), Sec. I (Theorems in Statics: The Pattern of Trade).

——, "The Proofs of the Theorems on Comparative Advantage," *Economic Journal* (March 1967).

BRANDIS, ROYALL, "The Myth of Absolute Advantage," *American Economic Review* (March 1967).

CAVES, RICHARD, *Trade and Economic Structure*, pp. 6–22. Cambridge: Harvard University Press, 1960.

HABERLER, GOTTFRIED, "A Survey of International Trade Theory," *Special Papers in International Economics*, No. 1, Chap. II, International Finance Section, Princeton University, 1961.

——, *The Theory of International Trade*, Chaps. X–XII. London: William Hodge & Company, 1936.

JOHNSON, HARRY, G., *Money, Trade, and Economic Growth*, Chap. II. Cambridge: Harvard University Press, 1962.

MACDOUGALL, DONALD, "British and American Exports: A Study Suggested by the Theory of Comparative Costs," *Economic Journal* (December 1951). Reprinted in AEA *Readings in International Economics*, eds. Richard Caves and Harry G. Johnson. Homewood, Ill.: Richard D. Irwin, Inc., 1968.

MEIER, GERALD, "The Theory of Comparative Cost Reconsidered," *Oxford Economic Papers* (June 1949).

STERN, ROBERT, "British and American Productivity and Comparative Costs in International Trade," *Oxford Economic Papers* (October 1962).

4

Production
and International Trade

In the previous chapter we analyzed the effects of cost differences between countries on the pattern of international trade. In the simple case of one factor of production we showed the relationship between factor inputs and products produced. But we refrained from showing the causes responsible for the shape of the production possibility curve in the event that more than one factor of production has to be considered. In this chapter we will look behind the production possibility curve and explain the different influences that determine its shape.

We know that international trade starts whenever the domestic price ratios of different commodities are not the same in the countries under consideration. Differences in production possibility curves for different countries constitute one important reason for these international price differentials that in turn lead to the emergence of international trade. It is therefore of the utmost importance to understand clearly the various factors that are responsible for the shape and position of the production possibility curve.[1]

At the same time we will make our theory more general by introducing a second factor of production. The two factors of production referred to may be any factors or factor bundles. In our examples we will usually refer to them as labor (L) and real capital (K).

To simplify the analysis we will initially assume in this chapter that demand patterns in the two countries under consideration are identical. This

---

[1] The reader unfamiliar with production theory is advised to read the appropriate material in the Appendix.

assumption enables us to eliminate any influence that different demand patterns might have on the structure of international trade. In the next chapter we will drop this assumption and analyze the effects of different demand patterns on trade.

There are three important conditions of production that will be singled out for treatment in the remainder of this chapter: the effects of differences in returns to scale, factor intensities, and factor endowments.

THE EFFECTS OF RETURNS TO SCALE

We will start our investigation with the effect of different returns to scale in production on the production possibilities of a country. To isolate the effects of the returns to scale we will assume that the factor intensities in the production of the two commodities are identical and that the factor endowments of the different countries are identical, too. As a consequence we will find that the Edgeworth Box diagrams for the two countries are of the same size and have a straight diagonal contract curve.

Constant Returns to Scale

A production possibility curve displaying constant opportunity costs of production is shown in Figure 4-1a. The quantities of the two outputs, cloth and wheat, are measured along the axes. The units of output of wheat shown along the horizontal axis are measured in such a way that the point R', denoting the maximum amount of output of wheat on the production possibility curve of Figure 4-1a, is vertically above point R, showing the same maximum level of wheat output in the Edgeworth Box depicted in Figure 4-1b. Similarly if all resources are devoted to cloth production, OM' of cloth and no wheat can be produced. Point M' in the output space corresponds to point M in the input space.

With this mapping technique it is possible to derive the whole production possibility curve from the contract curve. A decrease in cloth production will free resources for wheat production allowing for an expansion of this industry and vice versa. Different possible output combinations are given in Table 4-1 and are marked on Figure 4-1.

By now it should be clear that for each point on the contract curve there exists one corresponding point on the production possibility curve. If factors of production are reallocated between different employments, the output pattern will be changed accordingly.

All the points located on the contract curve represent technologically efficient production patterns, just as the corresponding points on the

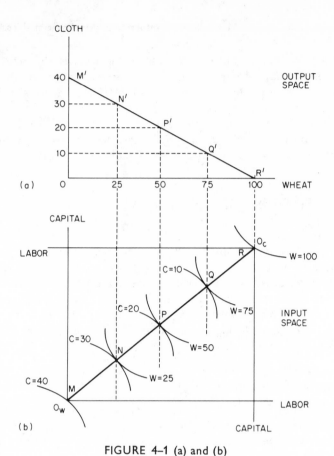

FIGURE 4–1 (a) and (b)

TABLE 4–1

POSSIBLE OUTPUT COMBINATIONS UNDER CONSTANT
RETURNS TO SCALE

Point	Change in Cloth Output	Total Cloth Output	Total Wheat Output	Change in Wheat Output
M		40	0	
	10			25
N		30	25	
	10			25
P	Constant R.T.S.	20	50	Constant R.T.S.
	10			25
Q		10	75	
	10			25
R		0	100	

52

production possibility curve represent technologically efficient production patterns. Similarly all points in the input space that are not actually located on the contract curve as well as their corresponding points in the output space are technologically inefficient.

Even with constant returns to scale there may still exist differences in the marginal rate of transformation (shown by the slope of the production possibility curve) in different countries, provided that the returns to scale differ in the sense that one country can produce with the same amount of resources a greater (or smaller) quantity of one of the commodities, that is, greater or smaller by a constant percentage, than the other country. In other words although the maximum cloth output in both countries may be forty units, one country may be able to produce one hundred units of wheat, but the other country can produce only eighty units of wheat. Both countries have constant opportunity costs, but they differ by a fixed factor.

Countries that have identical factor endowments, identical factor intensities, and are also subject to constant returns to scale may have different opportunity costs of production if the returns to scale are not identical.

Decreasing Returns to Scale

We can now relax the assumption of constant returns to scale by allowing decreasing returns to scale in the production of one commodity, say, wheat. The other commodity is still being produced under constant returns to scale, and all other assumptions remain intact. Table 4–2 shows possible output combinations that result from the shifting of equal amounts of resources. To move from M to N involves the same amount of resource shifting as the movement from N to P, from P to Q, or from Q to R.

Note that the resource shifts decrease cloth production each time by ten units—no matter at which level of output production is taking place. Wheat production, on the other hand, increases first by forty units, then by thirty, twenty, and ten units. The increments in output due to equal additions of resources become smaller and smaller as the output level increases, that is, we experience decreasing returns to scale.

In Figure 4–2 we plot the data supplied in Table 4–2 and find that the production possibility curve is concave viewed from the origin. Any increase in the production level of one of the two commodities will call for successively larger sacrifices of the other commodity, regardless of whether the expansion is in the production of the commodity that can be produced under decreasing or under constant returns to scale. For *both* commodities the opportunity cost of production increases.

Decreasing returns to scale in one commodity will tend to result in increasing opportunity costs of production for both commodities.

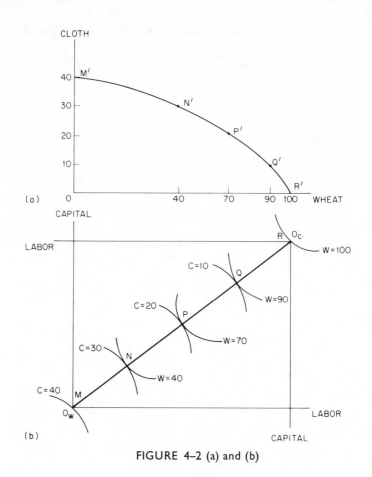

FIGURE 4–2 (a) and (b)

TABLE 4–2

POSSIBLE OUTPUT COMBINATIONS UNDER DECREASING
RETURNS TO SCALE IN THE PRODUCTION OF WHEAT AND
CONSTANT RETURNS IN CLOTH PRODUCTION

Point	Change in Cloth Output	Total Cloth Output	Total Wheat Output	Change in Wheat Output
M		40	0	
	10			40
N		30	40	
	10			30
P	Constant R.T.S.	20	70	Decreasing R.T.S.
	10			20
Q		10	90	
	10			10
R		0	100	

54

Increasing Returns to Scale

The case of increasing returns to scale is complementary to the decreasing returns to scale case treated above. Again we will assume that cloth is being produced under constant returns to scale, but wheat is now produced under increasing returns to scale. The data are shown in Table 4–3, and the relevant diagrams are drawn in Figure 4–3. The production possibility curve is convex toward the origin, indicating that the opportunity cost of production decreases.

Increasing returns to scale in one commodity will tend to result in decreasing opportunity costs of production for both commodities.

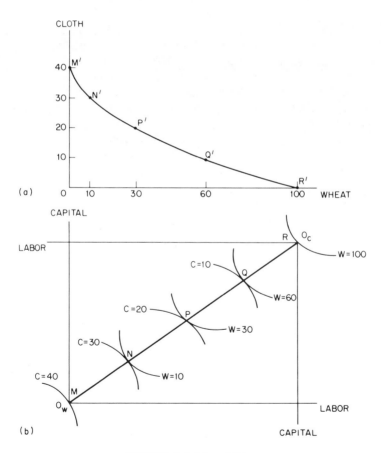

FIGURE 4–3 (a) and (b)

TABLE 4–3

POSSIBLE OUTPUT COMBINATIONS UNDER INCREASING
RETURNS TO SCALE IN THE PRODUCTION OF WHEAT

Point	Change in Cloth Output	Total Cloth Output	Total Wheat Output	Change in Wheat Output
M		40	0	
	10			10
N		30	10	
	10			20	Increasing
P	Constant R.T.S.	20	30	R.T.S.
	10			30
Q		10	60	
	10			40
R		0	100	

The Net Influence of Returns to Scale

Naturally it is also possible to find various combinations of the three cases described above. Returns to scale may differ in different output ranges of the same commodity, they may differ between commodities, and they may differ between countries. What is important for the pattern of international trade is the *net influence* that returns to scale exercise on the production possibility curve, that is, the countervailing or reinforcing influences resulting from different returns to scale. From the fact that there are increasing returns to scale in the production of one commodity, it cannot be inferred that the opportunity costs of production are decreasing. This is because there may be strongly decreasing returns to scale in the other commodity, more than offsetting the mildly increasing returns to scale in the first commodity. The net result would be increasing opportunity costs in the production of both commodities.

If the net influence varies in different output ranges, the opportunity costs of production may be increasing in some ranges of the production possibility curve while decreasing in other ranges. Such a situation is shown in Table 4–4 and Figure 4–4.

Although the production of wheat is subject to mildly decreasing returns to scale throughout the output range, cloth production shows first increasing and then decreasing returns to scale as we move from S to M. But although the decreasing returns in wheat production are very mild, the increasing returns in cloth production between Q and S are strong enough to predominate. As a result the production possibility curve has a roller coaster shape,

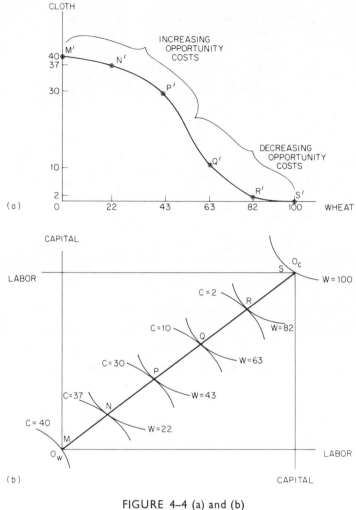

FIGURE 4–4 (a) and (b)

exhibiting increasing opportunity costs between M′ and P′ and decreasing opportunity costs between Q′ and S′. The number of different possible combinations is virtually unlimited, and there is nothing that we can say about the direction of trade on a priori grounds. All we know is that whatever commodity can be produced with a comparative advantage at home is likely to be exported, but the commodity with the comparative disadvantage is likely to be imported.

TABLE 4–4

POSSIBLE OUTPUT COMBINATIONS UNDER
VARYING RETURNS TO SCALE

Point	Change in Cloth Output	Total Cloth Output	Total Wheat Output	Change in Wheat Output
M		40	0	
	Decreasing R.T.S. 3			22
N		37	22	
	7			21
P		30	43	
	20			20 Decreasing R.T.S.
Q		10	63	
	Increasing R.T.S. 8			19
R		2	82	
	2			18
S		0	100	

THE EFFECTS OF FACTOR INTENSITIES

The second important parameter determining the shape of the production possibility curve is the factor intensity. By factor intensity we mean the *relative* amounts of the two factors that are used in the production of one commodity as compared to another commodity. Let us emphasize that the measure does not tell anything about the absolute amounts of the factors of production that are used. It is impossible to compare physical, absolute units of capital and labor because a common yardstick is missing. But relative comparisons are possible. For instance, we are able to say that cloth production uses relatively more capital than labor compared to wheat production. That is, the capital labor ratio in cloth production is greater than the one in wheat production: $(K/L)_{cloth} > (K/L)_{wheat}$. We will first look at the expansion path as the *level* of output is changed. In Figure 4–5 we show the isoquant maps for cloth and wheat and the expansion paths for one possible factor price ratio. At all output levels but given factor prices the capital/labor ratio for cloth production is greater than the capital/labor ratio for wheat production. If both production functions are homothetic,[2] one commodity will always be produced with a higher capital/labor ratio than the other one.

[2] For a definition see the appendix, p. 224.

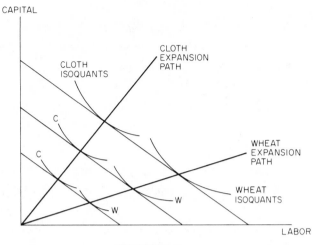

FIGURE 4-5

It is possible, however, for factor intensities to be reversed at different *output levels* and identical relative factor prices if at least one production function is not homothetic. Figure 4–6 shows the case of factor reversals in different ranges of the production function. At relatively low output levels cloth production is capital intensive compared to wheat production. At higher output levels, wheat becomes relatively capital intensive and cloth relatively labor intensive.

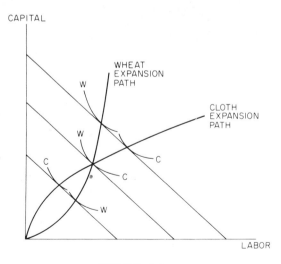

FIGURE 4-6

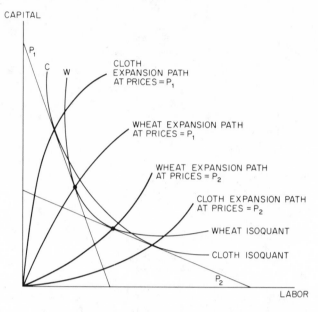

FIGURE 4–7

Next we will analyze the effect of different factor *prices*. Factor intensity reversals may occur at different relative factor prices. This case is illustrated in Figure 4–7. Only one cloth and one wheat isoquant is shown. If the factor price ratio is given by P_1, cloth production uses a higher capital/labor ratio than wheat. At the factor price ratio P_2 the reverse holds true: wheat is now relatively capital intensive when compared to cloth production. Let us note that factor intensity reversals due to factor price changes are possible even if both isoquant sets are homothetic. Factor intensity reversals will become important in Chapter 7, when we deal with the effect of international trade on the factor prices.

In order to focus attention solely on the role of the factor intensities we will first assume that both production functions are linear homogeneous, but not identical, for both commodities. As a consequence the contract curve is a curve, rather than a straight diagonal line, indicating different factor intensities for the two products. Due to the homogeneity assumption the contract curve will be located entirely on one side of the diagonal. No factor intensity reversals will occur.

Consider the customary Edgeworth Box diagram shown in Figure 4–8b. Production is thought of as taking place at point P. The quantities of the two inputs devoted to the production of each commodity are determined by the position of point P. Production of wheat utilizes PS of capital and SO_W of labor, resulting in a relative factor intensity of capital to labor of PS/SO_W. Production of cloth uses PT of capital and TO_C of labor, leading to a capital/labor ratio of PT/TO_C. The straight lines drawn from the origins to point P have the slopes PS/SO_W and PT/TO_C respectively. As is evident from the diagram the ratios PS/SO_W and PT/TO_C are not equal to each other, indicating that there are different factor intensities in the production of the two commodities.

If instead of using different factor intensities, we insist on operating with *identical* factor intensities in the manufacture of both commodities, production could take place on any point along the *diagonal* $O_W O_C$. Assume that the resources are evenly split between cloth and wheat production. This point is shown by R in the input space. A mapping of R in the output space yields point R', which is located on a straight line production possibility curve. The output levels associated with point R are fifty cloth and fifty wheat, due to our assumption of linear production functions.

However, instead of being limited to identical factor intensities, we do have the possibility of utilizing *different* factor intensities. Thus we are able

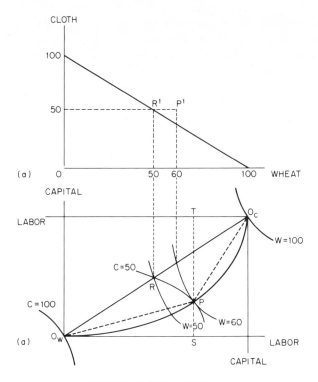

FIGURE 4–8 (a) and (b)

to produce at point P. Point P is located on the same cloth isoquant (cloth = 50) as point R. But P is located on a higher wheat isoquant (wheat = 60) than point R (wheat = 50). All we have to do is to mark the increased wheat output possible in the output space, and with the coordinate supplied by the unchanged cloth output (cloth = 50), we are able to map point P′ in the output space.

It should be pointed out that this mapping procedure from the input to the output space is applicable only to the case of linear homogeneous isoquants, as was initially assumed. The geometry becomes much more complex if we introduce nonlinear returns to scale.

The important result of this exercise is that we can show that point P′ is actually located above the straight line production possibility curve shown in Figure 4–8a. A complete mapping of all points on the contract curve of the Edgeworth Box into the output space leads to a production possibility curve that is concave if viewed from the origin. A concave production possibility curve is characterized by increasing opportunity costs of production.

Different factor intensities in the production of several commodities will tend to lead to increasing cost conditions in production. The greater the difference between the factor intensities, the more pronounced will be the curvature of the production possibility curve.

If we drop the assumption of homogeneity, it is possible that factor intensity reversals do occur. In that case the contract curve will no longer lie on one side of the diagonal only, but can meander across it. Depending on the scale of operations the commodity being produced may be labor intensive or capital intensive. We might envision a situation where labor intensive

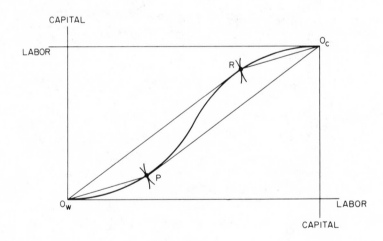

FIGURE 4–9

methods are used if the total output is relatively small, although capital intensive methods are more economical if the output level increases. Such a situation is shown in Figure 4–9. If production takes place at point P, wheat production is labor intensive and cloth is capital intensive, but the reverse holds true for production at point R.

THE EFFECTS OF FACTOR ENDOWMENTS

To isolate the effects of factor endowments we will assume that: (1) production functions are identical in both countries, (2) all isoquants are linear homogeneous, and (3) the factor intensities are identical for both commodities at any factor price ratio. Thus the only difference between the two countries lies in the relative amounts of factors of production that are available.

Let us assume that the United Kingdom is characterized by the factor endowments shown by the heavily lined box of Figure 4–10b. The contract curve is shown by the diagonal AB, and the corresponding production possibility curve is shown in Figure 4–10a by the line A'B'.

The United States, the second country of our example, is endowed with the same amount of capital as the United Kingdom, making the height of the box the same for both countries. Yet the United States has a larger amount of labor than the United Kingdom, which can be shown as an enlargement of the box to the right. The contract curve for the United States is shown by the line AC. It is clear that we have a set of wheat isoquants common to both countries; the U.K. wheat isoquant W^{UK} that goes through point B is the highest for the U.K., and the higher one W^{US} through C is the highest one for the U.S. Turning to cloth, we observe that the cloth isoquants are drawn with reference to origin O_C^{UK} for the United Kingdom and O_C^{US} for the United States. The highest attainable isoquants go through point O_W, showing that the United States can produce more cloth than the United Kingdom. We can conclude that in comparison to the United Kingdom, the United States can produce more of both commodities in exact proportion to the amounts that the United Kingdom can produce.

The production possibility curve of the United States (EF in Figure 4–10a), therefore, lies parallel to that of the United Kingdom (A'B'). The comparative cost ratios are the same in the two countries, thus eliminating the reason for the emergence of international trade.

If the factor intensities of all products produced by one country are the same, and the same holds true for the other country, then the two countries will not trade with each other even if the factor endowments differ.

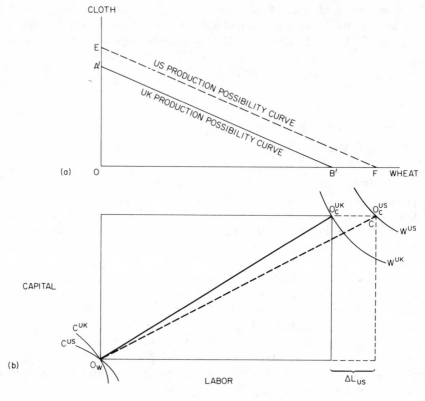

FIGURE 4–10 (a) and (b)

DIFFERENT FACTOR INTENSITIES AND ENDOWMENTS: THE HECKSCHER-OHLIN THEORY

One particular constellation of assumptions concerning the differences between countries has received a considerable amount of attention in the economic literature. The so-called Heckscher-Ohlin theory[3] of the emergence of trade assumes (1) that countries are characterized by different factor endowments, and (2) that there are different factor intensities between *products*. But the theory assumes that the factor intensities for each product

[3] Eli Heckscher presented the theory first in "The Effects of Foreign Trade on the Distribution of Income," *Economisk Tidskrift*, 1919. Reprinted in Howard S. Ellis and Lloyd A. Metzler, eds., *Readings in the Theory of International Trade* (Philadelphia: The Blakiston Company, 1950), Chap. XIII. This theory was elaborated on by Bertil Ohlin in *Interregional and International Trade* (Cambridge: Harvard University Press, 1933).

are the same in all countries for a given factor price ratio as are the returns to scale. Identical production functions are thus assumed for all countries.

It is important to stress that when we talk about differences in factor endowments, we refer to differences in *relative*, not absolute, endowments. Only the factor *proportions* are important for our analysis. A large country may well have the same factor proportions as a small country despite the fact that the absolute amount of her factors is much larger.

As the Heckscher-Ohlin trade model assumes different factor intensities between products and different factor endowments between countries, we will find that the differences between production possibility curves are the *net* result of the influence of these two factors. The different factor intensities between products will be mainly responsible for the degree of *curvature* of the production possibility curve, but the factor endowments are mainly responsible for the *position* of the curve.

Figure 4–11a illustrates the United Kingdom-United States case. The pretrade domestic production and consumption pattern is indicated by points D^{US} and D^{UK}. The United States is the relatively capital abundant country, and the United Kingdom is relatively labor abundant. From Figure 4–11b we see that although wheat production is relatively capital intensive, cloth production is relatively labor intensive. At each factor price ratio we will find that wheat production utilizes relatively more capital than labor. The country that is relatively abundant in capital, here the United States, can produce wheat relatively more cheaply. In the absence of unusually high demand for wheat in the United States the wheat price will be relatively low in the United States, resulting in a comparative advantage for the United States in wheat production. (Compare the slope of the U.K. production possibility curve at point D^{UK} with the slope of the U.S. production possibility curve at point D^{US}.) After trade opens up we will find that the United States exports wheat.

The reverse holds true for the United Kingdom. The United Kingdom is endowed relatively heavily with labor. Cloth production is relatively labor intensive, enabling the United Kingdom to produce cloth inexpensively. Consequently the U.K. enjoys a low cloth price and thus a comparative cost advantage in cloth.

In Figure 4–11a we also show a possible set of international terms of trade. The points of tangency of the production possibility curves with the international terms of trade denote the optimal production patterns P^{US} and P^{UK}. Two possible trade triangles are also shown in the figure, leading to the consumption points C^{US} and C^{UK}.

Given identical production functions but different factor endowments between countries, a country will tend to export the commodity that is relatively (to the other commodity) intensive in her relatively (to the other country) abundant factor.

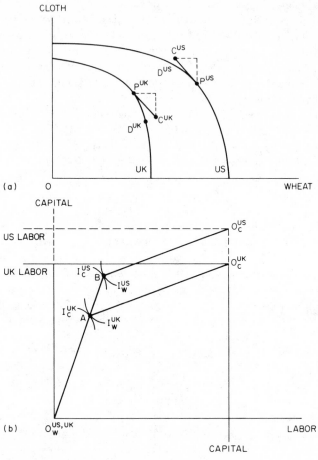

FIGURE 4–11 (a) and (b)

EMPIRICAL EVIDENCE

In this section the results of empirical research on the shape of production functions and the effects of factor intensities on patterns of international trade will be presented. We will focus attention on four questions. (1) Are production functions in different countries generally identical? (2) Are production functions characterized by increasing, constant, or decreasing returns to scale? (3) Are factor intensities different in the production of different commodities? And (4) what is the influence of factor endowments on international trade especially in the general framework of the Heckscher-Ohlin theory?

Production Functions

In a celebrated article Arrow, Chenery, Minhas, and Solow[4] reach the conclusion that production functions between countries are actually different. But they are found to differ only by a constant scale factor. This means that the production function for a commodity, say, automobiles in the United States, differs from the one in the United Kingdom by a fixed percentage. The scale factor will be different from industry to industry, and as a result we find that the production possibility curves for any pair of countries and commodities are different. These different production possibility curves will influence the emerging international trade patterns in the manner discussed above.

Returns to Scale

Evidence on returns to scale is available in a large number of econometric studies of cross-section and time-series data of industries and countries. Most of the results of these studies were conveniently summarized by A. Walters.[5] Surveying twenty-two *industry* studies, utilizing cross-section data obtained from individual firms that constitute each industry (excluding agriculture), Walters found that the evidence for *constant* returns to scale is very strong. The same applies to twenty-five studies pertaining to agricultural commodities. In four studies of the production function for individual industries, utilizing time-series estimates, he found widely different results. Yet in most of these cases the statistical procedure employed is open to serious criticism, and the most that we can say is that the results from time-series industry studies are inconclusive.

In fourteen studies of aggregate production functions for different *countries*, using time series, Walters found the linearity of the returns to scale remarkably consistent between countries. The same result is found in twenty-eight cross-section studies for countries that used industry-wide data. Again this would add to the evidence in favor of constant returns to scale.

For the *world* as a whole, Earl Thompson[6] finds that nineteen industries studied on a country cross-section basis conform to the constant returns to scale hypothesis. This result supports the evidence in favor of constant returns to scale.

[4] Kenneth Arrow, H. Chenery, B. Minhas, and R. Solow, "Capital-Labor Substitution and Economic Efficiency," *Review of Economics and Statistics*, August 1961.

[5] Alan A. Walters, "Production and Cost Functions: An Econometric Survey," *Econometrica*, January–April 1963.

[6] Earl Thompson, "The Estimation of Returns to Scale with International Cross Section Data" (unpublished manuscript).

Factor Intensities

The Walters study also sheds some light on the question of the relative intensity with which different factors of production are used in different industries. Taking data from twenty-two nonagricultural industry studies utilizing individual firm data and fourteen time-series and twenty-eight cross-section studies for countries utilizing industry-wide data we find that the share of labor coefficient generally varies between five- and nine-tenths, although the share of capital coefficient varies between one- and five-tenths. In other words the intensity with which labor and capital are used in production varies widely between different industries. Specialized factors of production, then, should be an important component in the determination of the shape of the production possibility curve in different countries.

Factor Endowments and the Heckscher-Ohlin Theory

One of the most widely publicized empirical tests in economics was undertaken by Wassily Leontief[7] in order to examine the validity of the basic Heckscher-Ohlin model of the determination of the structure of international trade. On the basis of the Heckscher-Ohlin theory one can predict that a country will tend to export the commodity that is relatively (to the other commodity) intensive in the relatively (to the other country) abundant factor.

To test this prediction Leontief makes use of a 1947 input-output table for the United States. This table gives detailed information on the capital and labor requirements for the production of any commodity group. Because such a table was available for the United States only, Leontief had to resort to the United States import-competing industries to estimate the capital and labor requirements for the production of a given batch of imports rather than using the corresponding requirements in the country of origin as a basis for comparison. This procedure is legitimate only if production functions in the United States and abroad are identical. This is an assumption that the Heckscher-Ohlin theory makes in its most rudimentary form. Products that are not produced in the United States, such as coffee, tea, and jute, are excluded. The same is true of service industries that do not enter into international trade, such as trucking, railroad transportation, warehousing, retail trade, banking, and so on. Also it must be assumed that the composition of exports and imports stays constant over the range of variations studied.

[7] Wassily Leontief, "Domestic Production and Foreign Trade: The American Capital Position Re-examined," *Proceedings of the American Philosophical Society*, September 1953.

Leontief then computes the capital and labor requirements for the production of 1 million dollars worth of United States exports and import-competing commodities. The results are summarized in Table 4–5.

The United States is generally acknowledged to be the most capital abundant country in the world. Consequently the Heckscher-Ohlin theory predicts that the United States will tend to export commodities that are intensive in her abundant factor, namely, capital, while importing commodities that could be produced at home only by the intensive utilization of

TABLE 4–5

DOMESTIC CAPITAL AND LABOR REQUIREMENTS
FOR PRODUCTION OF $1 MILLION U.S. EXPORTS
AND IMPORTS

	Exports	Imports
Capital (1947 prices)	$2,550,780	$3,091,339
Labor (man-years)	182	170
Capital	$13,991	$18,184
Labor	man-year	man-year

Source: W. Leontief, "Domestic Production and Foreign Trade," *Proceedings of the American Philosophical Society*, September 1953. With permission of the author and publisher.

her scarce factor of production, labor. The Leontief results contradict this prediction, however, because the United States is shown to export commodities that use only $13,991 of capital per man-year of labor, while importing commodities that require $18,184 of capital per man-year. The data could be interpreted to show that the United States tries to economize on the factor of production capital by trading internationally. These statistics seem to indicate that the Heckscher-Ohlin theory does not yield satisfactory predictions about the direction of trade in this particular case.

Leontief-type tests have been conducted for a number of other countries. R. Bharadwaj[8] found that India tends to export labor-intensive and import capital-intensive commodities. However, in trading with the United States, the most capital abundant country, India is found to export capital-intensive commodities to the United States while importing labor-intensive commodities in return.

[8] R. Bharadwaj, *Structural Basis for India's Foreign Trade*, Bombay, 1962, and "Factor Proportions and the Structure of Indo-U.S. Trade," *Indian Economic Journal*, October 1962.

M. Tatemoto and S. Ichimura[9] found that Japan, whose main economic problem for decades has been her excess population, exports capital-intensive commodities to the rest of the world, while importing labor-intensive commodities. However, this pattern is reversed for trade between Japan and the United States alone, where Japan is shown to export labor-intensive commodities.

In the case of Canada D. F. Wahl[10] found that Canadian exports are capital intensive and imports labor intensive. As most of her trade is with the United States, this is contrary to what would be expected on the basis of pure theory.

Finally W. Stolper and K. Roskamp[11] have investigated the nature of East German exports and imports. Compared to the rest of Eastern Europe East Germany may be considered capital abundant. It was found that her exports are capital intensive and her imports labor intensive.

Of all the empirical studies undertaken only the cases of direct trade between Japan and the United States and between East Germany and Eastern Europe can be taken to confirm the predictions of the Heckscher-Ohlin theory. In all other studies we find that the empirical evidence contradicts the predictions based on the most elementary version of the theory. We can conclude that in its simplest form the Heckscher-Ohlin theory is not supported by empirical evidence.

It should be noted here that much criticism can be leveled against the tests referred to. Many other factors determining the direction of trade can be allowed for in more complete models, based on the simple Heckscher-Ohlin model discussed here. These more sophisticated arguments will be taken up in Chapter 6.

SUGGESTED FURTHER READINGS

ARROW, KENNETH, H. CHENERY, B. MINHAS, and R. SOLOW, "Capital-Labor Substitution and Economic Efficiency," *Review of Economics and Statistics* (August 1961).

CAVES, RICHARD, *Trade and Economic Structure*, pp. 23–36 and Chap. VI. Cambridge: Harvard University Press, 1960.

[9] M. Tatemoto and S. Ichimura, "Factor Proportions and Foreign Trade: The Case of Japan," *Review of Economics and Statistics*, November 1959.

[10] D. F. Wahl, "Capital and Labour Requirements for Canada's Foreign Trade," *Canadian Journal of Economics and Political Science*, August 1961.

[11] W. Stolper and K. Roskamp, "Input-Output Table for East Germany with Applications to Foreign Trade," *Bulletin of the Oxford Institute of Statistics*, November 1961.

CORDEN, W. M., "Recent Developments in the Theory of International Trade," *Special Papers in International Economics*, No. 7, Chap. II, International Finance Section, Princeton University, 1965.

HABERLER, GOTTFRIED, "A Survey of International Trade Theory," *Special Papers in International Economics*, No. 1, International Finance Section, Chap. III, Princeton University, 1961.

HECKSCHER, ELI, "The Effects of Foreign Trade on the Distribution of Income," *Economisk Tidskrift* (1919). Reprinted in *Readings in the Theory of International Trade*, eds. Howard S. Ellis and Lloyd A. Metzler, Chap. XIII. Philadelphia: The Blakiston Co., 1949.

JONES, RONALD W., "Factor Proportions and the Heckscher-Ohlin Theorem," *Review of Economic Studies* (1956–1957). Reprinted in *International Trade*, ed. Jagdish Bhagwati. Baltimore: Penguin Books, Inc., 1969.

LANCASTER, KELVIN, "The Heckscher-Ohlin Trade Model: A Geometric Treatment," *Economica* (1957). Reprinted in *International Trade*, ed. Jagdish Bhagwati. Baltimore: Penguin Books, Inc., 1969.

LEONTIEF, WASSILY, "Domestic Production and Foreign Trade: The American Capital Position Re-examined," *Proceedings of the American Philosophical Society* (September 1953). Reprinted in *International Trade*, ed. Jagdish Bhagwati. Baltimore: Penguin Books, Inc., 1969, and AEA *Readings in International Economics*, eds. Richard Caves and Harry G. Johnson. Homewood, Ill.: Richard D. Irwin, Inc., 1968.

MINHAS, B. S., "The Homohypallagic Production Function, Factor-Intensity Reversals and the Heckscher-Ohlin Theorem," *Journal of Political Economy* (1962). Reprinted in *International Trade*, ed. Jagdish Bhagwati. Baltimore: Penguin Books, Inc., 1969.

OHLIN, BERTIL, *Interregional and International Trade*. Cambridge: Harvard University Press, 1933.

ROBINSON, ROMNEY, "Factor Proportions and Comparative Advantage," *The Quarterly Journal of Economics* (1956). Reprinted in AEA *Readings in International Economics*, eds. Richard Caves and Harry G. Johnson. Homewood, Ill.: Richard D. Irwin, Inc., 1968.

RYBCZYNISKI, T. M., "Factor Endowment and Relative Commodity Prices," *Economica* (November 1955).

SAVOSNICK, KURT, "The Box Diagram and the Production Possibility Curve," *Economisk Tidskrift* (1958).

5

Consumption
and International Trade

Preference patterns can be expressed by the graphical technique of indifference curves, whose nature and properties are discussed in the Appendix. It may suffice here to say that an *indifference curve* is defined as the collection of all commodity combinations that will yield the same amount of satisfaction or utility to the consumer.

Indifference curves are defined for individual persons, and our first problem is to derive an aggregate indifference curve for all residents of a given country, often referred to as a *community indifference curve*. Such a community indifference curve may then be used to represent the preference pattern for the country as a whole and will also allow us to draw certain welfare conclusions if the country moves from one community indifference curve to another. As the community indifference curve is to be used for these important purposes, it is imperative that we scrutinize carefully its derivation and theoretical foundation.

COMMUNITY INDIFFERENCE CURVES

Derivation of Community Indifference Curves

To derive the community indifference curves from the indifference curve maps of individual consumers we will start the analysis with the case of two consumers: Mr. Alpha and Mr. Beta. This can be extended afterward to cover any number of individuals.

Figure 5–1 shows the indifference curve set for Mr. Alpha in its customary

72

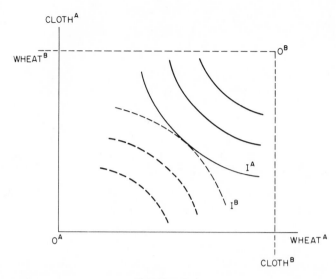

FIGURE 5–1

position. Quantities of the two commodities cloth and wheat are measured along the two axes. Superimposed on the diagram is Mr. Beta's coordinate system and indifference curve set (broken lines), but it is drawn upside down and the sides are reversed. Cloth for Mr. Beta is measured along the vertical axis but in the downward direction; wheat is measured along the horizontal axis in the leftward direction.

Now we arbitrarily pick two indifference curves that are tangent to each other, one for each consumer. Two such indifference curves might be I^A and I^B. At any point along one of these indifference curves the consumer experiences a constant level of utility. The tangency condition assures that no reallocation of resources could make one person better off without making the other one worse off. As far as the distribution of a given bundle of goods is concerned, the point of tangency represents an optimum.

It is now possible to slide the two indifference curves along each other in such a manner that the two coordinate systems always stay parallel to each other. This is done in Figure 5–2. The origin of Mr. Alpha's coordinate system, O^A, stays constant throughout this procedure. Initially the origin for Mr. Beta's coordinate system is located at O_P^B. Both persons consume quantities of cloth and wheat shown by point M, which is located on I^A and I_P^B respectively. Now we can move Mr. Beta's coordinate system and the indifference map belonging to it down and to the right. During this process we are careful to keep the two indifference curves I^A and I^B in a constant tangency position. One such new tangency position is shown by point N. At N both consumers are still on the same indifference curve as at M; however, the

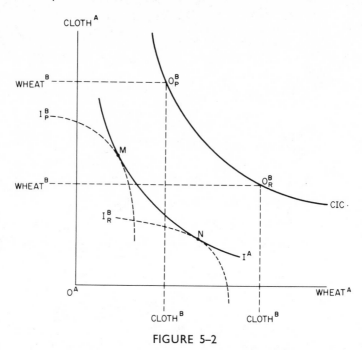

FIGURE 5–2

respective quantities of cloth and wheat consumed by each one of the persons has changed.

The *aggregate* quantities of cloth and wheat that both persons consume together is indicated by the respective points O^B with reference to the origin O^A. The moving point O^B (O^B_P, O^B_R, etc.) generates a path that shows the cloth/wheat combinations that are required to keep each one of the consumers on the same indifference curve. As each consumer individually stays on the same indifference curve during the process, the points generated by the moving origin describe commodity combinations between which the two consumers together are indifferent. The collection of all commodity combinations between which the consumers together are indifferent defines the *community indifference curve* (CIC) for these two consumers.

We can also draw some inferences about the *slope* of the community indifference curve. The slopes of the two individual indifference curves are equal to each other at point M (Figure 5–2). The marginal rates of substitution of cloth for wheat are the same for both consumers individually and, therefore, they also are the same as the rate for the two consumers together. Thus the slope of the community indifference curve of Mr. Alpha and Mr. Beta at point O^B_P is the same as the slope of the individual indifference curves at M. The same holds true for the slope of the community indifference curve at O^B_R and the individual indifference curves at N.

We are able to extend this analysis to any number of persons by sliding the indifference curves of successive individuals along the community indifference curve for Mr. Alpha and Mr. Beta. Any desired number of individual indifference curves can be added in this fashion.

A community indifference curve depicts all commodity combinations that will yield constant utility to the members of the community—individually and jointly.

Problems Associated with Community Indifference Curves

In Figure 5–3 we show two indifference curves that are tangent at point L. By sliding the indifference curves I_0^B and I_1^A along each other we generate the community indifference curve CIC_L. If we had picked instead the two indifference curves through point M, I_0^A and I_1^B, we would have generated the different community indifference curve CIC_M. Note that the initial total endowment of cloth and wheat is the same in both cases; the only difference is the *distribution* of cloth and wheat between Mr. Alpha and Mr. Beta. It is

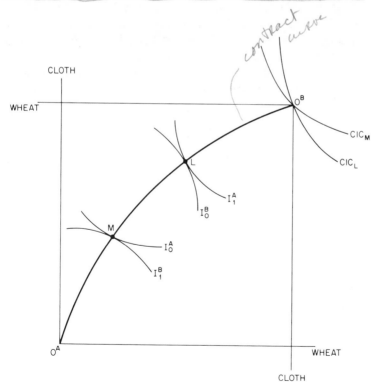

FIGURE 5–3

easily seen that because the slope of the common tangency of the two indifference curves at L is different from the one at M, the community indifference curves corresponding to the two income distributions have different slopes. More community indifference curves through point O^B with still different slopes can be generated by changing the income distribution anywhere along the contract curve $O^A MLO^B$.

We are able to derive by this method an infinite number of community indifference curves through point O^B. This, however, leads to an inconsistency. On the one hand we can say that a commodity combination represented by point O^B will yield a certain level of welfare; on the other hand we have different indifference curves through this point, and different indifference curves denote different levels of welfare. Only one of these two propositions can be true. Our results imply that changes in income distribution will lead to different community indifference curves or that the community indifference map is *not* independent of the income distribution within the community.

The dependence of the community indifference curve on the society's income distribution is explained by the fact that the utility measure used is *ordinal*. Ordinal utility allows only for "better than" or "worse than" comparisons but does not permit any statement of the numerical size of the utility gains or losses. Thus it is impossible to judge the net effect on society's utility level of a change that is due to an improvement in one person's utility and is accompanied by a decrease in another person's utility. This limitation of the analysis can cause community indifference curves to be inconsistent.

Justifications for Community Indifference Curves

Due to the importance of community indifference curves in analyzing the determination of equilibrium in international trade as well as for deriving welfare conclusions about the effects of free and restricted trade, it is worthwhile to make an effort to salvage the concept of community indifference curves for economic theory. There are various sets of assumptions that will permit the derivation of uniquely determined community indifference curves. Although all justifications presented are objectionable on certain grounds, it is still possible to see how closely the assumptions are actually approximated by real world conditions.

1. *One Inhabitant.* The simplest and most trivial justification of community indifference curves is that the entire population of the country in question is composed of a single individual. Robinson Crusoe on his island might serve as an illustration.

2. *Benevolent Dictator.* If there exists a benevolent dictator whose decisions reflect the preferences of the population, he may define a single set

of communal preferences. This uniquely defined preference set would have all the properties that individual preference sets have.

✳   *3. Same Incomes and Tastes.*   If all residents of the country have the same taste patterns and income levels, we are able to derive a single set of nonintersecting community indifference curves. The assumption of identical tastes is not altogether unreasonable, considering the general conformity created by the similarity of climate and cultural patterns that prevail among the residents of the same country. The assumption of identical incomes assures that all individuals are actually able to attain the same indifference curve. This can be achieved only through a completely egalitarian distribution. Specifying the income distribution excludes the possibility of intersecting community indifference curves. Furthermore it means that the community indifference curves are nothing but a blown-up version of the individual indifference curves.

✳ *4. Same Tastes and Homothetic Indifference Curves.*   The assumption of identical taste patterns and homothetic[1] indifference curves also allows us to draw up nonintersecting community indifference curves. The identical tastes assumption has already been discussed under 3. above.

Homothetic indifference curves are characterized by the fact that consumers, confronted with a certain set of relative prices, will buy the same proportion of the commodities, irrespective of their income level. The combination of the two assumptions assures that the contract curve in the box diagram showing two consumers will always be a diagonal straight line. Because of the homotheticity assumption all marginal rates of substitution along the contract curve are the same, irrespective of income distribution. It follows that the slope of the community indifference curve is uniquely determined. Intersecting community indifference curves are thus ruled out.

✳ *5. Same Incomes and Homothetic Indifference Curves.*   If all individuals have identical initial endowments (income), we know that they will start at the midpoint of the diagonal O^AO^B shown in Figure 5–4, which is labelled E. If we deal with homothetic indifference curves, for which the slope along any ray from the origin is the same, then there will be a unique point on the contract curve that will be reached if both individuals maximize their utility. This point is labelled F. Note that the homotheticity assumption ensures that the tangents to all indifference curves to the left of point F, such as shown by G, will be flatter than the price line PP. Hence these points cannot lie on the same price line as point E. Similarly to the right of point F the

---

[1] For the definition of *homothetic* see Appendix, page 224.

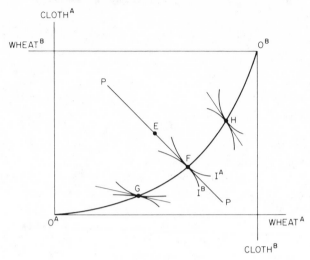

FIGURE 5-4

tangents will be steeper than PP, excluding again point E as the possible initial endowment from which a point such as H might be reached. We reach a unique point on the contract curve and thereby identify a unique, non-intersecting community indifference curve.

To summarize: Sections 3. through 5. showed that *any two* of the following three conditions will yield uniquely determined community indifference curves: identical tastes, identical incomes, or homogeneous indifference curves.

6. *Optimal Income Redistribution.* There is one other assumption that will allow us to justify the use of community indifference curves: it requires that the social utility of the last dollar of income be the same for all individuals. National income is distributed so that no reallocation of earnings could increase the recipient's welfare by more than it would decrease the welfare of individuals losing these earnings. From the standpoint of society as a whole income would be distributed in an optimal fashion because everybody derives the same marginal benefit from the last dollar he earns. Any deviation from the socially optimal income distribution has to be corrected by compensation payments by the gainers to the losers. The aggregate level of utility for society as a whole is not changed, because gainers are always compensating losers, and the original utility level can be maintained. The compensation payments assure that we move along one community indifference curve independent of the income distribution.[2]

[2] For a proof of this proposition, see Paul A. Samuelson, "Social Indifference Curves," *Quarterly Journal of Economics*, February 1956.

DIRECTION OF TRADE

In this section we will investigate the effects of different consumption patterns on international trade. To isolate the role of consumption we will assume throughout that the conditions of production are identical in all countries concerned. This assumption will be relaxed in Chapter 6, where we will analyze the conditions of general equilibrium.

A country in isolation has to produce all the commodities she wants to consume herself. The optimal commodity combination is defined by the con-

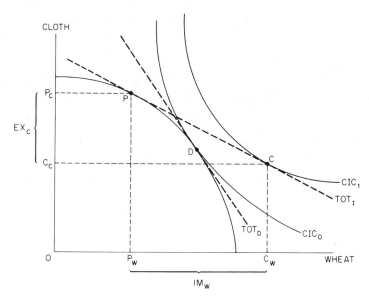

FIGURE 5–5

dition of equality of the marginal rates of substitution in consumption and the marginal rates of transformation in production for all commodity pairs. The equilibrium domestic exchange ratio is given by the slope of the tangent at the point at which the highest community indifference curve touches the production possibility curve. (For a more detailed review see Appendix.) Such a point of domestic equilibrium is given by point D in Figure 5–5, and the exchange ratio is shown by the slope of the line TOT_D.

If the country has the option of trading internationally at a given international exchange ratio (terms of trade) TOT_I, she will rearrange her consumption and production patterns accordingly. At this juncture we are not concerned with the determination of the international terms of trade themselves, and we will simply assume that they are given to the country.

The optimal production pattern for the country is attained when the marginal rate of transformation in production is equal to the international terms of trade. Under these conditions the country produces a commodity bundle that has the maximum possible value in international markets. Such an optimal production point, given the terms of trade TOT_I, is shown by point P in Figure 5–5. The possibility of trade at the international terms of trade will allow the country to modify the commodity bundle that it produces to suit domestic consumption patterns by exchanging some of the commodities produced against other commodities. Thus it is no longer necessary for the production pattern to coincide with the consumption pattern. The country will alter the composition of her commodity bundle until the highest possible community indifference curve is reached thereby attaining the greatest possible level of utility for the residents of the country. This condition is fulfilled when the marginal rate of substitution in consumption is equal to the international terms of trade. The community indifference curve CIC_1 is tangent at this point (point C in Figure 5–5) to the international terms of trade line TOT_I.

The modification of the commodity bundle produced (point P) into the commodity bundle consumed (point C) involves international exchange. The country will produce P_C of cloth and consume only C_C of it. It will also produce P_W of wheat yet want to consume C_W. In order to maintain the optimal production and consumption patterns the country will export $P_C C_C$ of cloth in return for which it receives $C_W P_W$ of wheat imports.

DETERMINATION OF INTERNATIONAL PRICES

To show the determination of the international exchange ratio we have to introduce a second country into our analysis. The two countries are assumed to have identical production possibility curves and different demand patterns. Two such countries, the United States and the United Kingdom, are depicted in Figure 5–6. The United States is shown to have a preference for wheat and the United Kingdom prefers cloth. After trade opens up the two countries will both produce at the same point on the production possibility curve, no matter what the consumption pattern. This is due to the fact that international exchange will result in a common set of terms of trade, represented by the line TOT. Because the two production possibility curves are identical, they can be tangent to the international terms of trade only at the same point. This point is the production point for both countries and is shown as point $P^{US,UK}$ on the graph.

However, the two countries have different preference patterns, and the

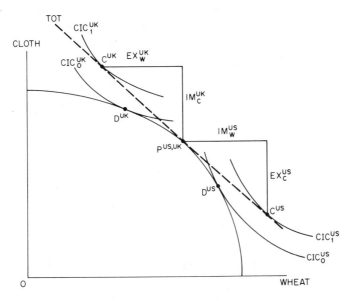

FIGURE 5-6

community indifference curves will therefore be tangent to the international terms of trade line at different points. Two possible equilibrium consumption points are shown by points C^{US} and C^{UK}.

If the terms of trade are to be equilibrium terms of trade, international trade must be balanced, meaning that the quantity of wheat that the United States wants to import must be exactly equal to the quantity of wheat that the United Kingdom wants to export. The reverse must hold true for cloth. Unless these conditions are met there will be forces set up that will tend to change the international terms of trade until equilibrium is restored.

Such a disequilibrium situation is shown in Figure 5-7. Here the quantity of cloth imports demanded by Britain exceeds the quantity of cloth exports supplied by the United States at the prevailing terms of trade. The reverse applies to wheat. There will be an excess demand for cloth and an excess supply of wheat. As a consequence the price of cloth will tend to rise while the price of wheat will tend to fall. Thus a smaller quantity of cloth will exchange for a given quantity of wheat. In the graph this price change would be represented by a counterclockwise rotation of the terms of trade line. The rotation will continue until all excess demands and supplies are eliminated, meaning that equilibrium has been restored.

In equilibrium the following conditions are fulfilled: (1) the marginal rate of substitution and the marginal rate of transformation are both equal to the international terms of trade, and (2) the quantities of the commodities traded are equal to each other.

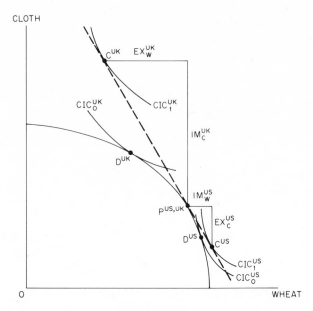

FIGURE 5–7

Trade will emerge when, irrespective of production costs, the domestic price ratios are different. A country will export (import) the commodity that is, relative to the other commodity, cheaper (more expensive) at home than abroad.

DEMAND REVERSALS

Clearly the pattern of trade depends both on the shape of the production possibility curve and the community indifference curves. Now the possibility arises that demand patterns reverse the direction of trade to be expected on the basis of cost considerations alone. This happens when residents of the country have a very strong preference for the commodity in which the country would otherwise enjoy a comparative advantage. In our example this would be the case if Americans have a strong preference for wheat and residents of the United Kingdom have a strong liking for cloth. If this is the case, the trade patterns that we might expect based on cost considerations alone may be reversed. Because extreme demand conditions play a crucial role, this case is referred to as a *demand reversal*.

Such a demand reversal is illustrated in Figures 5–8 and 5–9 where we show different increasing cost production possibility curves for the United States and the United Kingdom and draw the community indifference curves in such a way as to give expression to the strong American liking for wheat and British desire for cloth. As can be easily seen the trade patterns will

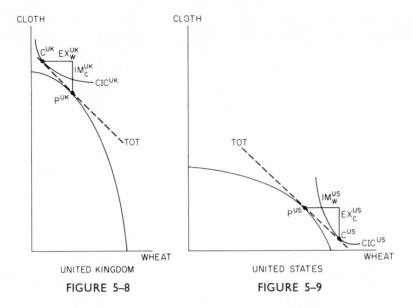

FIGURE 5–8   FIGURE 5–9

be reversed under these circumstances, with the United States exporting cloth and the United Kingdom exporting wheat. (Compare to Figures 3–12 and 3–13, where we show the normal case.)

As a practical example we might think of automobiles being imported into the United States in spite of the fact that we might have a comparative advantage based on cost considerations alone. But Americans have such a strong liking for automobiles that they will import Ferraris, Porsches, and Toyotas. Conversely countries in Asia that are able to produce rice at low cost will import additional quantities to satisfy the high demand for rice by their residents.

Of course there also exists the possiblity that domestic pretrade exchange ratios in the two countries are equal. In that case no trade will result, and both countries will remain self-sufficient.

Demand reversals may change the direction of trade to be expected on the basis of cost considerations alone.

THE OFFER CURVE

The construction of the equilibrium terms of trade presented in the previous section is rather cumbersome as it involves the constant adjustment of the terms of trade until a position is reached where the quantities traded balance. It is convenient to introduce here a tool of analysis that will allow us to determine the equilibrium terms of trade more directly and with greater precision. Because in this chapter we focus attention on the effects of consumption patterns on international trade, we will assume that each country is endowed with a certain fixed commodity combination. The way in which this initial commodity combination is obtained is of no immediate interest to us.

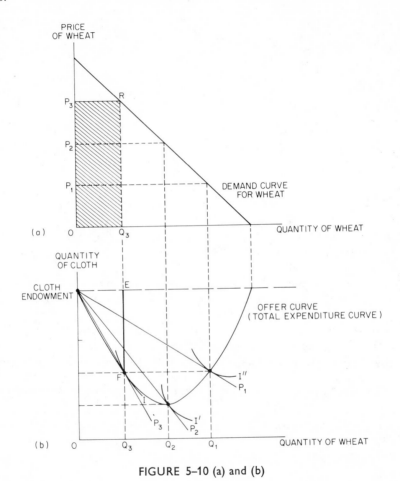

FIGURE 5–10 (a) and (b)

Figure 5–10a shows the familiar demand curve for wheat. We define the price of cloth as one. Given the price P_3 for wheat, people will demand the quantity Q_3. The total expenditures on the commodity are shown by the crosshatched area OP_3RQ_3. If there are only two commodities, this means that this country is willing to spend (or offer) OP_3RQ_3 of cloth for wheat. This information can also be seen in the lower part of the diagram.

In Figure 5–10b we show the quantity of cloth along the vertical axis and the quantity of wheat along the horizontal axis. Given the price of wheat (in terms of cloth) indicated by the price line P_3, the country will be willing to give up EF of cloth in exchange for OQ_3 of wheat. The *area* OP_3RQ_3 in Figure 5–10a is equal to the *distance* EF in Figure 5–10b.

Note that point F is depicted as an equilibrium point, given the price line P_3. This must mean, however, that a wheat/cloth indifference curve (indifference curve I in Figure 5–10b) is tangent to the price line at point F. Only then would point F be the most preferred point anywhere along P_3.

Similarly given any other price of wheat, such as P_1 or P_2, we are able to find the quantity of wheat demanded at that price and the quantity of cloth offered in exchange. Given any price ratio, the amounts of cloth offered in exchange for wheat delineate the *offer curve* for the country in question. The offer curve may also be described as the line connecting all points at which an indifference curve is tangent to a price line.

OFFER CURVES AND INTERNATIONAL PRICE DETERMINATION

To show the determination of the terms of trade between two trading partners, we must reintroduce the United Kingdom into our analysis.

In Figure 5–11 we reproduce the offer curve diagram from Figure 5–10b for the United States. In the same figure we also show the offer curve diagram for the United Kingdom, but it is shown upside down and with the sides reversed. The origin for the coordinate system of the United Kingdom is labeled O^{UK}, wheat is measured in the horizontal direction to the left, and cloth in the vertical direction downward. The offer curve of the United Kingdom is labeled OC^{UK}.

Note that the United States has an initial cloth endowment of AO^{US}, and the United Kingdom has an initial wheat endowment of AO^{UK}. Both countries are willing to modify their initial commodity bundle by exchanging any commodity combination that is located on their offer curve. By trading they try to reach the highest possible community indifference curve for each country.

Given the way the offer curves are drawn, there is only one point at which the quantities that the two countries want to exchange are consistent with each other. This is the point of intersection of the two offer curves: point B. This point determines the terms of trade TOT. The United States wants to export AC_B of cloth in exchange for BC_B of wheat, while the United Kingdom wants to export AW_B of wheat in exchange for BW_B of cloth. The quantities that the two countries wish to exchange at this set of terms of trade match exactly, and the international markets will be cleared at this price ratio.

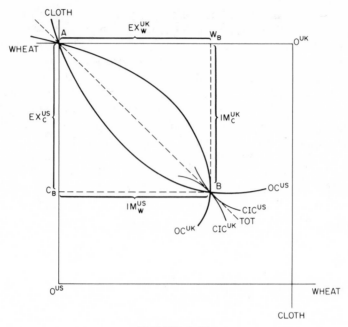

FIGURE 5–11

Any other terms of trade line will lead to surpluses or shortages in international markets, and market forces will tend to restore equilibrium. A detailed discussion of the stability of equilibrium is deferred to Chapter 6.

The intersection of the offer curves of the two countries determines the equilibrium terms of trade. The quantities of the two commodities that the countries wish to exchange will match exactly.

EMPIRICAL EVIDENCE

In this chapter we have demonstrated how different demand patterns in different countries can theoretically constitute a cause for the emergence of international trade, even if the production possibilities of the countries involved are identical. Consequently it is important to know whether demand patterns in different countries tend to be sufficiently different to account for the emergence of international trade.

In his survey of household expenditure patterns Hendrik Houthakker[3]

---

[3] Hendrik S. Houthakker, "An International Comparison of Household Expenditure Patterns, Commemorating the Centenary of Engel's Law," *Econometrica*, October 1957.

found that the income elasticities of the demand for different commodity classes—such as food, clothing, housing, and other expenditures—were similar but not identical between different countries. The income elasticities for food consumption ranged generally between .3 and .7; those for clothing, between 1.0 and 1.5; those for housing were usually slightly less than 1.0; and those for other expenditures were generally above 1.4. Thus the expenditure patterns in different countries varied, but the variation is—perhaps surprisingly—small. National differences in climate, cultural patterns, and social organization are apparently not large enough to cause significantly different income elasticities between countries. Within the same country expenditure patterns were found to be very similar.

Other studies[4] of expenditure patterns shed more light on the relationship between income and expenditures on consumption. It is generally found that the percentage of food expenditures declines as the income level goes up. A semilogarithmic function seems to explain the relationship between income and food expenditures rather well. On the other hand most other commodities are best characterized by a double-logarithmic function.

Although it is true that income *elasticities* do not vary greatly between countries, we can conclude that countries with widely different per capita income *levels* will typically exhibit dissimilar demand patterns. In addition demand will be a fairly important factor in the determination of the structure of international trade between countries with different per capita income levels, although for countries with similar per capita income levels it will be of minor importance. Of course demand is only one factor determining the direction of trade.

SUGGESTED FURTHER READINGS

BAUMOL, WILLIAM, "The Community Indifference Map," *Review of Economic Studies* (1949-1950).

CAVES, RICHARD, *Trade and Economic Structure*, Chap. VII. Cambridge: Harvard University Press, 1960.

HOUTHAKKER, HENDRIK, "An International Comparison of Household Expenditure Patterns," *Econometrica* (October 1957).

LEONTIEF, WASSILY, "The Use of Indifference Curves in the Analysis of Foreign Trade," *Quarterly Journal of Economics* (May 1933). Reprinted in *International Trade*, ed. Jagdish Bhagwati. Baltimore: Penguin Books, Inc., 1969.

[4] S. J. Prais and H. S. Houthakker, *The Analysis of Family Budgets* (Cambridge: Harvard University Press, 1955).

LERNER, ABBA, "The Diagrammatical Representation of Demand Conditions in International Trade," *Economica* (August 1934).

SAMUELSON, PAUL A., "Social Indifference Curves," *Quarterly Journal of Economics* (February 1956).

VANEK, JAROSLAV, *International Trade: Theory and Economic Policy*, Chap. XIII. Homewood, Ill.: Richard D. Irwin, Inc., 1962.

6

Equilibrium
in International Trade

In this chapter we will consider the interaction of the different variables that were discussed in the previous chapters in determining international equilibrium. The analysis of the previous chapters was limited in the sense that we were holding constant some of the variables affecting international equilibrium in order to allow us to analyze the influence of the other variables step by step. We are now ready to assemble the individual building blocks and to analyze the model in general equilibrium terms, considering the interaction of all the variables at once.

CONSUMPTION, PRODUCTION, AND INTERNATIONAL TRADE

As we showed at the end of the previous chapter it is possible that in countries where there are differences *both* in consumption and cost patterns among commodities, demand patterns tend to make one commodity the export commodity, and production cost patterns tend to make the other commodity the export commodity. Which of the two commodities will actually be exported and which will be imported will depend on the relative strength of the effects. Naturally it is also possible for the two effects to work in the same direction thus reinforcing each other. The net result cannot be predicted from either the community indifference curves or the production possibility curves for the two countries in isolation.

In Figure 6–1 we show the production possibility curves for both the United Kingdom and the United States. Only the final equilibrium situation

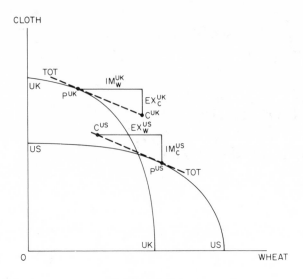

FIGURE 6–1

is shown, where the United Kingdom consumes and produces at points C^{UK} and P^{UK} respectively, while the United States is at points C^{US} and P^{US}. The amounts traded are indicated by the vertical and horizontal differences between the consumption and production points for each of the two countries. The international terms of trade are shown tangent to the production possibility curve and an indifference curve for each country. The terms of trade lines are parallel, indicating that one common world exchange ratio has been established.

The construction employed is rather cumbersome, and it takes a lot of trying before a set of equilibrium terms of trade can be found at which the quantities that the two countries wish to export and import match exactly. Our next task, therefore, will be to adapt the offer curve technique to the problem of general equilibrium in international markets. This will allow us to condense the relevant information contained in the community indifference curves and the production possibility curve.

THE INTERNATIONAL TRADE OFFER CURVE

To derive a technique allowing us to depict the various amounts of international trade that a country is willing to undertake at different terms of trade we must first find the foreign trade indifference curves for the country concerned.

The Trade Indifference Curve

The tool that enables us to summarize the information contained in the domestic community indifference curves and production possibility curves is the *foreign trade indifference curve*. This new construct shows the different amounts of foreign trade, that is, export-import combinations, that will yield the same level of utility to one country. In other words it is the collection of all foreign trade combinations to which the country is indifferent.

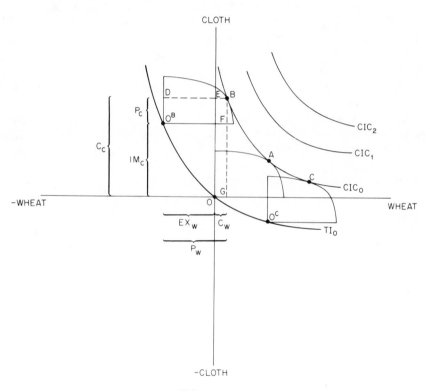

FIGURE 6–2

In Figure 6–2 we show the coordinate system for the country under consideration. In the horizontal direction we measure quantities of wheat, with points to the left of the origin indicating negative quantities of wheat. Similarly the vertical axis measures quantities of cloth, with points below the origin indicating negative quantities. A set of community indifference curves is drawn in the customary position in the northeastern quadrant. The production possibility curve is also shown and is tangent to the highest possible community indifference curve at point A, which describes the production and consumption pattern for the country in isolation.

Now it is possible to slide the production possibility curve along the community indifference curve CIC_0 so that the country will remain on the utility level it is able to reach in isolation. This is done in such a fashion that the production possibility curve always stays tangent to the community indifference curve CIC_0. Note, too, that the coordinate system with reference to which the production possibility curve is drawn is shifted together with the production possibility curve. The points A, B, and C in Figure 6–2 are points of tangency between the sliding production possibility curve and the community indifference curve CIC_0. It is important to keep the coordinates of the shifting production possibility curve always parallel to the original coordinate system.

Let us single out one possible position of the production possibility curve and analyze the production, consumption, and trade patterns that it implies. If the production possibility curve is tangent to the community indifference curve CIC_0 at point B, the country will consume OG of wheat and OE of cloth. Note that all quantities *produced* are measured with reference to the *new origin* of the production possibility curve, namely, point O^B. The country produces now DB of wheat and BF of cloth. It is clear that the country produces too large a quantity of wheat and too small a quantity of cloth to reconcile production and consumption. As consumption and production are not identical, this country will have to engage in foreign trade to make her consumption and production patterns consistent. This adjustment can be accomplished by exporting DE of wheat and importing FG of cloth in exchange. Note that although the wheat exports are measured in the negative direction, indicating that we give up this commodity, the cloth imports are measured in the positive direction, indicating that we supplement our domestic production by imports. Because the points A, B, and C lie on the same indifference curve as point P, the country is indifferent between the three positions.

By sliding the production possibility curve along the community indifference curve CIC_0 we are now able to generate a whole series of points (O^C, O, and O^B) that show combinations of exports and imports between which the country is indifferent in the sense that all of them will enable the country to reach the same utility level. The line connecting all points of indifference between different amounts of international trade to be undertaken is the *trade indifference curve* (TI_0).

In a similar fashion we are now able to derive a whole set of trade indifference curves, each one corresponding to a different level of utility for the residents of the country. Each one of these trade indifference curves is generated by the same process of sliding the production possibility curve along a community indifference curve and letting the origin of the production possibility curve's coordinate system trace out the trade indifference curve. In Figure 6–3 we show a set of trade indifference curves generated in the manner

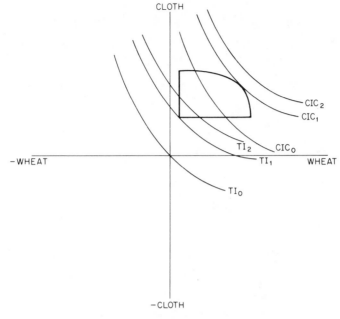

FIGURE 6-3

described. One such curve, TI_1, was obtained by sliding the production possibility curve along the community indifference curve CIC_1.

A trade indifference curve shows all export-import combinations that, given a production possibility curve, will allow the country to reach a certain community indifference curve thus permitting her to maintain a constant level of utility.

Slope of the Trade Indifference Curve

A direct relationship exists between the slope of the community indifference curve, the production possibility curve, and the trade indifference curve. These relationships are illustrated in Figure 6-4. Consider the shift of the production possibility curve from tangency position R to tangency position P. The origin of the production possibility curve moves from point T to point S, involving greater imports of e of cloth and greater exports of f of wheat. The consumption pattern will change from point R to point P, resulting in increased cloth consumption of b and decreased wheat consumption of a. At the same time the production pattern is being rearranged. From production pattern R, measured with reference to origin T, we change to production pattern P with reference to origin S. To allow for better comparison the location of production point P is also shown with reference to origin T. This

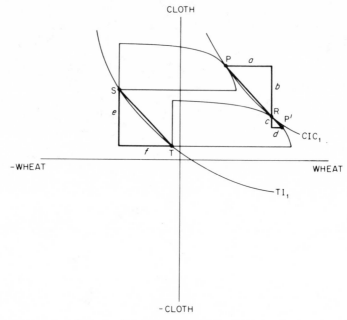

FIGURE 6–4

point is labeled P'. The rearrangement of production patterns involves in this case a movement from point R to point P' (measured in the same coordinate system), resulting in a decreased cloth production of c and an increased wheat production of d.

The total increase in cloth imports of e is due to (1) an increase in cloth consumption by b and (2) a decrease in cloth production of c. The total increase in wheat exports of f is made possible by (1) a decrease of wheat consumption of a and (2) an increase in wheat production of d. Therefore it holds that:

$$b + c = e \quad \text{and} \quad a + d = f$$

A line between P and P' would be parallel to ST. But PP' is made up of the two segments PR and RP'. If we talk about very small, or infinitesimally small, shifts in the production possibility curve, we find that the slopes of the lines PR and RP' tend to approximate the slope of the straight line PP'. Also the slope of PR and RP' will approximate the slope of the tangency at these points. For very small shifts of the production possibility curve we can therefore conclude that the slope of the community indifference curve is equal to the slope of the production possibility curve, which is also equal to the slope of the trade indifference curve.

At "corresponding" points on the community indifference curve, the production possibility curve, and the trade indifference curve, it holds that the marginal rate of substitution in consumption is equal to the marginal rate of transformation in production is equal to the marginal rate of export-import substitution.

From the Trade Indifference Curve
to the Trade Offer Curve

An *offer curve* shows the various quantities of two commodities that the economic unit wishes to exchange, given different prices. That is, for each

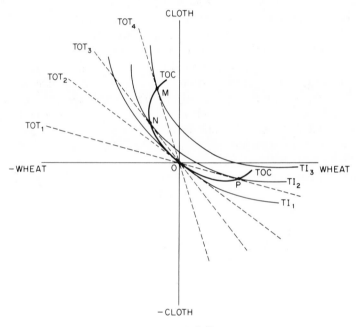

FIGURE 6–5

and every price the offer curve shows how much of one commodity the economic unit—here a country—is willing to exchange against how much of the other commodity. We will apply this concept now to international exchange, allowing for a rearrangement of both production and consumption patterns at once.

In Figure 6–5 we show a set of trade indifference curves and different terms of trade. Given the terms of trade TOT_2 the highest possible trade indifference curve that the country can reach is TI_1. The point of tangency is the origin O. Given the terms of trade TOT_3 and TOT_4 the country is able to attain tangency positions to TI_2 and TI_3 at points N and M respectively.

All the points of tangency of a trade indifference curve to a given terms of trade line show the optimal export-import pattern for the country. This optimal pattern will allow the country to reach the highest utility level consistent with her consumption and production patterns as well as with her trading opportunities. The collection of all points denoting the optimal trade pattern for each possible terms of trade is the *international trade offer curve*. The line through point M, N, O, and P shows such a trade offer curve (TOC).

Given any set of trade indifference curves we are able to derive a trade offer curve by finding the trade patterns that will allow the country to attain the highest possible utility level under all possible terms of trade.

The trade offer curve is a helpful tool in international trade analysis because it allows us to tell at a glance the different commodity combinations a country is willing to trade at any given exchange ratio. For this reason we find the trade offer curve often referred to as a "willingness to trade curve." It also shows the total expenditures (exports in our case) of one commodity that a country is willing to make at any given exchange ratio in order to obtain a certain quantity of the other commodity (here, imports). Therefore it gets the name "total expenditure curve." Finally the curve shows the demand for each commodity in terms of the other commodity, hence the name "reciprocal demand curve."

The usefulness and applicability of the tool to a wide variety of problems is foreshadowed by this long list of names, which directs our attention to the different purposes for which the trade offer curve can be used.

Elasticity of the Trade Offer Curve

In this section we will derive a geometric measure for the demand elasticity of the trade offer curve. It is very easy to make a statement about the elasticity of the trade offer curve. Let us remind ourselves first of the elementary definition of elasticity. A demand curve for a commodity is called elastic if a lowering of the price of that commodity results in an increase of expenditures on the good. It is unit elastic if total expenditures stay constant and inelastic if total expenditures fall in response to a fall in price.

In Figure 6–6 we show the trade offer curve of a country that imports cloth and pays for these cloth imports with wheat exports. Hence our expenditures are measured in terms of wheat exports. Note that cloth imports are measured along the positive part of the ordinate in Figure 6–6, and wheat exports are indicated along the negative portion of the abscissa.

The trade offer curve is elastic as long as total wheat exports (or expenditures) increase as the quantity of cloth imported increases subsequent to a fall in the relative price of cloth. In Figure 6–6 this is true in the range between

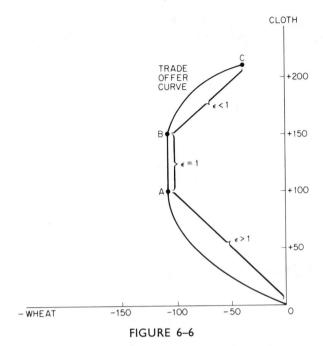

FIGURE 6–6

O and A. Expenditures in terms of wheat exports stay constant at one hundred units in the range AB, indicating unitary elasticity of the demand for cloth imports. Finally in the range BC the trade offer curve is inelastic because increasing quantities of cloth can be had for smaller and smaller total expenditures in terms of wheat exports. When we remember that the trade offer curve is also called the total expenditure curve, the elasticity definition becomes immediately clear. Also it is important to keep in mind that it is expenditures in terms of wheat exports that we incur to pay for the cloth imports demanded.

TABLE 6–1

THE ELASTICITY OF THE TRADE OFFER CURVE

Range	If Cloth Price Falls, Total Expenditures in Terms of Wheat	Elasticity of Trade Offer Curve
OA	Increase	Elastic
AB	Stay constant	Unitary
BC	Decrease	Inelastic

We may now derive formally the elasticity measure of the demand for cloth imports. Let us define:

C   The quantity of cloth imports demanded
W   The quantity of wheat exports supplied
W/C   The price of cloth, expressed in number of wheat units to be paid for one unit of cloth
ϵ The elasticity of the trade offer curve

We know that the elasticity is given by the percentage change in quantity demanded over the percentage change in price.

$$(6\text{–}1) \qquad \epsilon = \frac{dQ/Q}{dP/P} = \frac{dC/C}{d\left(\dfrac{W}{C}\right)\Big/\left(\dfrac{W}{C}\right)}$$

Expanding by W/C we obtain

$$\epsilon = \frac{dC}{C}\cdot\frac{W}{C}\Big/ d\left(\frac{W}{C}\right) = \frac{W\cdot dC}{C^2}\Big/ d\left(\frac{W}{C}\right) = \frac{W\cdot dC}{C^2}\Big/ \frac{C\cdot dW - WdC}{C^2} =$$

$$(6\text{–}2) \quad \epsilon = \frac{WdC}{CdW - WdC} = \frac{1}{(C/W)(dW/dC) - 1}$$

We may now interpret Equation (6–2) in terms of Figure 6–7. Measuring the elasticity of the trade offer curve at point E we find that C/W corresponds to EH/HO. Also dW/dC is equal to HK/EH. Substituting these new terms into Equation (6–2) we obtain:

$$(6\text{–}3) \quad \epsilon = \frac{1}{(EH/HO)(HK/EH) - 1} = \frac{1}{\dfrac{HK}{HO} - 1} = \frac{1}{\dfrac{HK - HO}{HO}} = \frac{1}{\dfrac{KO}{HO}}$$

and

$$(6\text{–}4) \qquad\qquad\qquad \epsilon = \frac{HO}{KO}$$

Hence in order to derive the point elasticity of a trade offer curve at any point, say E, we have to first draw a line through point E perpendicular to the horizontal axis and mark the point H. Then we have to draw a tangent to the trade offer curve at E and mark the point at which this line cuts the horizontal axis K. The measure HO/KO gives the elasticity of the trade offer curve at

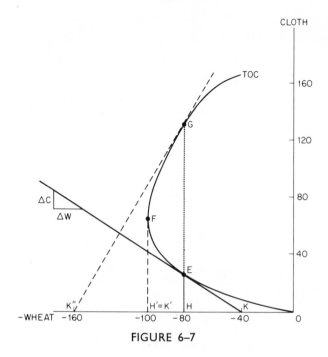

FIGURE 6–7

point E. In Figure 6–7 the trade offer curve at E is clearly elastic. Our numerical elasticity formula (6–4) yields an elasticity figure of $\epsilon = HO/KO = 80/40 = 2$ at point E.

In the same manner we are able to derive the elasticity at alternate points, such as F and G. At F the elasticity formula yields: $\epsilon = H'O/K'O = 100/100 = 1$, the unitary elasticity of the vertical trade offer curve. At G we obtain $\epsilon = HO/K''O = 80/160 = \frac{1}{2}$, the inelastic number to be expected in the backward bending part of the trade offer curve.

The simple geometric device of drawing a tangent and dropping a line perpendicular to the horizontal axis allows us to evaluate the elasticity of a trade offer curve. The elasticity of the offer curve will become important in connection with the stability conditions of equilibria for the terms of trade.

Also for the country under consideration the elasticity of its trade offer curve is of great importance. It shows the policy makers how exports and imports will behave if the country is faced with a change in the terms of trade. The desired export performance is especially important in this context. If the offer curve is elastic, this means that additional imports will have to be paid for by a greater quantity of exports. If, however, the country should have an inelastic offer curve, changes in the terms of trade will allow the country to import a *larger* quantity of cloth in exchange for an absolutely *smaller* quantity of wheat exports.

THE TERMS OF TRADE

Equilibrium Terms of Trade

We have shown the quantities of the two commodities that one country is willing to trade as the collection of all points on the trade offer curve. To

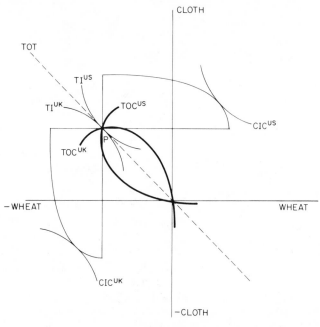

FIGURE 6-8

show which particular set of terms of trade will lead to equilibrium in international markets we have to introduce a second country, say, the United Kingdom.

In Figure 6–8 we draw the United Kingdom domestic indifference curve set in the lower left quadrant, exactly opposite the United States domestic indifference curve set, which lies as usual in the upper right quadrant. Utilizing the same technique we developed for the derivation of the United States trade indifference curves we now derive the United Kingdom trade indifference curves. After drawing in the trade offer curves for both countries, TOC^{US} for the United States and TOC^{UK} for the United Kingdom, we are able to derive point P as the point of intersection of the trade offer curves for the two countries. At point P we will have an international trade equilibrium. The following conditions are fulfilled at this point: (1) we have one common exchange ratio of the two commodities as indicated by the terms of trade line TOT; (2) both countries have attained the highest possible trade indifference curve consistent with these terms of trade; and (3) the cloth imports by the United States are exactly equal to the exports of the same commodity by the United Kingdom, and the wheat exports by the United States are equal to the imports of the same commodity by the United Kingdom. With these offer curves any other set of relative prices would result in different terms of trade, and at these different terms of trade one country would prefer to export more of a commodity than the other country would want to import, and vice versa. Such a situation could not provide an equilibrium solution. There would be forces in existence that would tend to return the terms of trade lines to their equilibrium position.

Demand Reversals and the Direction of Trade

It was pointed out above that the direction of trade is determined by the interaction of both supply and demand conditions. A change in demand patterns alone could be responsible for a change in the direction of trade.

A *demand reversal* was previously defined as a condition where the commodity that a country is expected to export according to cost considerations alone is actually imported because it is so highly demanded at home that the country will want to supplement its domestic production by imports.

It may be true, for instance, that cloth is so highly demanded in the United Kingdom that, despite a comparative cost advantage in its production, the price will be driven up to a level higher than in the United States. As a consequence the United Kingdom will tend to import cloth from the United States. This pattern of trade is a reversal of the one that would be predicted by taking cost considerations alone into account.

A demand reversal situation is shown in Figure 6–9, where the United States exports cloth at the equilibrium terms of trade TOT, and the United Kingdom exports wheat.

Finally the possibility exists that the forces of supply and demand in each of the two countries balance each other in such a fashion that the same relative prices prevail. The slopes of the production possibility curves and the indifference curves are identical, and as a consequence the slopes of the trade indifference curves are also the same in the no-trade situation. Because all prices are already equalized, there is no reason for the emergence of international trade. Such a situation is shown in Figure 6–10.

Countries with widely different production possibility curves and indifference curve patterns will not trade with each other if the relative price ratios of the different commodities in the countries in isolation are identical.

Note that in all three cases, as shown in Figures 6–8, 6–9, and 6–10, the terms of trade are identical, as are the production possibility curves of the two countries. The only variable that is changed is the pattern of demand. As it changes so does the direction of trade, as outlined above.

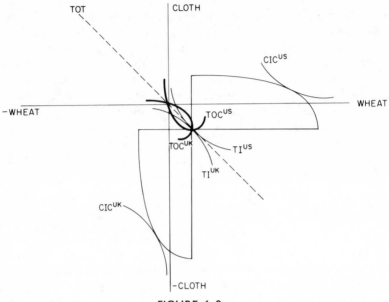

FIGURE 6–9

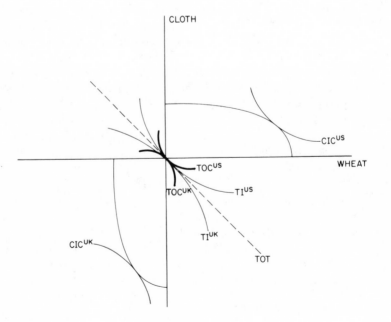

FIGURE 6–10

Multiple Equilibria and Stability Conditions

1. *Multiple Equilibria.* It is possible that several different terms of trade exist that are consistent with equilibrium. One such situation is illustrated in Figure 6–11, where we show the offer curves TOC^{US} and TOC^{UK}, representing the willingness to trade of the United States and the United Kingdom. A few of the international trade indifference curves belonging to each country are also shown. It will be noted that there are three points at

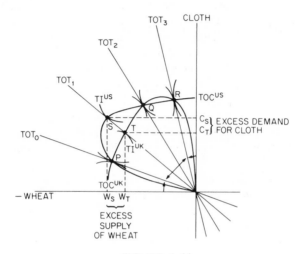

FIGURE 6–11

which the two trade offer curves intersect. These points are labeled P, Q, and R. The volume of exports will be equal to the volume of imports at any one of these three points; we also find at each point two trade indifference curves that are tangent to each other.

2. *Stability Conditions.* There is nevertheless a substantial difference in the *type* of equilibrium that prevails at points P and R on the one hand and point Q on the other. To show the difference in the types of equilibrium it will be useful to investigate what will happen if there is the slightest disturbance to the equilibrium situation. If there is a tendency for the same equilibrium to be restored after a disturbance, we will refer to this type of equilibrium as *stable*. If, however, a slight disturbance of the equilibrium will set up forces that will lead us even further away from equilibrium, we shall classify this situation as an *unstable equilibrium*.

Consider the terms of trade TOT_2, shown in Figure 6–11. Now let a disturbance of the initial equilibrium prices result in the new terms of trade TOT_1. Let us investigate whether there is a tendency of the terms of trade to return to their initial TOT_2 position. In the situation shown in the figure the United States exports wheat and imports cloth. The opposite applies to the United Kingdom. At the terms of trade TOT_1 the United States will find a trade indifference curve tangent to its terms of trade line at point S. She will therefore be willing to export W_SO of wheat and to import C_SO of cloth. Similarly the United Kingdom will find one of its trade indifference curves tangent to the terms of trade line at point T, making it want to export C_TO of cloth and to import W_TO of wheat. From the graph it is apparent that the quantity of wheat exports by the United States is greater than the quantity of wheat imports by the United Kingdom. Also the quantity of cloth exports by the United Kingdom is smaller than the quantity of cloth imports by the United States. There will be an excess supply of wheat and an excess demand for cloth. As a consequence the price of wheat will tend to fall, and the price of cloth will tend to rise. Wheat will become cheaper in terms of cloth, which finds its expression in a counterclockwise rotation of the terms of trade line. Thus the terms of trade line TOT_1 will move *away* from the original terms of trade TOT_2. As there is no tendency for the equilibrium at point Q to be restored, we can conclude that point Q represents an *unstable* equilibrium.

We have shown that the terms of trade TOT_1 will be inclined to rotate counterclockwise. The process will come to a stop when the new equilibrium terms of trade TOT_0 are reached. At point P it will once again be true that the equilibrium conditions are fulfilled. There will be no tendency for the terms of trade to move beyond TOT_0. If they should, forces will be set in action that will tend to push the terms of trade back to their equilibrium at TOT_0. Thus point P represents a stable equilibrium point.

A similar argument applies to the equilibrium point R. It is also true here that if the equilibrium terms of trade are disturbed, there will be a tendency for the terms of trade to return to their original position, restoring equilibrium at point R.

We can conclude that points P and R are stable equilibria, and that Q is unstable. A stable equilibrium is characterized geometrically by the trade offer curves of the two countries cutting each other from below (or from the inside, viewed from the origin). Unstable equilibria have trade offer curves cutting each other from above (or the outside). In general we will find that every unstable equilibrium point is surrounded by two stable equilibrium points.

We are able to derive formal criteria for the stability of an equilibrium. Consider Figure 6–12. The trade offer curves are drawn so that they have the same slope at the point of equilibrium, point P. The elasticity measure derived previously allows us to calculate the elasticities of the offer curves. The trade offer curve of the United States shows a demand elasticity that is equal to $\epsilon_{US} = HO/KO$. The United Kingdom trade offer curve's elasticity

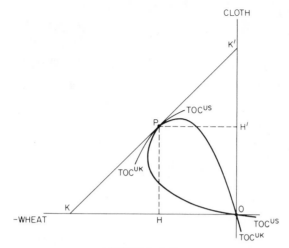

FIGURE 6-12

is given by $\epsilon_{UK} = H'O/K'O$. As the U.K. elasticity measure is expressed in terms of cloth, we will have to convert it first into wheat terms to render it comparable to the U.S. elasticity measure. This transformation can be accomplished by considering similar triangles:

$$\frac{H'O}{K'O} = \frac{PH}{K'O} = \frac{KH}{KO} \qquad (6\text{-}5)$$

The sum of the elasticities of the trade offer curves at point P for the two countries together is

$$\epsilon_{US} + \epsilon_{UK} = \frac{HO}{KO} + \frac{KH}{KO} = 1 \qquad (6\text{-}6)$$

If the slopes of the trade offer curves at the point of equilibrium are identical, the sum of the elasticities will be equal to one.

Remembering that if the trade offer curves cut each other from the inside we will have a stable equilibrium, we can conclude that if the sum of the elasticities of the trade offer curves at the equilibrium point is larger than one, we have a stable equilibrium. Such a situation is shown in Figure 6-13, where the trade offer curves TOC^{US} and TOC_2^{UK} cut each other from below. Conversely if the sum of the elasticities of the trade offer curves is smaller than one, we have an unstable equilibrium. Trade offer curves TOC^{US} and TOC_1^{UK} may serve as an illustration. The borderline case of elasticities summing to one, which served as the starting point of this analysis, will occupy our attention somewhat more in the following section.

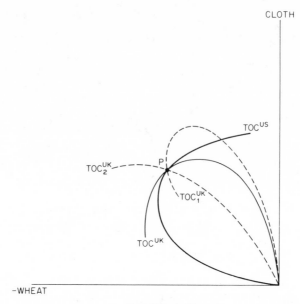

FIGURE 6–13

3. *Regions of Indeterminacy.* The possibility arises that the trade offer curves of the two countries may overlap in a region. This case is shown in Figure 6–14. The offer curves of the United States and the United Kingdom have the same slope and therefore coincide in the region between points V and W. The elasticities will sum to one. *Any* terms of trade line that crosses the trade offer curves between these two points will represent a stable set of prices. A movement of the terms of trade line, such as from TOT_0 to TOT_1, will not set in motion any forces that would tend to turn the terms of trade line even further or to return it to the original position. Thus we have a region of indeterminacy, within which we cannot decide how the terms of trade will adjust themselves. International exchange may take place at any one of an infinite number of terms of trade.

4. *Relevance to Policy Decisions.* The question of multiple equilibria and stability of these equilibria is of great importance in policy decisions of individual countries. Consider the position of the United States in the multiple equilibria case discussed in Section 1. above and illustrated by Figure 6–11. If the United States faces the terms of trade TOT_0, she will export and import a commodity combination depicted by point P. Slight disturbances of equilibrium will lead to a re-establishment of the stable equilibrium terms of trade TOT_0. A study of the situation will reveal that point P is optimal in the sense that all conditions for the best possible allocation of resources are fulfilled.

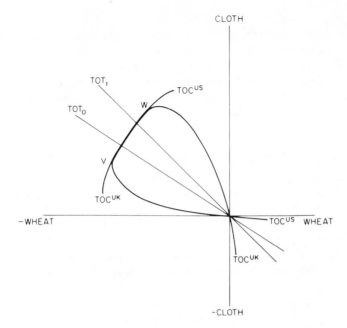

FIGURE 6–14

However, there exists the stable equilibrium point R, which can be reached if the terms of trade change drastically. A big push is needed to change the terms of trade beyond the point at which they would return to the original equilibrium position at P. If the country succeeds in pushing the terms of trade beyond TOT_2, they will be moved on to TOT_3 by market forces. Once the position R has been reached, the United States could import a much *larger* quantity of cloth for a *smaller* quantity of wheat exports than before.

For the policy maker it is therefore important not to focus attention solely on the fulfillment of the optimum *marginal* conditions but to look out also for the *total* conditions of the situation at hand. Only a knowledge of the full trade offer will permit the policy maker to render a judgment.

Similarly if the country should be faced with the terms of trade TOT_2, which were identified as being unstable equilibrium terms of trade in our example, any attempt to maintain these terms of trade is doomed to fail. The slightest disturbance in international markets will move the equilibrium terms of trade all the way to P or R. If the policy makers realize early enough that the situation they face is an unstable one, they might take action that would make it possible to reach the more favorable of the stable terms of trade that surround the unstable equilibrium.

Finally if the country should find herself in a zone of indeterminacy, as depicted in Figure 6–14, it would be possible to move the terms of trade at will to any position within the zone. Naturally the country would want to take the opportunity to influence the terms of trade in order to import the greatest quantity of commodities in exchange for exporting the smallest possible quantity. Only if the country actually realizes that it is operating in such a zone of indeterminacy will it be able to take full advantage of the situation. Otherwise the country might assume that the terms of trade are in a stable equilibrium position and fail to take any action.

THE CONSTANT COST CASE

In the previous analysis we assumed throughout that the country experiences increasing opportunity cost in the production of both commodities. In the case of constant opportunity costs of production we are able to observe some interesting phenomena that will lead to important policy conclusions concerning the effect of country size on international trade. Some of the results to be derived have already been foreshadowed in Chapter 3.

Constant Cost Offer Curve

In the upper right quadrant of Figure 6–15 we show the familiar domestic community indifference curve CIC_0 and the production possibility block NMO, exhibiting constant opportunity costs. When we start to slide the production possibility curve along the indifference curve in order to generate the international trade indifference curve, we observe that the point of tangency, P, does not immediately change its position on the indifference curve. As a result we find that the trade indifference curve will be a straight line in the segment RS, which lies parallel to the line NM. Only after the production possibility curve touches the indifference curve with one of its endpoints N or M will the international trade indifference curve assume the familiar curvature.

As soon as either one of the endpoints of the production possibility curve touches the indifference curve the country is completely specialized. No further increase of production of one commodity is possible, and the trade indifference curve will run parallel to the community indifference curve, where the displacement is given by the size of the production possibility curve.

Given a set of trade indifference curves, such as shown in Figure 6–16, we are able to derive the trade offer curve of the country. This is done by the familiar method of taking the points of tangency of different trade indifference curves to all possible terms of trade lines. In the region OA the terms of trade line TOT_0 coincides with the slope of the trade indifference curve TI_0. The trade indifference curve is therefore identical to the trade offer curve in the OA segment. Given the terms of trade TOT_1, tangency will occur at point B,

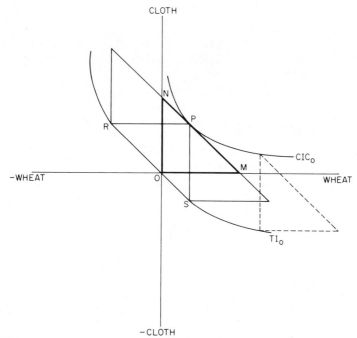

FIGURE 6–15

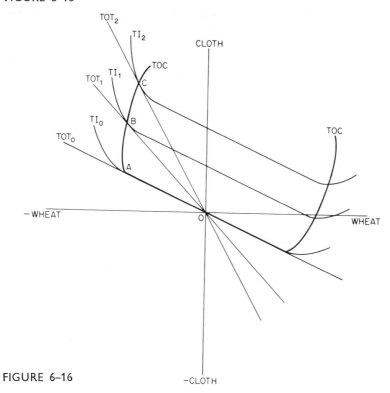

FIGURE 6–16

109

although the terms of trade TOT$_2$ allow for tangency at point C. The line connecting OABC is the trade offer curve for the constant cost case.

The trade offer curve of a country that experiences constant cost in production is characterized by a linear segment.

Effects of Country Size on Trade and Specialization

We can make some interesting observations on the patterns of international trade and specialization that evolve as a consequence of size differ-

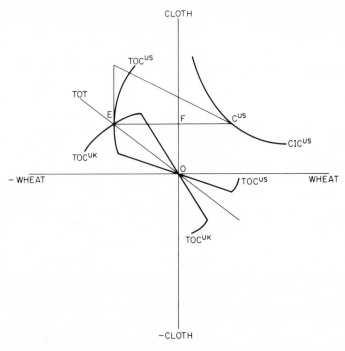

FIGURE 6–17

ences between countries. We will use the constant cost case to illustrate the principles involved, although similar patterns of complete and incomplete specialization can also be found in the increasing and decreasing cost cases. In constant cost situations we find the analysis particularly straightforward and unambiguous.

1. *Two Large Countries.* In Figure 6–17 we show the trade offer curves for the United States and the United Kingdom, which are both assumed to be large countries. The trade offer curves intersect at point E, which defines the

equilibrium terms of trade and the quantities that each country wishes to export and import at this international exchange ratio. Point E is located in the curved section of the offer curves of the two countries, indicating that both countries are completely specialized in production.

Let us focus attention on the United States case. The United States wishes to import OF of cloth in exchange for EF of wheat exports. She wants to do this in order to be able to attain consumption point C^{US}, which is located on the highest community indifference curve that can be reached: CIC^{US}. The production possibility curve of the country touches the community indifference curve with one of its endpoints at C^{US}. The country specializes completely, producing EC^{US} of wheat. Only FC^{US} of the total wheat production is consumed at home, leaving EF for export purposes.

It will be noted that the pretrade United States exchange ratio coincides with the slope of the production possibility curve. The same is true of the United Kingdom. Demand patterns of the two countries are influential in determining the precise position of the terms of trade line between the limits set by the pretrade domestic exchange ratios.

We can conclude that under constant cost conditions countries whose trade offer curves intersect in the curved segments specialize completely in the production of one commodity.

2. *A Large Country and a Small Country.* In Figure 6–18 we show the trade offer curves of a large country, say, the United States, and a small country, say, the United Kingdom, which acts like a price taker. If the trade offer curves of the two countries intersect in the straight segment of the trade offer curve of the larger country, the small country will specialize completely, but the large country will continue to produce both commodities. In our example the trade offer curve of the United Kingdom intersects the trade offer curve of the United States at E. The United States will produce EG of wheat and $C^{US}G$ of cloth. She will export EF of her total wheat production in exchange for FO of cloth, allowing her to consume the commodity bundle depicted by point C^{US}.

Note that the international terms of trade coincide with the domestic terms of trade of the large country. This is because production takes place under constant cost conditions and the large country continues to produce both commodities. As the large country is presumably able to produce additional wheat or cloth under the same cost conditions under which she is currently producing, any changes will not disturb the exchange ratio prevailing in the market.

If countries are of unequal size, the small one will specialize completely, but the large one may continue to produce both commodities. The international terms of trade will coincide with the pretrade domestic exchange ratio of the larger country if specialization is incomplete.

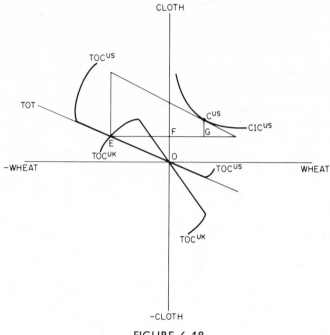

FIGURE 6–18

MULTI-COUNTRY AND
MULTI-COMMODITY CASES

Up to now we have limited ourselves to the two-country, two-commodity case. In this section we will extend the analysis to cover any arbitrary number of countries and deal with the many-commodity case.

Previously we derived the international trade offer curve for a country. We will recall that the offer curve shows the quantities of the commodities that the country in question is willing to trade at any given set of terms of trade. If we want to extend our analysis to include more than two countries and commodities, we must devise a technique that will allow us to aggregate the offer curves.

Many Countries

Let us first turn to the case of many countries and two commodities and assume that production is carried on under conditions of constant costs. By aggregating the trade offer curves for all countries we are able to derive a world trade offer curve for the two commodities. There are some countries that wish to import wheat in exchange for cloth. These countries will generate an aggregate trade offer that crosses the trade offer curve of the cloth-importing countries. The intersection will determine the world terms of trade between cloth and wheat. As long as there are any countries that

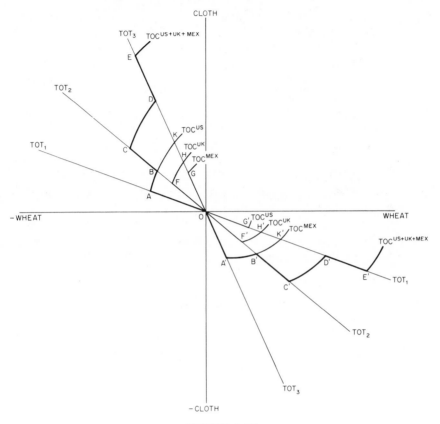

FIGURE 6–19

have excess demands or excess supplies at the world terms of trade, the terms of trade will continue to adjust until all such excess demands and supplies are eliminated.

To find the amounts that individual countries will want to trade once the world terms of trade are set we have to go back to each country's trade offer curve and check the amounts that the country wants to export and import at the price ratio set in the world market. The countries in our example are the United States, the United Kingdom, and Mexico. Their individual trade offer curves are shown in Figure 6–19 and are labelled TOC^{US}, TOC^{UK}, and TOC^{MEX} respectively. Let us consider first which countries will want to export wheat and import cloth. That is, we will try to derive the aggregate trade offer curve in the northwest quadrant. At the terms of trade TOT_1 only the United States will be willing to export wheat in exchange for cloth. The same holds true for all terms of trade up to TOT_2 (but not including the latter). Hence the aggregate trade offer curve showing wheat exports for cloth imports is identical to the U.S. trade offer curve OAB for all terms of trade lines flatter than TOT_2.

At the terms of trade TOT_2 the price of wheat has risen sufficiently so that the United Kingdom is also willing to export wheat. We must now add the U.K. trade of OF to the U.S. trade volume of OB. In Figure 6–19 we show the new trade volume OC as the sum of the U.S. trade OB and the U.K. trade of OF = BC. Finally at the terms of trade TOT_3 Mexico will also enter the group of wheat exporters, and hence its trade volume of OG (= DE) will be added to that of the U.S. and the U.K., resulting in a total trade volume of OE at the terms of trade TOT_3. The resulting aggregate trade offer curve for the three countries in the northwestern quadrant is OABCDE.

In a similar fashion we can derive the trade offer curve for cloth exports and wheat imports in the southeastern quadrant. Note that Mexico is now the first cloth exporter, and only when cloth prices rise relative to wheat prices do we find that first the United Kingdom and then the United States joins the group of cloth exporters and wheat importers. The final aggregate trade offer curve for the three countries together is given by the line EDCBAOA'B'C'D'E'. The pattern of comparative advantage in the production of cloth and wheat finds expression in the aggregate trade offer curve. The United States has the greatest comparative advantage in wheat and the least in cloth production. Hence she is the first wheat exporter in our group. The United Kingdom occupies an intermediate position, and Mexico has the greatest comparative advantage in cloth and the least in wheat production, making her the first cloth exporter. We may schematize as follows:

To determine which countries will actually export cloth and which will export wheat we have to rotate the bottom half of the aggregate trade offer curve of Figure 6–19 by 180 degrees, so that it will also lie in the northwestern quadrant. This is done in Figure 6–20. Note that the sequence of the linear segments indicates the ranking of the countries according to their comparative advantage in the two commodities. That is, the trade offer curve TOC_A, which shows willingness to export wheat and import cloth, ranks the countries in the order U.S., U.K., and Mexico, although the trade offer curve TOC_B, showing potential cloth exporters and wheat importers, ranks them in the order Mexico, U.K., and U.S.

In Figure 6–20a the equilibrium terms of trade are TOT_2, which happen

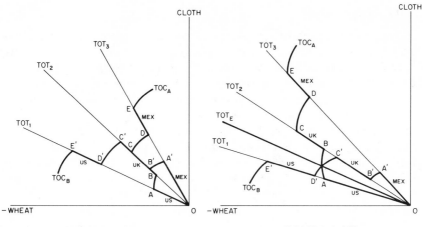

FIGURE 6–20a   FIGURE 6–20b

to be the pretrade domestic terms of trade of the United Kingdom. In this
example the United States specializes completely in the production of wheat
and Mexico specializes completely in the production of cloth. The United
Kingdom will produce somewhere between points B′ and C and may therefore
be completely specialized in one or the other commodity or continue to produce both goods. If the aggregate trade offer curves intersect in one of the
linear segments, one country may not be completely specialized.

Another possible configuration is shown in Figure 6–20b, where the trade
offer curves intersect in the *curved* segments. Under these conditions all
countries will be completely specialized. The U.S. will specialize in and export
wheat, although the U.K. and Mexico specialize completely in and export
cloth. The international terms of trade TOT_E are given by the intersection
of the two aggregate offer curves.

Of course there exists a large number of possible varieties of intersecting
aggregate trade offer curves, and we were able to illustrate the possible cases
with only two examples. Let us keep in mind that the cases discussed here
refer to constant costs of production only. Linear segments of the aggregate
trade offer curve can be found only in the constant cost case. But as the
number of countries in our example increases, the linear segments of the
aggregate trade offer curve will become relatively smaller and smaller and
the aggregate trade offer curve will approach a smooth curve.

Let us note, too, that in the case of increasing costs of production the
aggregate trade offer curve will be smooth throughout, and individual
countries may or may not be specialized completely in production. Complete
specialization will occur only in the rare case that the world price of a
commodity is higher than the marginal cost incurred by moving the very last
resources into the production of that commodity.

Many Commodities

Under constant cost conditions it is also possible to extend the analysis to the many-commodity case. For simplicity's sake we will assume that there are only two countries, each with resources that can be grouped into homogeneous "bales," which are in turn able to produce certain commodities in a fixed ratio. Thus one bale might be used to produce x units of cloth, y units of wheat, or z units of pizza. After we have decided how many bales of resources are to be devoted to the production of each commodity we can draw up a trade offer curve for the different commodities that can be produced with the bales at hand. The cost of the commodity in terms of bales of resources is shown by the slope of the trade offer curve. The number of linear segments of the trade offer curve coincides with the number of commodities under consideration. The country will be the sole producer of all commodities that lie below the point of intersection on the aggregate trade offer curve and will *not* produce any commodities that lie above it. The country will share in the production of any commodities whose linear segment happens to lie at the crossing point of the two trade offer curves. Conditions for complete or incomplete specialization in commodities are identical to the ones discussed for different countries in the preceding section. All we have to do is replace the word *country* with *commodity*.

EMPIRICAL EVIDENCE

A theory as general as the one outlined in this chapter is not very useful for policy purposes. Economic policy is concerned with the economic effects of a change in the parameters that can be influenced by governmental authorities. The theory presented here essentially predicts that anything can happen. A change in any one parameter can always be offset by a change in the opposite direction of another parameter.

For this reason it is difficult to test the theory empirically. Few, if any, testable empirical propositions can be derived that can be either rejected or validated by the data available.

The usefulness of the general equilibrium model lies, therefore, not so much in its ability to generate empirically useful predictions, but in the help it provides in understanding the interaction of the variables of the economic system. Only if one has a firm grasp of the interdependency of the different variables is one able to take account of a whole multitude of possible reactions.

The two most popular theories of the structure of trade, the comparative cost theory and the simple Heckscher-Ohlin theory, restrict themselves to the supply side only, assuming no international differences in tastes. One of the outstanding characteristics of the general equilibrium trade model that grew out of the simple Heckscher-Ohlin model is that it takes into account demand and supply patterns at the same time.

From all the empirical evidence available on consumption patterns we concluded (see Chapter 5) that demand is an important factor in determining the structure of international trade between countries with widely different per capita income levels. It was pointed out, too, that there exists the possibility of demand reversals, which would invalidate the predictions of the Heckscher-Ohlin theory.

Some of the disappointing results of the empirical verification of the Heckscher-Ohlin model (see Chapter 4) may be explained by the existence of these demand reversals. As the likelihood of demand reversals increases with increasing disparity in the per capita income levels between countries, we should expect that countries with widely different per capita income levels will be affected by demand reversals. These conditions are fulfilled for two of the three cases in which the simple Heckscher-Ohlin theory yielded unsatisfactory predictions. The large income differential between the United States and the rest of the world, as well as the more specific instance of India and the United States are cases in point. These two cases involve probably the largest per capita income differentials of any of the studies, and the chance for a demand reversal is therefore great.

Note that we are not able to state definitely that it is demand reversals that are actually responsible for the perverse predictions, as there is no evidence to compel us to exclude other factors that might have influenced the empirical results actually obtained. Nevertheless these findings are important because they present evidence that foreign trade cannot be explained in terms of supply conditions alone, and show that demand may be just as important a factor influencing the pattern of world trade. The basic framework of the Heckscher-Ohlin model does valuable service in that it pinpoints many of the crucial variables that are relevant to the problem of determining the direction and composition of trade.

SUGGESTED FURTHER READINGS

BECKER, GARY, "A Note on Multi-Country Trade," *American Economic Review* (September 1952).

ELLIOTT, GEORGE, "The Theory of International Values," *Journal of Political Economy* (February 1950).

GRAHAM, FRANK, "The Theory of International Values Re-examined," *Quarterly Journal of Economics* (November 1923). Reprinted in *Readings in the Theory of International Trade*, eds. Howard S. Ellis and Lloyd A. Metzler, Chap. XIV. Homewood, Ill.: Richard D. Irwin, Inc., 1949.

KLEIMAN, E., "Comparative Advantage, Graham's Theory, and Activity Analysis," *Economica* (August 1960).

MEADE, JAMES, *A Geometry of International Trade*, Chaps. I–IV. London: George Allen & Unwin, 1952.

METZLER, LLOYD, "Graham's Theory of International Values," *American Economic Review* (June 1950).

VANEK, JAROSLAV, *International Trade: Theory and Economic Policy*, Chap. XIV. Homewood, Ill.: Richard D. Irwin, Inc., 1962.

WHITIN, THOMAS, "Classical Theory, Graham's Theory, and Linear Programming in International Trade," *Quarterly Journal of Economics* (November 1953).

7

Effects of International Trade on the Factors of Production

In Chapters 4 and 6 we had occasion to refer to the interrelationships between factors of production and the production possibilities of a country. But we refrained from making any specific statements about the effects of international trade on factor prices and factor quantities supplied. In this chapter we will analyze these effects.

DEFINITION OF A FACTOR OF PRODUCTION

The definitions of a factor of production, factor abundance, factor scarcity, and comparative cheapness of a factor are important. Much confusion about the effects of international trade on factor prices and factor supplies stems from the fact that people associate different concepts with the same words.

Often the definition of a factor of production is not entirely unambiguous. We will classify as one factor of production all resources composed of individual units that can be exchanged against each other in any production process without resulting in a change in the output level. In other words only resources that are perfect substitutes for each other will be classified under the same factor of production heading.

It is clear that the time element plays a crucial role in the definition of a factor of production. In the short run much capital is embodied in its present use in the sense that it cannot be shifted into another use. Capital equipment is characterized by the fact that it tends to wear out in use. Once a piece of

119

capital equipment is fully physically depreciated, it has to be replaced by a new piece of equipment. At this time we have the choice of building a different piece of capital equipment. In the long run then we have a choice between one piece of capital equipment and another. The crucial observation to be made is that in the long run capital is more homogeneous than in the short run. In the long run capital can be shifted between different production processes without affecting the output level, although this is not possible in the short run when much of the capital is embodied.

Similar considerations apply to the factor of production labor. Workers have to be retrained before they can be employed in different production processes, and often the retraining process is very costly. Again in the long run these shifts are easier. New entrants into the labor force can choose between different occupations, and they are very mobile before they have started their training process. Once the training process has started, it is more difficult to change over to a different occupation.

The other concepts that need careful definition are abundance, scarcity, and relative cheapness of a factor. We will use the words *abundance* and *scarcity* only when we are talking about *physical* factor endowments. The words *cheapness* and *expensiveness* will be referred to in connection with *values* of factors of production. Physical measures of amounts of factors of production take account of supply conditions of the factors only; value measures reflect the interaction of supply and demand. Quite often we will find that physical abundance and cheapness coincide. But there are cases where demand for the physically abundant factor is so high that it actually becomes the relatively expensive factor in value terms. Because it is difficult to compare physical abundance of different factors of production in the absence of a common measuring rod, we will always talk about the relative abundance of capital and labor in one country as opposed to another country. In other words we will be primarily interested in comparing capital/labor ratios in different countries.

FACTOR PRICE CHANGES CAUSED BY TRADE

Figure 7–1 depicts a production possibility curve and an Edgeworth Box showing isoquants for the two commodities cloth and wheat.[1] We will assume that the country shown in the diagram is relatively (to the other country) labor abundant and capital scarce, and that all production functions are linear homogeneous and identical among countries, with no factor intensity reversals.

[1] These basic concepts are reviewed in the Appendix.

In isolation the country will produce at point A (Figure 7–1a), where her production possibility curve is tangent to the community indifference curve CIC_0. The relative price ratio of wheat to cloth is given by the slope of the

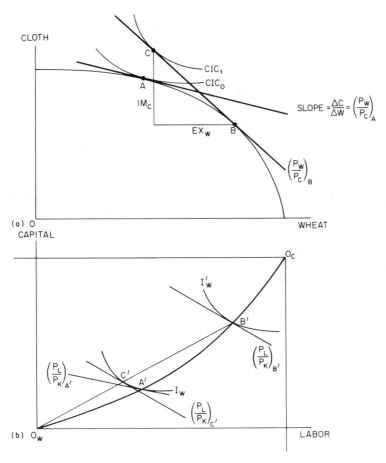

FIGURE 7–1 (a) and (b)

common tangency at point A. The optimal factor utilization pattern associated with the production pattern A is given by point A′ in Figure 7–1b. Point A′ is a point on the contract curve, characterized by the tangency of a wheat isoquant to a cloth isoquant (not shown in the diagram). The slope of the common tangency to the two isoquants at point A′ shows the ratio at which capital can be substituted for labor and is equal to the relative price ratio of labor to capital.

Let us assume that the international terms of trade at which the country may trade are given by the product price ratio $(P_W/P_C)_B$. Ruling out the possibility of demand reversals, the country will tend to export wheat, the commodity that is intensive in the country's abundant factor of production: labor. Wheat production will expand at the expense of cloth production, as is shown in Figure 7–1a by the movement from A to B.

As wheat production expands, resources have to be taken out of cloth production and transferred to wheat production. But the factors are not released in the contracting cloth industry in the same proportion as they are needed in wheat production. As a consequence the price of the factor that is used intensively in the expanding wheat industry, namely, labor, will be driven up relatively to the price of capital. In Figure 7–1b resource use patterns change from point A′ (before trade) to B′ (after trade). The tangent to the isoquants at point B′, $\left(\dfrac{P_L}{P_K}\right)_{B'}$, is steeper than the tangent to the isoquants at A′, $\left(\dfrac{P_L}{P_K}\right)_{A'}$, indicating that the price of labor has increased relatively to the price of capital.

The relative steepness of the tangents (factor price lines) at A′ and B′ follows immediately from the homothetic assumption that underlies our model. Homothetic isoquants have equal slopes along any ray from the origin. The slopes of the two wheat isoquants shown are the same at points B′ and C′. As point A′ is located on the same isoquant, to the right of point C′, and as isoquants are convex to the origin, the slope of the isoquant must be flatter at point A′ than at C′. And as the slope at C′ is equal to the slope at B′, the slope at A′ must be flatter than at B′. The steeper slope of the factor price line at B′ indicates that the P_L/P_K ratio has increased, which means that the price of labor has increased relatively to the price of capital.

It is possible to condense much of the information contained in Figures 7–1a and 7–1b into one diagram. This is done in Figure 7–2. Later this translation will allow us to derive more readily the conditions for complete factor price equalization in different countries.

Along the vertical axis of Figure 7–2a we measure the slope of the *product* price line, which shows the price of wheat over the price of cloth, P_W/P_C. On the horizontal axis we measure the slope of the *factor* price line, showing the price of labor over the price of capital, P_L/P_K. In the diagram we plot the slopes of the corresponding product and factor price ratios of Figures 7–1a and 7–1b. The two points A″ and B″ show the price ratios corresponding to points A and B (product price ratio) and A′ and B′ (factor price ratio). By plotting all possible price ratios we are able to generate the line RR′, which shows the commodity-price factor-price relations prevailing in the country.

In Figure 7–2b we go one step further and relate the factor price ratio (P_L/P_K), plotted along the horizontal axis, to the physical capital labor ratio

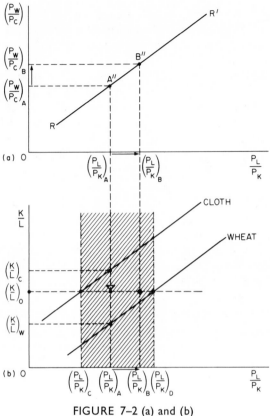

FIGURE 7-2 (a) and (b)

(K/L) shown along the vertical axis. The overall capital/labor ratio of the country, that is, the factor endowment ratio of the country is marked $(K/L)_0$ in Figure 7–2b. This overall endowment ratio is given by the size of the Edgeworth Box of Figure 7–1b. The optimal capital/labor ratios for different labor/capital price ratios are shown in Figure 7–2b for the commodities cloth and wheat. Note that the relatively capital-intensive commodity cloth uses a higher capital/labor ratio at each factor price ratio than does wheat. The line for cloth always lies above the line for wheat, indicating that cloth production is always more capital intensive than wheat production.

Individual countries must decide on an optimal pattern of production and specialization. If a country decides to trade internationally, she will have to rearrange her production patterns to adjust herself to the new situation. Two parameters are especially important in the country's decision: (1) her overall capital/labor endowment ratio, and (2) the world price ratio of the commodities she produces or is interested in trading.

For any given product price ratio P_W/P_C we have a unique factor price ratio P_L/P_K. These two variables are plotted in Figure 7-2a. In our example the two ratios always change in the same direction. If P_W/P_C rises, so does P_L/P_K. This is due to the fact that an increase in the price of the factor of production (say, labor), which is used intensively in a product (wheat), will increase the price of this product more than the price of the other product (cloth). In the previous diagram (Figure 7-1b) this was indicated by an increasing slope of the factor price ratio. It will also be true that an increased product (say, wheat) price will attract new factors of production into the industry. But proportionately more of the factor of production (labor) that is intensive in the expanding industry is required. This increased labor can be hired only at higher wages, thus increasing the labor/capital factor price ratio. In Figure 7-1b this was indicated by an increasing slope of the factor price ratio P_L/P_K as we moved from point A′ to point B′.

Figure 7-2b shows how much of a country's resources are devoted to the production of each one of the two commodities. The overall capital/labor ratio for a country is given and is labeled $(K/L)_0$.

If the factor price ratio were equal to or any lower than $(P_L/P_K)_C$, the country would find it advantageous to produce only cloth, although at any factor price ratio greater than or equal to $(P_L/P_K)_D$ the country would specialize completely in wheat production. Factor prices are free to change between the limits set by $(P_L/P_K)_C$ and $(P_L/P_K)_D$. We might want to call this zone the *feasible region* for factor price changes.

After the country enters into international trade the product price ratio will change from $(P_W/P_C)_A$ to $(P_W/P_C)_B$, the international terms of trade. As there is a direct relationship between the product price ratio and the factor price ratio, the prices of factors of production will adjust to take account of the product price change. In Figure 7-2a we move from point A″ to B″, which implies a move in the factor price ratio from $(P_L/P_K)_A$ to $(P_L/P_K)_B$. The factor price change is accompanied by a shift in the production pattern from cloth to wheat production. This result conforms to the one obtained from Figures 7-1a and 7-1b.

Let us point out, too, that the overall capital/labor ratio of the country, $(K/L)_0$, is a weighted average of the individual capital/labor ratios in the production of the two commodities. For instance at point A and the corresponding labor/capital price ratio $(P_L/P_K)_A$ we use a capital/labor ratio of $(K/L)_C$ in the production of cloth and a capital/labor ratio of $(K/L)_W$ in the production of wheat. The overall capital/labor ratio is a weighted average of the capital/labor ratios of the two commodities. Obviously if the factor price ratio reaches one of the limits of the feasible zone, such as at $(P_L/P_K)_C$, and only cloth is being produced, then the overall capital/labor ratio is the same as the capital/labor ratio in cloth production.

FACTOR PRICE EQUALIZATION

We will return to our two-country model to show the effects of international trade on the prices of the factors of production. Of special interest is the possibility of factor price equalization as a result of free international trade. Under certain assumptions it is possible to show that absolute factor prices will in fact be equalized if the countries engage in free international trade.

It is customary at this juncture to restate the whole list of assumptions that assure factor price equalization in our model. The assumptions are:

1. Two countries
2. Two commodities and two factors of production
3. Perfect competition
4. Linear homogeneous production functions
5. Identical production functions in different countries
6. Diminishing marginal productivity of factors
7. Absence of complete specialization
8. Absence of factor intensity reversals
9. Perfectly inelastic factor supply curves for each country
10. Absence of tariffs and transport costs

Below we will try to relax these assumptions and see which ones can be done without while the others remain sufficient to guarantee the validity of the factor price equalization theorem.

Factor price equalization relies on the existence of several important links: for one we must have completely free international trade, so that the prices of the traded products will be equated in all countries. Also prices of commodities must accurately reflect the cost of producing them. From this it follows that the marginal cost of producing a given traded commodity is the same in all countries. Finally because production functions in the different countries are identical, the relationship between factor earnings and product cost is the same in all countries. The link between equal product prices and equal factor earnings is therefore established.

A word of caution may be in order: in the previous paragraph we asserted that the "marginal cost of [production] . . . is the same in all countries." Note that this statement refers to the production costs of the very last unit of each commodity that the country produces after trade has started. If additional units could be produced at a (relatively) lower cost than in the other country, the country would actually produce them and export them to the other countries. Differences in relative production costs are a precondition for the emergence of international trade, but the rise of international trade will eliminate any existing differences. Pre-trade factor prices (just like product prices) are different, but post-trade prices are identical.

The wheat/cloth price ratios that prevail in each country before trade are shown in Figure 7–3a as $(P_W/P_C)_{US}$ and $(P_W/P_C)_{UK}$. In Figure 7–3b we show

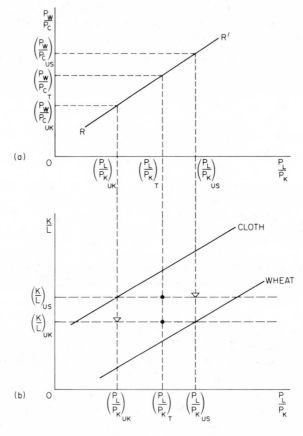

FIGURE 7–3 (a) and (b)

the capital/labor endowment ratios $(K/L)_{US}$ and $(K/L)_{UK}$ for the United States and the United Kingdom respectively. These conditions imply a set of factor price ratios (shown along the horizontal axis of both figures) of $(P_L/P_K)_{US}$ and $(P_L/P_K)_{UK}$. Britain will tend to export her relatively cheap commodity, wheat, and the United States will tend to export cloth. International trade will equalize the product prices, and, because the product prices are related directly to the factor prices, these will be equalized, too. The final world product price ratio with trade is shown as $(P_W/P_C)_T$, and the factor price ratio is $(P_L/P_K)_T$. Note that the overall physical capital/labor endowment ratios in the two countries do not change at all. The only variables free to adjust to the product price changes are the factor prices and the factor quantities devoted to the production of the two commodities.

We can conclude that under certain assumptions international trade will lead to absolute factor price equalization.

It may be worth our while to note here that the changing factor prices imply that the income distribution within each country will change. Some factors of production will receive a higher remuneration, although others will experience a drop in their earnings. The consequences of the factor price changes for the income distribution will be spelled out in greater detail in Chapter 11.

Demand Reversals and Factor Demand Reversals

In previous chapters we dealt with the consequences of demand reversals, that is, demand conditions that lead to a reversal of the trade pattern to be expected on the basis of cost considerations alone. The high demand for the product will lead to a high derived demand for the factor that is used intensively in its production, thus raising the factor's price to a comparatively high level despite its relative abundance in physical terms. A *factor demand reversal* results.

Figure 7–4 illustrates such a case. The product price ratio (P_W/P_C) is higher in the United Kingdom than in the United States, the result of the great demand for wheat in Britain. Correspondingly the factor price ratio (P_L/P_K) is very high in the United Kingdom, too. The high value attached to labor stands in contrast to the relative physical abundance of labor that exists in Britain. Before trade the United Kingdom specializes almost completely in wheat, the commodity that is intensive in her physically *abundant* factor—labor. Similarly the United States specializes in cloth, which is intensive in her abundant factor—capital.

Free international trade will lead to product price equalization, which in turn will equalize factor prices. The important observation to be made is that the *direction* of trade is reversed: the United Kingdom imports wheat, the commodity that is intensive in her physically abundant factor—labor. However, labor is relatively expensive in value terms in Britain. The United States imports cloth, which is intensive in her physically abundant factor— capital, which is the factor that is relatively expensive in value terms.

The pattern of international specialization is dictated not by physical abundance ratios, but by the criterion that a country tends to export (import) the commodity that is intensive in her relatively cheap (expensive) factor of production.

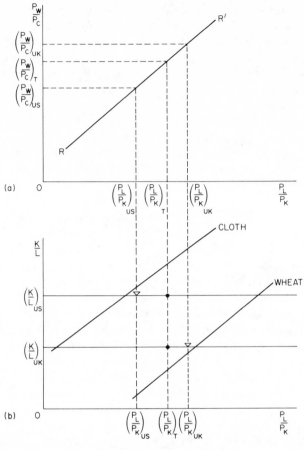

FIGURE 7–4 (a) and (b)

Obstacles to Factor Price Equalization

In this section we will critically evaluate the assumptions underlying the factor price equalization theorem.

1. *Many Countries.*   There is no reason why we cannot generalize the factor price equalization theorem to any number of countries. As long as the production functions are identical in all countries, and all the other assumptions are fulfilled, we will find that international trade will equalize commodity prices and thereby induce factor price equalization in all countries.

2. *Many Products and Factors of Production.*   We are able to extend the factor price equalization theorem to the many-product, many-factor case,

as long as for each factor price that has to be determined there is at least one product price to determine it. To put the matter the other way around: if the number of factors should exceed the number of products, then we do not have enough information contained in the product prices to allow us to determine all the factor prices. The system would be undetermined. But as long as the number of factors does not exceed the number of products, factor price equalization will be guaranteed.

3. *Imperfect Competition.* As soon as the assumption of perfect competition is dropped, the identity of marginal unit cost and product price is destroyed. Also factors of production will no longer be paid the value of their marginal product. As the direct link between product prices and factor earnings is broken, we can no longer say that product price equalization will lead to factor price equalization. The assumption of perfect competition cannot be relaxed if we are to guarantee factor price equalization.

4. *Increasing Returns to Scale.* As soon as there are increasing returns to scale in the production of one commodity, perfect competition will break down. We have shown already in Section 3. that the assumption of perfect competition cannot be relaxed. Therefore increasing returns to scale will invalidate the factor price equalization theorem.

5. *Different Production Functions in Different Countries.* The factor price equalization theorem will be invalidated if the relationship between product prices and factor prices is no longer the same in all countries as a result of different production functions. This assumption cannot be relaxed either without invalidating the theorem.

6. *Increasing Marginal Productivity of Factors.* If production functions exhibit increasing marginal productivity for individual factors of production, it will no longer be true that the wage paid to the factor is equal to the marginal revenue product. Again the direct link between factor productivity and factor remuneration required for factor price equalization will be broken.

7. *Complete Specialization.* One of the conditions for complete factor price equalization is that all countries will continue to produce all commodities after the introduction of international trade. In other words complete specialization by a country will rule out the possibility of complete factor price equalization.[2]

Complete specialization will occur if the feasible regions of factor price changes for the two countries do not overlap. Such a case is illustrated in

[2] Except in the borderline case where factor price equalization would be reached at precisely the same price ratios that would yield complete specialization.

Figure 7–5. Here the physical capital/labor endowment ratios in the United States and the United Kingdom differ markedly. Production and consumption patterns are such that the factor price ratios in the United States $(P_L/P_K)_{US}$ and the United Kingdom $(P_L/P_K)_{UK}$ are well within the feasible

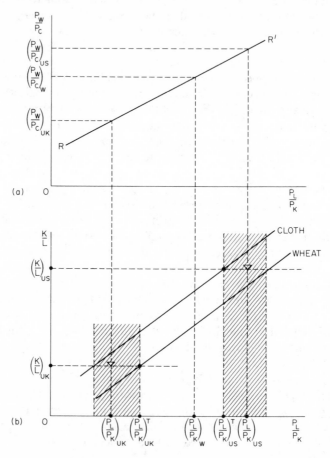

FIGURE 7–5 (a) and (b)

region before trade starts. After the opening up of trade relations a world commodity price ratio $(P_W/P_C)_W$ will be established, and factor prices will *tend* toward equalization, which should occur at the factor price ratio $(P_L/P_K)_W$. However, due to the physical capital/labor ratios prevailing in the two countries, the movements of the factor prices toward equalization will stop short of complete equalization. The factor price ratios are limited to the feasible regions indicated in Figure 7–5b, and as soon as the limits of the feasible regions are reached, the factor prices will stop moving. The new factor price ratios with trade are $(P_L/P_K)^T_{US}$ and $(P_L/P_K)^T_{UK}$ respectively. Both countries are completely specialized: the United States produces only cloth, and the United Kingdom produces only wheat.

After complete specialization is reached the factor price ratios in the countries concerned can no longer adjust themselves to the ratio necessary for the attainment of complete factor price equalization.

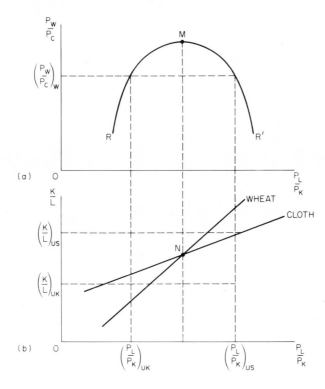

FIGURE 7–6 (a) and (b)

8. *Factor Intensity Reversals.* It is possible for the factor intensities to be different in the relevant ranges of the production functions of the countries under consideration. This possibility was alluded to already in Chapter 4. Figure 7–6 illustrates this possibility. The factor intensity reversal occurs at point M in Figure 7–6a. Up to that point the product price ratio P_W/P_C increases as the factor price ratio P_L/P_K increases. With further increases in the factor price ratio the product price ratio falls. Point N in Figure 7–6b marks the factor price ratio at which wheat production becomes capital intensive when compared to cloth production. After trade opens up both countries will trade at the common product price ratio $(P_W/P_C)_W$. But in the

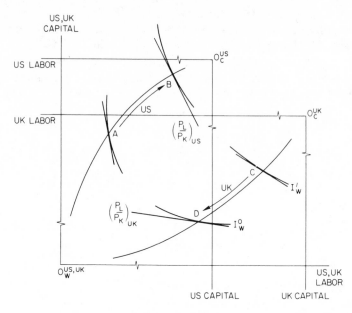

FIGURE 7-7

two countries we will have divergent factor price ratios. The post trade equilibrium factor price ratios are marked in Figure 7-6b.

Figure 7-7 shows Edgeworth Box diagrams for the United States and the United Kingdom. United States wheat production is shown as being capital intensive and cloth production is labor intensive. The reverse holds true for the United Kingdom: wheat production is labor intensive and cloth production is capital intensive.

Let us assume that after the opening of trade relations the United States exports wheat and the United Kingdom exports cloth. This means that resources in the United States have to be reallocated from the contracting cloth industry to the expanding wheat industry. In the Edgeworth Box of Figure 7-7 this is shown by the move from A to B. If the isoquants are homothetic, the price of the factor capital, which is used intensively in the expanding wheat industry, will increase. This is indicated by the slope of the price line tangent at B, which is flatter than the one at A.

At the same time the United Kingdom will expand her cloth production, which will drive up the price of capital because British cloth production is capital intensive. The slope of the price line tangent to the isoquants at point D is flatter than the one at point C. We can conclude that in the United Kingdom, just as in the United States, the price of capital has increased relatively to the price of labor. Because the factor price ratio moves in the same direction in both countries, it is in general not possible to determine whether the factor price gap will widen or narrow with the introduction of international trade.

The case discussed here represents only one of many different possibilities that may arise if there are factor intensity reversals. Under certain circumstances a larger number of reversals will lead again to the narrowing of factor price gaps. But there is also the possibility that factor price differentials will increase after trade starts.

If there are factor intensity reversals between the two countries' initial factor prices, there may be a tendency for the factor price gap either to widen or narrow, but complete equalization is ruled out.

9. *Variable Factor Supplies.*   If the quantity of factors of production supplied is a function of the rate of return that these factors are able to obtain, factor price equalization will still take place after the markets have reached the new equilibrium point. This case will be discussed in greater detail below. Similarly international factor mobility will be no obstacle to factor price equalization. As a matter of fact if factors can move internationally in response to factor price differentials, these factor movements in themselves will tend to equalize factor prices. International trade is no longer necessary to produce factor price equalization, which can be accomplished directly by the factor movements.

10. *Tariffs and Transportation Costs.*   Tariffs and transportation costs are similar in their effect on product price equalization. We noted earlier that free international trade will lead to the establishment of identical product prices for all traded commodities. Tariffs and transportation costs will tend to make the prices paid by the residents of the exporting country lower than the prices paid by residents of the importing country. Product prices in different countries are no longer completely equalized by international trade. It follows that factor prices cannot be completely equalized either, because different product prices imply (given all our assumptions) different factor prices. We can say that with tariffs and transportation costs, there is still a *tendency* toward factor price equalization, without its being complete.

FACTOR QUANTITY CHANGES
CAUSED BY TRADE

We showed the influence of international trade on factor prices. We assumed that the supply of the factors of production is perfectly inelastic. Changes in factor prices were not to influence the quantity of the factors of production supplied. Now we will assume that the factor supply curves are *not* perfectly inelastic. Under this new and less restrictive assumption we can analyze the changes in the quantities of the factors that result from factor price changes induced by international trade.

Except under circumstances of a demand reversal or factor intensity reversal we find that the country exports the commodity that is intensive in her abundant factor. In the last section we saw that the price of the factor of production that is used relatively intensely in the export commodity will tend to rise. It follows that the price of the relatively abundant factor of production will tend to increase after trade starts.

If we assume now that factor quantities supplied are positively correlated with factor prices, we can conclude that increases in the factor prices will bring forth increases in the factor quantities supplied. As the factor prices of the already relatively abundant factor increase, the growing supplies of this factor will make it even more abundant.

Assuming homothetic production functions, Figure 7–8b may help to illustrate the point. For the sake of clarity we will assume that the quantity of capital remains constant. The graph shows the familar box diagram, measuring quantities of inputs along the axes, and the line connecting all points of tangency for the different isoquants, namely, the contract curve. Let us assume that labor is the relatively abundant factor of our example. Free trade will lead to further specialization in the commodity that is intensive in the abundant factor, namely, wheat, and we will move from point A' to point B', where TOT_B is the given international price ratio. The labor/capital factor price ratio given by the slope of isoquants increases as we move from A' to B'. The higher price of labor will attract more workers, which represents a growth of the labor supply. Let us say that the box diagram increases by ΔL, moving the origin for cloth production to the new point O'_C.

We now have to find the point on the new contract curve (dashed line) at which the country will produce. To do this we recall that the factor price equalization theorem postulates a direct relationship between product prices and factor prices. The free trade product price ratio that corresponds to the factor price ratio at B' is the same as that which prevails after the factor supply adjustment has taken place.[3] Therefore the factor price ratio will be the same at the new point C' as it was at B'. Note that B' and C' are located on the same ray from the origin O_W. In a homogeneous isoquant set this assures identical factor price ratios.

As we move from B' to C' we find that wheat production expands and cloth production contracts. This is also shown in Figure 7–8a, which shows the production response to the factor price changes. We move from point A to point B before the factor quantity adjustment and on to point C after the factor quantity has adjusted fully.

---

[3] This holds true in a strict sense only if the country under consideration is relatively small. The assumption will be dropped in the following chapter.

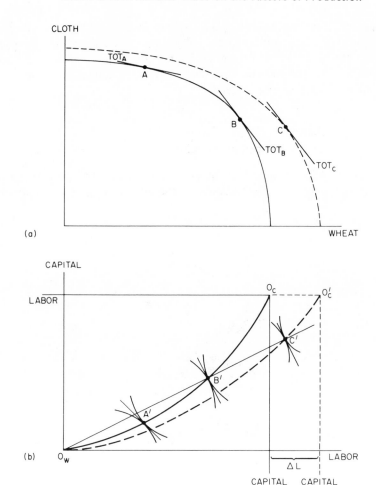

FIGURE 7–8 (a) and (b)

Specialization in production will be even stronger if we allow factor supplies to vary in response to induced factor price changes.

At first this may seem a surprising result, but when we consider that international trade tends to increase the price of the abundant factor, and that factor quantity changes help to keep this very factor price low, it is clear that a much greater expansion of the export industry's product is possible.

A few additional observations are in order. First of all, not only will the abundant factor of production expand in quantity, but the scarce factor, here capital, will tend to contract because its wage falls. Second, effects of trade on factor supplies will be similar in the other countries. Third, we can expect that product prices will not stay constant after the factor supplies have changed. It is not possible to make any generalizations about the direction of the product price changes and their consequent effect on factor supplies. Some of the problems that come up in this connection will be discussed in Chapter 8, where we deal with problems of autonomous factor changes and their effects on international trade.

Effects of Changing Factor Supplies on the Production Possibility Curve

If we allow for the possibility of induced factor quantity changes, we have to address ourselves to the question of the effects of these factor quantity

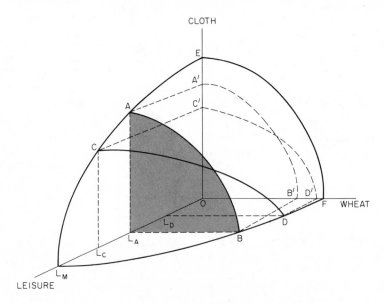

FIGURE 7–9

changes on the production possibility curve. We might be especially interested in the question of the position of the production possibility curve with constant factor supplies as opposed to the one with variable factor supplies.

In addition to the two commodities measured along the axes of the production possibility curve diagram we introduce now a third variable: the changing factor supply. In order to keep the diagram to three dimensions we will limit ourselves to the case of one factor of production only. In Figure 7–9 we measure leisure, denoting all time not worked, along the third axis. Cloth is measured in the usual vertical direction and wheat in the horizontal direction. If the residents of the country should decide to consume all leisure available, that is, 24 hours a day, 365 days a year, there would be no labor services provided at all, and, consequently, production will be equal to zero. The point in the figure corresponding to this state of affairs is L_M, where people consume the maximum amount of leisure possible. The production possibility curve has been reduced to a point. If, however, the residents of the country should work without interruption, consuming no leisure at all, we would find ourselves at the origin of the diagram. Under these circumstances it is possible to produce anywhere on the production possibility curve EF.

In reality we will find neither one of these two extreme possibilities. Let us start with the assumption of *fixed* factor supplies. The country's residents may want to consume OL_A of leisure and spend $L_A L_M$ of their total time on work. The production possibility curve corresponding to this work effort is labeled AB. Its projection on the cloth-wheat plane (dashed lines) is labeled A'B'. For each factor supply we can construct a corresponding production possibility curve, which can be visualized as a "slice" of the grand production possibility surface shown in Figure 7–9.

If we now allow for factor quantity changes in response to factor price changes induced by international trade, we may find that the total quantities of leisure demanded will vary between L_C and L_D. Corresponding to the varying amounts of work effort (equal to total time minus leisure time) are different points on the production possibility surface L_MFE that are most preferred by the country. A set of such points is shown by the line CD. Note that at any point on CD the number of hours worked will be different. A projection of the variable factor supply production curve CD on the cloth-wheat plane will generate C'D'.

The important observation to be made is that we are not able to make any general statements of the relationship of the fixed factor supply production possibility curve A'B' to the variable factor supply production possibility curve C'D'. These relationships will depend crucially on the trade-offs between cloth, wheat, and leisure that characterize the residents of the country.

The variable factor supply production possibility curve may lie wholly inside or wholly outside the fixed factor supply production possibility curve, or the two curves may intersect.

Two important policy conclusions emerge from the analysis in this chapter. For one, international trade will tend to eliminate factor price differentials that might exist between countries. Free international trade may thus serve as a full substitute for international factor movements, which would presumably also eliminate factor price differentials. Two, international trade tends to accentuate, rather than diminish, the relative domestic factor endowment ratios between countries. The relatively abundant factor of production will become even more abundant as a result of international trade. These two statements are not mutually inconsistent, as they might appear at first sight. The first statement refers to factor movements *between* countries, and the second is concerned with factor quantity changes *within* the same country. These latter factor *quantity* changes are caused by the very factor *price* changes that are the result of international trade.

EMPIRICAL EVIDENCE

The most important problem discussed in this chapter is the possibility of international trade leading to factor price equalization. Much of the empirical evidence relevant for factor price equalization has been discussed in previous chapters, yet it might prove useful to assemble briefly the various bits of evidence that are of importance in this connection. We will concentrate attention on the assumptions that cannot be relaxed without invalidating the factor price equalization theorem.

1. *Perfect Competition.* Even casual armchair empiricism tells us that there are many industries that are not characterized by perfect competition. For this reason alone we should not expect complete factor price equalization to take place.

2. *Returns to Scale.* Evidence compiled by A. Walters and discussed in Chapter 4 led us to the conclusion that the empirically relevant ranges of the production function are probably characterized by constant returns to scale. No obstacle to factor price equalization should be expected on this account.

3. *Production Functions in Different Countries.* Arrow, Chenery, Minhas, and Solow[4] found that production functions tend to differ between countries by a constant scale factor. As a result factor price equalization cannot be expected to be complete in *absolute* terms. Yet, as the relative factor proportions used in the production of various commodities tend to be the same in different countries, we could still get an equalization of relative factor prices between countries. In other words factor prices in different countries would differ by a constant factor, although their relative position to each other would be identical.

4. *Marginal Productivity of Factors.* There is no empirical evidence available that would point to the existence of increasing marginal productivity of factors of production, and we need expect no obstacle to factor price equalization from this source.

[4] Kenneth Arrow, H. Chenery, B. Minhas, and R. Solow, "Capital-Labor Substitution and Economic Efficiency," *Review of Economics and Statistics*, August 1961.

5. *Complete Specialization.* There is a small number of commodities that are produced almost exclusively by one country. In most cases this is due to a virtual monopoly of resources required for their production. But patents or limited availability of relevant techniques and skills may also preserve the monopolistic position of one or a group of a few countries. Again in these cases factor price equalization is not likely to occur.

6. *Factor Intensity Reversals.* Another important question, studied by B. S. Minhas,[5] is whether or not factor intensity reversals actually do occur within the empirically relevant ranges of the production function. For the United States Minhas found that these reversals do take place within the empirically relevant ranges thus eliminating the possibility of factor price equalization.

From all the evidence presented it is clear that complete factor price equalization is unlikely. The most we can hope for is a *tendency* toward factor price equalization. But we must remember that we do not live in a static world where most variables do not change. The other factors at work may tend to increase, rather than narrow, the existing factor price gaps. The effect of international trade may be considered as a "leaning against the wind," in that factor price differentials would be even larger in the absence of trade.

SUGGESTED FURTHER READINGS

BALASSA, BELA, "The Factor Price Equalization Controversy," *Weltwirt-schaftliches Archiv*, No. 1 (1961).

BHAGWATI, JAGDISH, "Protection, Real Wages and Real Incomes," *Economic Journal* (December 1959). Reprinted in *International Trade*, ed. Jagdish Bhagwati. Baltimore: Penguin Books, Inc., 1969.

HECKSCHER, ELI, "The Effect of Foreign Trade on the Distribution of Income," *Economisk Tidskrift* (1919). Reprinted in *Readings in the Theory of International Trade*, eds. Howard S. Ellis and Lloyd A. Metzler, Chap. XIII. Homewood, Ill.: Richard D. Irwin, Inc., 1950.

JOHNSON, HARRY G., "Factor Endowments, International Trade, and Factor Prices," *The Manchester School of Economic and Social Studies* (September 1957). Reprinted in AEA *Readings in International Economics*, eds. Richard Caves and Harry G. Johnson. Homewood, Ill.: Richard D. Irwin, Inc., 1968.

[5] B. S. Minhas, "The Homohypallagic Production Function, Factor Intensity Reversals, and the Heckscher-Ohlin Theorem," *Journal of Political Economy*, April 1962.

LANCASTER, KELVIN, "Protection and Real Wages: A Restatement," *Economic Journal* (June 1957).

OZAWA, TERUTOMO, "The Rybczynski Theorem: A Diagrammatic Note and a Corollary Proposition," *Economica* (August 1970).

RYBCZYNSKI, T. M., "Factor Endowment and Relative Commodity Prices," *Economica* (November 1955). Reprinted in AEA *Readings in International Economics*, eds. Richard Caves and Harry G. Johnson. Homewood, Ill.: Richard D. Irwin, Inc., 1968.

SAMUELSON, PAUL A., "International Trade and the Equalization of Factor Prices," *Economic Journal* (June 1948).

————, "International Factor-Price Equalization Once Again," *The Economic Journal* (June 1949). Reprinted in AEA *Readings in International Economics*, eds. Richard Caves and Harry G. Johnson. Homewood, Ill.: Richard D. Irwin, Inc., 1968.

VANEK, JAROSLAV, "An Alternate Proof of the Factor Price Equalization Theorem," *Quarterly Journal of Economics* (November 1960).

8

Economic Growth
and International Trade

In the last chapter the effects of international trade on the factors of production were analyzed. We focused attention on changes in factor prices and factor supplies caused by the rearrangement of the production patterns taking place after international trade is taken up. In this chapter we will follow the reverse procedure and take factor supply changes as given and study their effect on the pattern of international trade. In this context we will also investigate the question of what factor supply changes must take place if specific changes in trade patterns are to be achieved. This last area is particularly important in countries that are expanding and wish to ascertain whether economic growth will make them more or less dependent on international trade. To simplify the analysis we will assume throughout this chapter that factor prices stay constant.

There are two sets of assumptions that play an important part in the outcome of our analysis: (1) the familiar difference between large and small countries and (2) economic growth caused by changes in the quantity or the quality of factors of production, that is, changes in factor endowments or production functions.

THE SMALL COUNTRY AND
ECONOMIC GROWTH

1. *Consumption Effects.* A small country faces a given set of terms of trade at which she is able to exchange commodities. Let us assume initially that the country is characterized by constant cost conditions. Under these

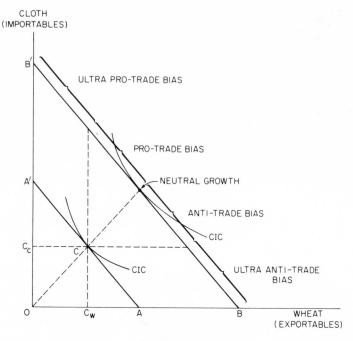

FIGURE 8-1

circumstances the country will specialize in the commodity in which she has a comparative advantage, say, wheat, and exchange some of her wheat output at the world terms of trade against cloth imports.

Before there is any economic growth the country is producing OA (Figure 8-1) of wheat. The international terms of trade are given by the slope of the line AA′, and in order to reach the highest possible community indifference curve the country will modify her commodity bundle by exporting C_WA of wheat in exchange for C_WC of cloth. Thus she is able to attain commodity bundle C.

Now let economic growth occur, which will allow the country to produce the larger quantity of wheat OB. The now-attainable commodity combinations are delineated by the line BB′, which describes the trading opportunities newly open to the country. The commodity bundle on BB′ that will actually be chosen is, as usual, the one at which a community indifference curve is tangent to the price line.

The growth pattern of the country can be classified conveniently by using the relative size of the foreign trade sector as a yardstick. If its size in relation to total national output stays the same, we will speak of *neutral* economic growth. If it increases, we will speak of *pro-trade biased* economic growth.

Conversely a decrease in relative size will be referred to as an *anti-trade biased* growth. Finally there is the possibility that not only the relative, but the *absolute*, size of the foreign trade sector increases more than the increase in national output. This will be called an *ultra pro-trade bias*. An absolute *decrease* in the foreign trade sector concomitant with economic growth will be referred to as an *ultra anti-trade bias*.

We may also use average and marginal propensities to consume importable commodities as a classification scheme. The various possibilities are summarized in Table 8–1, which corresponds to the cases shown in Figure 8–1. Marginal propensities to import are denoted by MPI and average propensities to import by API.

TABLE 8–1

GROWTH AND BIASES IN CONSUMPTION

Bias	Demand Propensities for Importables	Income Elasticities of Demand for Importables
Ultra pro-trade	MPI > 1	$\epsilon_y > 1$
Pro-trade	MPI > API	$\epsilon_y > 1$
Neutral	MPI = API	$\epsilon_y = 1$
Anti-trade	MPI < API	$\epsilon_y < 1$
Ultra anti-trade	MPI < 0	$\epsilon_y < 0$

Alternatively we may utilize the income elasticity of the demand for importables as the basis for our classification system. If the demand for importables increases in the same proportion as total income, we obtain an income elasticity ϵ_y of the demand for importables of unity. If the income elasticity is larger than one, we have a pro-trade bias, and if the income elasticity is smaller than one, we find an anti-trade bias.

In the cases of pro-trade, neutral, and anti-trade biased growth, part of the increase in income due to economic growth will be spent on the imported commodity. An ultra pro-trade bias occurs if the imported commodity is a superior good. Superior goods are characterized by the fact that people spend more than their income increase on the commodity. Similarly the ultra anti-trade bias is the result of the imported commodity being an inferior good; that is, people spend an absolutely smaller amount on this commodity.

2. *Production Effects.* Up to now we assumed that the growing country experiences constant opportunity costs in production, resulting in complete

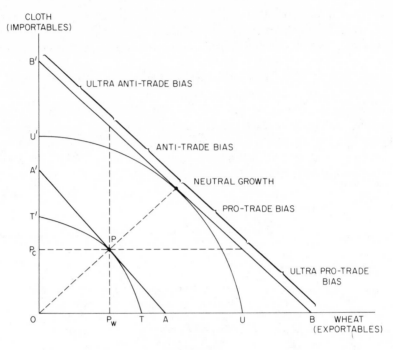

FIGURE 8–2

specialization in the commodity in which the country enjoys a comparative advantage. We will drop now the constant cost assumption and assume instead that the country is characterized by increasing costs in production. This time we will attempt to isolate the effects of production patterns on economic self-sufficiency in the context of growth.

As before the assumption crucial to our argument is that the terms of trade are given for the country in question. This given set of terms of trade is indicated by the slope of the line AA′ in Figure 8–2. Given the initial production possibility curve TT′ the country will produce at point P. Economic growth will lead to an outward shift of the production possibility curve. Again a tangency position of the production possibility curve to the terms of the trade will be found. If the new bundle of commodities to be produced contains more of the commodity that the country formerly imported, the country has become more self-sufficient. This growth pattern would therefore have had an *anti-trade* bias, because the volume of international trade has become smaller, relative to the total output. Again there exists the possibility of an *ultra anti-trade bias*, which will occur if the production of the importable commodity increases so strongly that the production of the other commodity actually decreases in absolute terms. In other words, if less than OP_W of wheat is produced as a result of economic growth, then growth is characterized by an ultra anti-trade bias. That is, of course, if cloth is the imported commodity. *Neutral* production increases take place if the output pattern does not change at all with economic growth. This case is illustrated by the production possibility curve UU' in Figure 8–2. The relative shares of cloth and wheat produced stay constant. Finally there remains the possibility of pro-trade biased growth. A *pro-trade bias* results when a country produces a relatively (to total output) smaller amount of the imported commodity herself; an *ultra pro-trade bias* implies that the country produces an absolutely

TABLE 8–2

GROWTH AND BIASES IN PRODUCTION

Bias	Supply Propensities of Importables	Income Elasticity of Supply of Importables
Ultra pro-trade	$MSI < 0$	$\sigma_y < 0$
Pro-trade	$MSI < ASI$	$\sigma_y < 1$
Neutral	$MSI = ASI$	$\sigma_y = 1$
Anti-trade	$MSI > ASI$	$\sigma_y > 1$
Ultra anti-trade	$MSI > 1$	$\sigma_y > 1$

smaller amount of the imported commodity after economic growth takes place. Thus the country becomes less self-sufficient, and hence the name pro-trade bias.

Again we may classify the various possibilities in terms of propensities and elasticities. However, this time we deal with *production* data. The average supply of importables as a fraction of total production is denoted by ASI and the marginal supply response to production changes as MSI. The supply elasticities with respect to production changes are labelled σ_y.

3. *Net Effects of Growth.*   Neither production effects nor consumption effects alone decide whether economic growth occurring in a country is going to be neutral, biased, or even ultra biased. To determine the final effects of growth one has to take both consumption and production patterns of the growing country into consideration. The *net effect* of changes in consumption and production patterns due to economic growth will determine the effects of growth on the size of the foreign trade sector.

Figure 8–3 shows some of the relevant magnitudes. In the graph the production pattern before the occurrence of economic growth is given by D, and a neutral growth pattern brings us to point D' after growth has occurred. Similarly there is a movement from consumption point C to C' due to

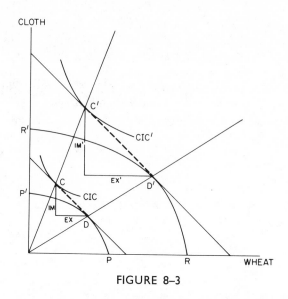

FIGURE 8–3

growth. The net effect in the example shown is that trade expands in exact proportion to the growth in national income. The dashed lines show the exports and imports traded by the country at the different levels of total output.

The only observation that can be made regarding the size of the foreign trade sector is that essentially anything is possible. Even an ultra pro-trade biased growth in consumption might be turned by a strongly ultra anti-trade biased growth in production into an ultra anti-trade bias as far as the net results are concerned. Only if more specific assumptions as to the likely magnitude of the different effects are made will it be possible to narrow down the range of possible outcomes. To give a complete taxonomy of all the possible cases would, however, lead us too far astray.

FACTOR QUANTITY CHANGES

Hitherto we have not specified precisely how economic growth in the country occurred. Here two basic types of economic growth may be distinguished: (1) an increase in the factor quantities available, and (2) a technological advance, allowing production of a larger output with the same quantity of resources. It is very important to distinguish between these two cases, because factor quantity changes and changes in the production functions lead to very different results in our simple two factor models. Basically the difference arises due to the assumption that additional factors of production will receive a wage equal to their marginal revenue product, although technological improvements are assumed to be exogenous to the system—and are available for free. Under this latter assumption the gains due to technological innovations will accrue to *other* factors of production. If we were to recognize explicitly the role of research and development as a factor of production that receives a remuneration, we would introduce a third factor of production into our model.

We will deal first with the simpler case of an exogenous increase in the physical quantity of the factors of production. We still maintain the small country assumption of fixed commodity prices at which the country may trade in world markets.

1. *Ultra-biased growth.* Let us first consider the case of an autonomous increase in one of the factors of production, and let us suppose that the labor force of the country increases due to population growth. In Figure 8–4b the size of the box diagram will increase by the increase in the labor force (shown as dashed lines).

Before the increase in the labor force, the country is confined to the production possibility curve PP' (Figure 8–4a). Given the international terms of trade TOT, the country produces a commodity bundle A'. This output combination of 60 units of wheat and 30 units of cloth implies a resource allocation pattern indicated by point A in Figure 8–4b.

The increase in the work force will cause a shift in the production possibility curve from PP' to RR'. Given these expanded production possibilities, the country will again equate the terms of trade with the marginal rate of transformation. The new production point is B', where 100 units of wheat and 20 units of cloth are being produced.

At first it may seem surprising that economic growth of a factor of production will lead to a *decrease* in the output level of one product, although output of the other product increases, that is, to an ultra-biased change in the production pattern. Our assumption that the country in question is so small that she faces a given set of world market prices, namely, the terms of trade TOT, is crucial here. We know that under our usual set of assumptions, including linear homogeneous production functions, a unique relationship exists between product prices and factor prices. Therefore, because product prices do not change as a result of economic growth, the factor prices will have to stay the same, too. This, however, means that the factor intensities must also stay constant. In the Edgeworth Box shown in Figure 8–4b, the new equilibrium point B will have to lie on the same ray from the wheat origin as does point A. For the shifting origin of the isoquant system for cloth production this condition is to be replaced by the requirement that the two rays depicting the factor intensities, that is, AO_C and BO'_C, are parallel to each other. The only possible intersection of the factor intensity rays, namely, point B, will lie on a higher wheat isoquant and a lower cloth

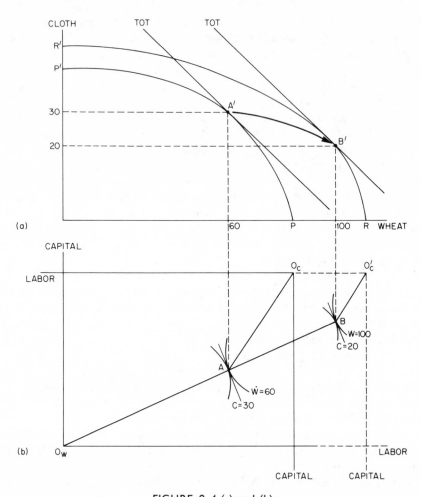

FIGURE 8-4 (a) and (b)

isoquant. The output of one commodity will therefore increase, while the output of the other will decrease in absolute amount.

We can go one step further and infer which product will experience a production increase and which a decrease. In our example wheat is relatively labor intensive, and cloth is relatively capital intensive. The additional workers have to be absorbed by the economy at the going wage for the reasons stated above. This can come about only if the additional workers are employed in the industry that uses labor intensively, and if *in addition* there is a decrease in the output level of the capital intensive industry. This latter decrease in output level will free relatively more capital than labor, and this capital can then be used together with the previously unemployed workers in the expanding wheat industry. The factor intensities can be maintained, too, because the expanding wheat industry uses relatively little capital. Thus it is clear that only an actual contraction of the cloth industry can free the capital required in the expanding wheat industry, such that the additional workers due to the labor force increase can find employment at the going wage.

An increase in one factor of production will lead to ultra biased growth, favoring the industry that uses the growing factor intensively.

2. *Biased growth.* Next we come to the case of biased economic growth. Actually we will concentrate on the borderline case between ultra biased and biased growth, that is, the case of an increase in the output level of one product only. This kind of growth is of great importance for a country wishing to pursue a development policy designed to increase output of only one commodity or group of commodities.

After the case of ultra-biased growth the answer to this problem is simple. We know that product prices will have to stay constant, and, consequently, factor prices cannot change either. In order to increase the output of one industry only, without affecting factor prices, factor quantities must be increased in precisely the same proportion as they are used in the industry in which expansion is to take place. Only under these conditions will there be no incentive for factors to migrate between the different industries.

Consider Figure 8–5. Production takes place initially at point A′, and resource allocation patterns are depicted by point A. The aim is to expand output to a point like A″, where only cloth output is increased while wheat output remains the same as at point A′. It is necessary to stay on the same wheat isoquant in Figure 8–5b, while moving to a higher cloth isoquant. This must be done without changing the factor proportions used in either industry. The only way to accomplish this feat is to increase capital and labor by the amounts of ΔC and ΔL, which are exactly proportional to the factor intensity in the cloth industry. As a consequence the origin for cloth production O_C in the Edgeworth Box will be displaced to O_C'. The cloth isoquant through point A will now denote a higher cloth output level because it is drawn with reference to an origin that is farther removed than it was before. The higher cloth isoquant denotes the new output level for cloth, shown by point A″ in the upper portion of the diagram.

An increase in factors of production in the same proportion as they are used in one industry will lead to an increase in the output level of that industry alone.

3. *Neutral Growth.* For various reasons it may be desirable to increase the outputs in exactly the same proportion as they are being produced at present. In other words it may be desirable for economic growth to occur in a balanced or neutral pattern.

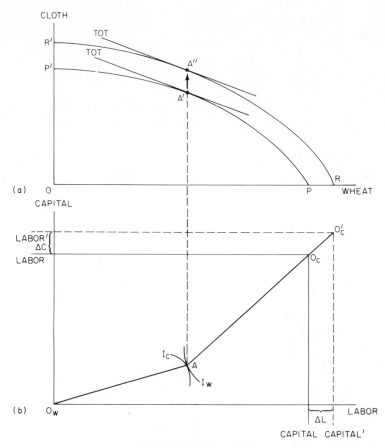

FIGURE 8–5 (a) and (b)

Again product and factor prices will be the same before and after economic growth takes place. Thus the factor intensities in the production of both commodities cannot be affected. If, in addition, both outputs are to increase in exactly the same proportion as they did before economic growth occurred, the factors must be increased in accordance with a weighted average of their use in the two industries. This weighted average is provided by the *overall* capital/labor ratio that prevails in the country. All that is required to attain neutral economic growth is an increase of factors in exactly the proportion in which they are already applied in the country.

Figure 8–6 illustrates the point. The initial factor endowments are given by the solidly lined box. Production takes place at A. The two factors of production are expanded in exactly the same proportion as they are used before economic growth occurs. The three points O_W, O_C, and O'_C are all

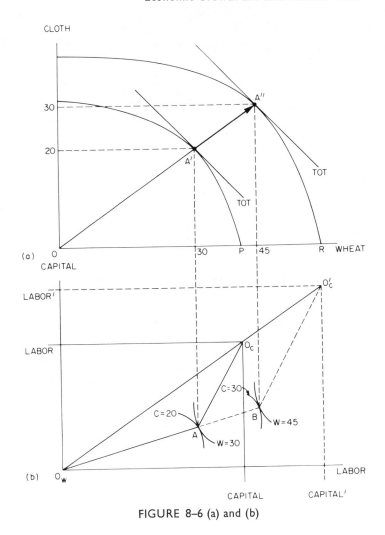

FIGURE 8–6 (a) and (b)

located on a straight line. The condition of constancy of the factor prices requires again that the factor intensities stay the same, and the new resource allocation point B (Figure 8–6b) can be found by extending O_WA beyond A and drawing a line parallel to O_CA from the new origin O'_C. The intersection point of these two lines, point B, denotes the new resource allocation pattern. Given linear homogeneous production functions, the increase in the output of each one of the two commodities will be proportional to their original output level.

An increase of all factors of production in the proportion in which they are found in the economy will result in neutral economic growth.

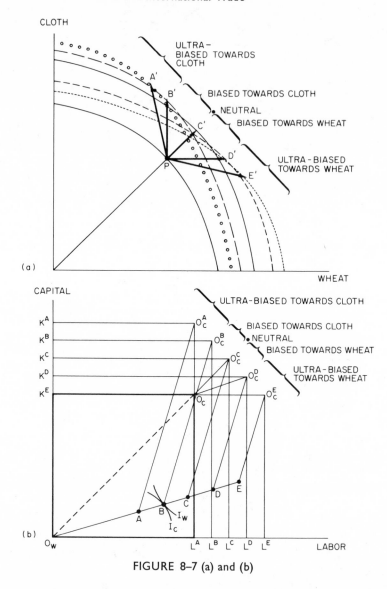

FIGURE 8–7 (a) and (b)

4. *The General Case.* All possible cases of growth due to factor quantity increases are summarized in Figure 8–7. The initial Edgeworth Box is the heavily lined rectangle $O_W K^E O_C L^A$ in Figure 8–7b. Production takes place at point B, resulting in an output pattern P in Figure 8–7a. The cases discussed previously may now be classified in the two diagrams. Capital/labor augmentation in proportion to the overall capital/labor ratio leads to growth pattern C, which is of course the case of neutral growth. The two

ranges of biased growth in favor of either cloth or wheat come about if factors increase less than in the proportion in which they are used in either one of the two industries. The bias will be in favor of the industry whose capital/labor ratio comes closest to the increase in the capital/labor ratio. Finally ultra-biased growth results if the incremental capital/labor ratio falls outside the range provided by the capital/labor ratios of the two industries.

TABLE 8–3

FACTOR CHANGES AND OUTPUT CHANGES

Case (compare Figure 8–7)	Factor Changes	Output Changes
A	$\dfrac{\Delta K}{\Delta L} > \left(\dfrac{K}{L}\right)_C$	$\Delta Y > 0;\ \Delta W < 0$
B	$\dfrac{\Delta K}{\Delta L} = \left(\dfrac{K}{L}\right)_C$	$\Delta Y > 0;\ \Delta W = 0$
C	$\dfrac{\Delta K}{\Delta L} = \left(\dfrac{K}{L}\right)_{overall}$	$\Delta Y > 0;\ \Delta W > 0$
D	$\dfrac{\Delta K}{\Delta L} = \left(\dfrac{K}{L}\right)_W$	$\Delta Y = 0;\ \Delta W > 0$
E	$\dfrac{\Delta K}{\Delta L} < \left(\dfrac{K}{L}\right)_W$	$\Delta Y < 0;\ \Delta W > 0$

The various growth patterns that may result from factor endowment changes shown in Figure 8–7 may be summarized in Table 8–3.

The changes in the capital/labor ratios are indicated by $\Delta K/\Delta L$, and the original factor ratios are given by K/L. The subscripts refer to the various industries. For instance, case A shows that a change in the K/L ratio that is greater than the K/L ratio existing in the C industry will lead to an increase in C output and a contraction in W output.

TECHNOLOGICAL PROGRESS

The second type of economic growth that we have to consider is due to technological progress. *Technological progress* is generally defined as a change in production techniques that allows us to produce the same quantity of output with a smaller quantity of resources or, alternatively, a larger output with the same resources. Technological progress denotes a change in production functions.

We will assume here that technological progress occurs exogenously. That is, we will assume that the new information becomes available free of charge to the producers of the commodities that may benefit from it. Alternatively we could have assumed that technological progress is produced by engaging in research and development and that certain economic units have property rights like patents or copyrights in the new processes. In that case we would be introducing in effect a third factor of production into our two factor model. We will not follow this route and will assume that technological progress occurs exogenously.

We may distinguish two cases: (1) technological progress occurring in *both* industries in the same degree, and (2) technological progress occurring only in one industry.

Technical Improvements in Both Industries

Let us define as *neutral* technological progress an improvement in technology that saves all factors of production to the same extent. If such neutral technological progress takes place simultaneously in both industries, we find that each isoquant in Figure 8–8b is now associated with a higher level of output than before. The same amount of resources can produce a larger quantity of output no matter in which industry the resources are employed. The result is that output levels of both industries increase proportionally. In Figure 8–8a we move from point A′ to point A″. Given the assumption of fixed world prices the production pattern of the country will expand in a neutral fashion, that is, the wheat/cloth output mix will be unaffected. Note that although world *prices* have remained constant, factor prices will increase proportionally if we assume linear homogeneous production functions. But as the profitability of both industries increases to the same extent, there is no incentive to shift resources from one industry to the other.

Neutral technological progress in all industries will lead to a proportional expansion of all industries.

Technical Improvements in One Industry

1. *Neutral Progress.* The situation is quite different if the neutral technological progress occurs in only one industry. (See Figure 8–9). In this case the *cost* of production will decrease in this industry alone, although world *prices* remain unchanged. The result is that only in the industry experiencing technological progress are profit margins increased, although they remain at their old level in the other industry. The industry that experiences the technological progress will expand. The higher returns will attract additional factors of production. In the expansion process the price

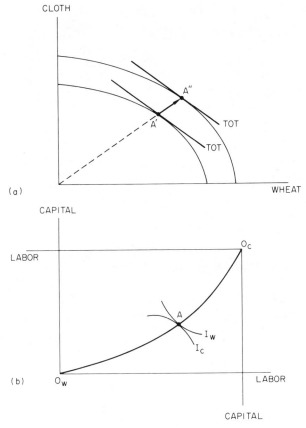

FIGURE 8–8 (a) and (b)

of the factor that is used intensively in the expanding industry will be bid up. (The factor price ratio in Figure 8–9b increases as we move from point A to B.) Because technological progress is neutral, the contract curve will remain unchanged with only the output levels associated with the various isoquants changing. The movement from A to B represents complete adjustment to neutral technological progress in the wheat industry.

Neutral technological progress in one industry alone will lead to an expansion of this industry, while the other industry will contract.

2. *Biased Progress.* In the case of biased technological progress, the situation is different. The word *biased* refers here to an improvement in technology that economizes on the use of the factors of production in different proportions. We will assume that the biased technological progress occurs only in the wheat industry, which is assumed to be labor intensive.

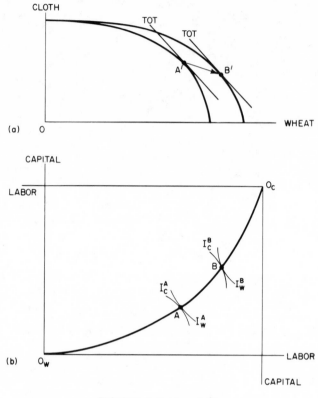

FIGURE 8–9 (a) and (b)

If we would also stipulate that the factor prices are not to be changed, this would mean that the cloth industry, where no technological change has occurred, would continue to operate at the same capital/labor ratio as before. In other words the cloth industry would be confined to the factor intensity ray that emanates from O_C and passes through A (see Figure 8–10b).

Now let us turn to the wheat industry and assume that the biased technological progress is of the labor-saving variety. As this factor is saved some of the workers in the wheat industry will no longer be able to find employment at the going wage. The wheat industry will want to employ a larger quantity of capital in conjunction with each worker.

This point is illustrated in Figure 8–10b where production is assumed to take place initially at point A, leading to a cloth output of 20 units and a wheat output of 30 units. After the labor-saving technological improvement occurs the new (dashed) isoquants will represent the production function for wheat. Point B is an efficient point of production now, because it shows a point at which a new wheat isoquant is tangent to a cloth isoquant. However, point B violates one of our initial stipulations, that the factor price ratio

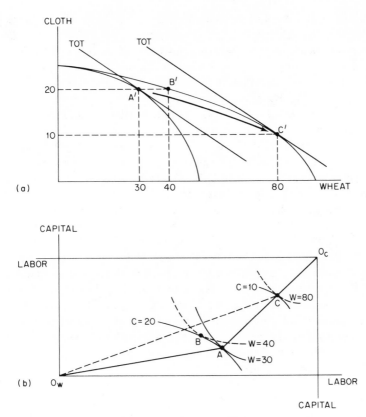

FIGURE 8–10 (a) and (b)

remain unchanged. Also the factor intensity ratio in the cloth industry is different from the initial situation.

To restore the original factor price ratio the workers who were "saved" in the wheat industry due to the technological advance must get the same proportion of capital to work with as before. This required capital can be obtained only through a contraction of the capital-intensive cloth industry. As the cloth industry contracts, it releases relatively more capital than labor. This capital can be used in the wheat industry, which is expanding, in order to restore the marginal productivity—and by this the wage—of the factor labor.

The final point of equilibrium is shown by C, which is the point of tangency of a cloth isoquant (C = 10) and a new wheat isoquant (W = 80). The factor price ratio at C is the same as at A, because both are located on the same ray from the origin O_C. The homogeneity assumption about the isoquants assures that all the cloth isoquants have the same slope at the point at which they are cut by the ray. After the labor-saving technological improvement the wheat industry will use *relatively* less labor. The absolute amount of both factors of production in the wheat industry will increase, as will the output level.

Technological progress that saves the factor of production used intensively in that industry will lead to ultra-biased growth of this industry.

There is one other case that should be examined in this context. If technological progress in the wheat industry saves the factor of production that is used relatively little, that is, capital, it will be found that this capital can be absorbed at the going wage only in the other industry. The cloth industry that uses capital intensively will therefore expand. The wheat industry, in which the technological progress occurs, is also likely to expand somewhat. In general, however, it will not be possible to say whether the resulting economic growth is biased in favor of one or the other industry.

Technological progress that saves the factor of production that is not used intensively in that industry may lead to any kind of growth pattern.

Let us note again that there is a difference between growth due to factor quantity changes and technological changes. For instance in the case of factor endowment changes in exact proportion to the endowments already existing in the wheat industry, we will find that just the output of the wheat industry expands, while cloth output stays constant. The increased revenues from the additional output will be paid to the two factors of production, labor and capital. There is no further incentive to reallocate resources. The case was illustrated in Figure 8–5 above.

Contrast this to the situation that results after technological progress that saves the two factors of production in exact proportion as they are used in the wheat industry. The two factors, labor and capital, will continue to be paid the same amount. But as output increases with unchanged total costs, we find that the entrepreneurs start to make profits. Under competitive conditions the excess profits earned will lead to an expansion of the wheat industry, and resources will be bid away from the cloth industry that will contract. Figure 8–9 illustrated this case.

The crucial difference lies in who is the recipient of the additional revenues from the output expansion. In the case of factor quantity changes, the factors receive the funds. In the case of technological progress, it is assumed that the entrepreneur receives the additional revenues in the form of profits. If we were to expand our model into a three-factor case, with the third factor being research and development that generates the technological change, the additional revenues would accrue to research and development.

THE LARGE COUNTRY AND ECONOMIC GROWTH

Throughout the preceding discussion we assumed that the country is relatively small and faces a given set of terms of trade at which it can trade any quantity of commodities desired. This condition will be replaced now by the assumption that the country plays a large role in the relevant markets so that international terms of trade will in fact be influenced by her actions. Most of the conclusions established in the preceding pages must be modified to take account of the changing international commodity prices caused by economic growth.

Here we will deal only with the net effects of economic growth on the country. Pro-trade biased economic growth is again taken to mean that the country will tend to trade a larger percentage of its national product. As the trade volume expands, the price of imports will be driven up and the price of exports will fall. The terms of trade turn "against" the country, because only a smaller quantity of imports can now be obtained for the same (or even larger) quantity of exports.

With an anti-trade bias it is possible for the terms of trade to turn either in favor of or against the growing country. The criterion in this case is whether the *absolute* quantity of trade tends to increase or to decrease concomitantly to economic growth. The final result will depend on the elasticities of the domestic and foreign supply and demand curves.

Even with neutral economic growth there exists the possibility that the terms of trade may turn so strongly against the growing country that she will actually wind up on a lower indifference curve than she could attain before economic growth. This case of *immizerizing growth*,[1] as it is often called, is illustrated in Figure 8–11. Production takes place initially at point P_1, and the country consumes the commodity combination C_1. Thus she is able to reach the community indifference curve CIC_1. After economic growth occurs production changes to P_2, and as the terms of trade change to TOT_2 the best possible consumption point is C_2. Point C_2, however, is located on the community indifference curve CIC_0, which is located below the community indifference curve CIC_1 and therefore denotes a lower attainable welfare level. The country will be worse off as a consequence of economic growth.

We should point out, though, that it is always possible for the growing country to levy an appropriate tariff, which will protect the country from welfare losses it would otherwise experience. This becomes clear when we recall that the offer curve of the trading partner has not changed at all because of the economic growth in the large country. Foreigners will always be willing to continue to exchange the same quantity of commodities at the old terms of trade.

Economic growth in a large country that increases the volume of trade may lead to a deterioration of the terms of trade. The terms of trade may deteriorate to such an extent that the country is worse off as a result of growth. This, however, can always be avoided by the imposition of an appropriate tariff.

The policy implications of this conclusion can be observed frequently. To avoid the deterioration of the terms of trade caused by the sale of larger

[1] Jagdish Bhagwati, "Immerizerizing Growth," *Review of Economic Studies*, June 1958.

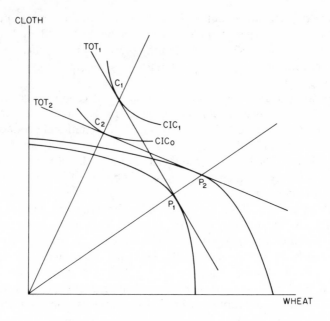

FIGURE 8-11

quantities of the export commodity of a country, especially in the face of inelastic demand curves, the country can assess export duties on the commodity. Quantitative restrictions are employed frequently with the same result. Because home demand for the commodities involved may be insufficient, it may even be rational from the viewpoint of the exporting country to place limitations on the production of the commodity or, if it is a perishable commodity and has been produced already, to destroy it.

EMPIRICAL EVIDENCE

The basic question of this chapter is whether the foreign trade sector tends to grow proportionally faster or slower than national output as a whole. Does economic growth make a country more dependent on foreign trade, or less?

Empirical evidence on this topic is hard to come by, and the few available studies present only fragmentary evidence. In several time series studies of the share of foreign trade in national income Karl Deutsch and Alexander Eckstein conclude that there is a tendency for international trade to expand relatively to national income in the early stages of industrialization.[2] After

[2] Karl Deutsch and Alexander Eckstein, "National Industrialization and the Declining Share of the International Economic Sector, 1890–1959," *World Politics*, January 1961.

this, however, there seems to be a persistent decline in the percentage of foreign traded commodities. The peak in the size of the foreign trade sector seems to come for most countries with the completion of industrialization. For most of the European countries it can be placed in the late nineteenth and early twentieth centuries.

This evidence on the share of foreign trade in world income is supported by the finding that the growth rate of exports lags persistently behind the growth rate for national income for ten countries that account for more than 50 per cent of total world trade.

We are able to assemble some evidence on why the share of foreign trade relative to income tends to decline. For one, agricultural products are characterized by inelastic demand patterns, as was pointed out in Chapter 5. As income levels go up the demand for these items increases less than proportionally, and to the extent that they are traded internationally, trade will tend to decrease relatively to national income.

A second important influence is the tendency for services to increase more than proportionally as the income level goes up. As the bulk of all services is of the domestic variety, an increase in the service sector implies a decline of the foreign trade sector in percentage terms.

Finally industrial growth tends to occur in most countries at a more rapid rate than the increase in demand.[3] As a consequence we find that countries will tend to substitute their own industrial products for imports. The result is a further decline in the importance of the foreign trade sector in relation to total national income. Chenery found that even in Japan, one of the countries most successful in expanding exports, 40 percent of industrial growth was due to import substitution while only 10 percent was due to increased exports.

The post World War II period, however, brought a sharp turnabout in the historical pattern. The volume of world trade increased from $53 billion in 1948 to $279 billion in 1970—an increase of 523 percent over a twenty-two year period. Thus world trade grew at a much faster rate than national incomes. The income elasticity of the demand for foreign goods (see Chapter 2) also has values substantially above unity in most countries.

It is clear that the increasing importance of the foreign trade sector came about largely as a result of continuing trade liberalization policies adopted by most countries in the post World War II period. The General Agreements on Tariffs and Trade (GATT) provided the framework within which much of the tariff reductions and removals of export and import quotas were negotiated. Another powerful influence in expanding world trade was exercised by the various regional common markets that were established and within which trade is not hampered by tariff barriers. The European

[3] H. Chenery, "Patterns of Industrial Growth," *American Economic Review* September 1960.

Economic Community, initially composed of France, Germany, Italy, Belgium, Luxembourg, and the Netherlands, was enlarged to include Denmark, Iceland, and the United Kingdom. The Latin American Free Trade Association formed by Brazil, Argentina, Chile, Mexico, Uruguay, Paraguay, and Peru and the Central American Common Market are the most prominent examples. New negotiations about the formation of new unions in Asia are under way.

Hence the evidence on the rising or declining importance of world trade is far from compelling and much further research needs to be done before we can hope to state the relationship between economic growth and international trade in a more definite manner.

SUGGESTED FURTHER READINGS

BHAGWATI, JAGDISH, "Immizerizing Growth," *Review of Economic Studies* (June 1958). Reprinted in AEA *Readings in International Economics*, eds. Richard Caves and Harry G. Johnson. Homewood, Ill.: Richard D. Irwin, Inc., 1968.

———, "Optimal Policies and Immizerizing Growth," *American Economic Review* (December 1969).

FINDLAY, R., and H. GRUBERT, "Factor Intensities, Technological Progress, and International Trade," *Oxford Economic Papers* (February 1959). Reprinted in *International Trade*, ed. Jagdish Bhagwati. Baltimore: Penguin Books, Inc., 1969.

JOHNSON, HARRY G., *International Trade and Economic Growth*, Chaps. III and IV. London: George Allen & Unwin, 1958.

———, *Money, Trade, and Economic Growth*, Chap. IV. Cambridge: Harvard University Press, 1962.

KEMP, MURRAY, *The Pure Theory of International Trade*, Chap. VII. Englewood Cliffs, N.J.: Prentice-Hall, Inc., 1964.

KINDLEBERGER, CHARLES, *Foreign Trade and the National Economy*, especially Chap. XI. New Haven: Yale University Press, 1962.

MEIER, GERALD, *International Trade and Development*, Chap. II. New York: Harper & Row, 1963.

MUNDELL, ROBERT, "International Trade and Factor Mobility," *American Economic Review* (June 1957).

RYBCZYNSKI, T. M., "Factor Endowments and Relative Commodity Prices," *Economica* (November 1955).

9

Tariffs
and International Trade

One of the most important tools of foreign economic policy is the tariff. Tariffs allow the country levying them to influence the pattern and volume of her trade with the outside world. By imposing different tariffs on different commodities the country is able to change the relative prices of the commodities, which will result in a different trade pattern than would occur in the absence of the tariffs. In other words the commodity composition of international trade will change. The country is also able to determine, within limits, the absolute volume of international trade. By increasing the tariff the volume of international trade undertaken will generally fall. There will always be one tariff so prohibitively high that international trade will cease altogether. On the other hand a decrease of the tariff rate will usually lead to a rise in trade volume. A negative tariff, or subsidy, will generally lead to an expansion of international trade over and above the free trade volume.

ARGUMENTS FOR PROTECTION

There are several noneconomic arguments that might make it desirable for a country to trade less and to move to a position of greater autarky. The desire to preserve a certain way of life, isolated from foreign influences, may be so strong that a country is willing to pay a certain economic price for the attainment of this social objective. Greater self-sufficiency is also often a military objective. The manufacture of arms and heavy industrial equipment as well as the production of agricultural commodities are examples of industries that can be important for national defense. In all these cases the benefits to be derived from greater protection should always be weighed against the additional costs incurred by the protective policy.

Alternatives to protecting the industry against foreign competition must be considered, too. Stockpiling of the commodities deemed essential for the defense effort is one alternative. Other possibilities include the support of the armament industry by policies other than the restriction of foreign trade, such as tax advantages or outright subsidies.

Economic arguments for protection are often built on the divergence of private and social benefits and costs. Private and social benefits can diverge if certain benefits from the production process accrue to society as a whole yet not to the entrepreneur who is unable to charge an appropriate price— quite often because the relevant markets have not been formed or cannot be formed without undue costs. It is also possible that private and social costs are not identical. Producers may, for instance, be able to avoid paying certain costs by imposing them on other members of society.

Frequently tariff protection is advocated for so-called infant industries. This term refers to a newly established industry that has not yet reached an output level allowing it to benefit from certain economies of scale which may exist at higher output levels. A protective tariff may help such an industry to get off the ground and achieve levels of production at which the industry can be competitive in the world market. As soon as this competitive level is achieved the tariff can be removed, and the industry is then forced to compete with the most efficient outside producers in order to ensure its own efficiency. Again it is desirable to investigate alternative courses of action. A state-guaranteed loan, a tax advantage, or an outright subsidy may help the industry at a smaller cost to society as a whole than a tariff. Also the amount of direct or indirect subsidy that the industry receives makes the costs incurred by society more apparent than they will be when a tariff is imposed, thereby forcing the decision makers to take a stand on whether or not the cost is worthwhile.

EFFECTS OF A TARIFF

Several economic effects of a tariff deserve mentioning. It is important to realize that the imposition of a tariff on commodities imported from abroad[1] will affect not only the economy of the country imposing the tariff but will also have profound effects on her trading partners.

Let us consider first the case of a small country that faces given prices in world markets. We will concentrate on one commodity, cloth, and assume

---

[1] In this discussion we will concentrate on tariffs levied on imports. It should be pointed out, however, that export tariffs are perfectly symmetrical to import tariffs in their economic effects.

that cloth production is vertically integrated both here and abroad. Also the domestically produced cloth is assumed to be a perfect substitute for foreign cloth.

In Figure 9–1 we show the domestic U.S. supply and demand curves for cloth and the world market supply curve, S^W. If the United States does not impose a tariff on the importation of cloth, the domestic and the world market price of cloth will be PO. Domestic producers will supply PC (= OG)

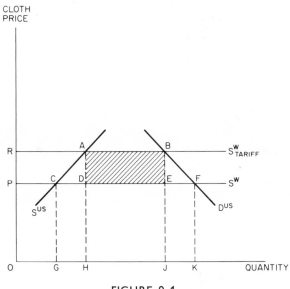

FIGURE 9–1

of cloth, and CF (= GK) will be purchased by Americans in the world market. Hence total U.S. consumption will amount to PF (= OK) units of cloth.

Now let us assume that a tariff is imposed at the per unit rate RP. The *nominal* or *ad valorem* tariff rate expresses the per unit tariff RP as a percentage of the price PO. Hence the nominal tariff rate in our example is RP/PO. In the following discussion we will always be concerned with nominal tariff rates.

Economists distinguish among the following effects of the tariff. First of all there is a *consumption effect* with respect to cloth. In the United States the consumption of cloth will decrease from OK to OJ. Decreased cloth consumption in the United States is due to the rise in price that follows directly from the imposition of the tariff. Second there is a *production effect* of the tariff. The increased protection afforded the cloth industry in the United States leads to an expansion of domestic output from OG to OH. Third there

revenue effect

redistribution effect

is a *revenue effect* consisting of a change in government receipts because of the tariff. In our example there is initially a zero tariff, naturally bringing no revenue. Then a tariff of RP, multiplied by the quantity of imports after the imposition of the tariff, namely AB, gives the total amount of tariff revenue. The total government receipts are indicated by the shaded area ABED. Finally there is a *redistribution effect*, reflecting the fact that producers now receive a price for their commodities that is above their increase in production costs. This amount, RPCA, now accrues to producers in the form of economic

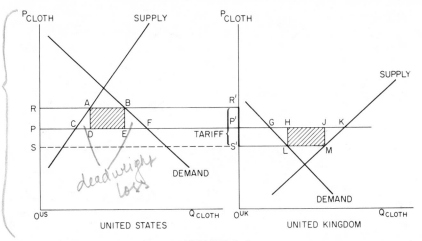

deadweight loss

FIGURE 9–2

rent, but it used to be part of the consumer's surplus that the residents derived because they were able to purchase the commodity at the low pretariff price, yet derived from it utility equal to the area under the demand curve. In addition there will be a net loss of consumers' surplus equal to BEF as well as additional production costs equal to ACD due to the inefficiencies introduced by the tariff.

It is clear that the magnitude of the effects described depends on the size of the tariff as well as on the elasticities of the supply and demand curves involved. This is easy to see when we change the shape of some of the curves in Figure 9–1 and observe the changes in the size of the areas discussed.

The analysis is not changed much when we remove the small country assumption in our model and replace it with the large country assumption that a country will influence the world prices. In Figure 9–2 we show the domestic supply and demand curves for cloth in the United States and the United Kingdom. In the absence of international trade the price of cloth will be determined by the intersection of the supply and demand curves in each country. In our example the cloth price in the United States will be above the price in the United Kingdom. As soon as free international trade starts one world price will be established for both countries together, excluding transport costs. We recall the necessary condition for the new world price to be an equilibrium price—that trade between the two countries must be balanced. This condition is fulfilled in Figure 9–2, where the United States imports CF of cloth and the United Kingdom exports GK at the going world price PO^{US} ($= P'O^{UK}$).

Now let us suppose that the United States imposes a tariff of the magnitude RS on her cloth imports from the United Kingdom.[2] As a result the price of cloth in the United States increases to RO^{US}, and the price in the United Kingdom decreases to $S'O^{UK}$. For the new prices to be equilibrium prices the condition that exports equal imports must be fulfilled. Cloth imports of AB by the United States are matched by cloth exports of LM by the United Kingdom. Note that the tariff will affect the prices in both the United States and the United Kingdom. The nominal tariff rate is RS/SO^{US}.

The consumption, production, and redistribution effects are defined as before. But note that the governmental tariff revenue is now composed of two areas: ABDE and HJML. The product of the import volume AB ($= LM$), the price increase to American consumers of RP, and the price decrease for British producers of P'S' make up the revenue of the tax authorities. The tariff revenue is shown by the shaded area.

THE TERMS OF TRADE

Traditionally the effects of a tariff on the terms of trade have been studied with great care, and they will occupy our attention for the remainder of this section. In Figure 9–2 we show that a tariff of the size RS increases the domestic price of the commodity by only a fraction of this amount, namely, RP, while simultaneously lowering the foreign price of the commodity by PS. Note that the United States is now able to buy the imports at the *lower* price $S'O^{UK}$ from the United Kingdom, but that the domestic price in the United States, after the duty has been collected by the United States government, is now at the higher level RO^{US}. The difference between the different prices can also be brought out in the traditional international offer curve diagram.

In Figure 9–3 we show the free trade offer curves of the United States and the United Kingdom, TOC^{US} and TOC^{UK} respectively. The free trade terms of trade, TOT, are determined by the intersection of the trade offer curves of the two countries. If the United States imposes a tariff on the importation of cloth, *and the tariff is levied in terms of wheat* by the United States

[2] It is possible to substitute "an export tariff by the United Kingdom" at this juncture without affecting any of the following conclusions, except that the U.K. collects all the tariff revenues.

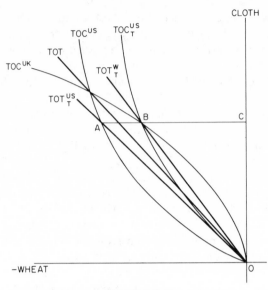

FIGURE 9-3

government, then the new U.S. offer curve, including the tariff, is TOC_T^{US}. This offer curve, including the tariff, represents a displacement of the free trade offer curve TOC^{US} by the amount of the tariff, here shown as AB. The tariff rate is given by $t = AB/BC$. The total tariff *revenue* (in terms of wheat) is equal to AB.

The intersection of the new trade offer curve TOC_T^{US} and the British trade offer curve TOC^{UK} determines the new global terms of trade TOT_T^{W}. It now takes a smaller quantity of wheat exports to import the same quantity of cloth than it did before the tariff was imposed by the United States. This change will be referred to as a "favorable" movement in the terms of trade for the United States. As seen from the viewpoint of the United States consumer, however, the terms of trade have worsened because of the tariff. This is so because the domestic resident now faces a set of terms of trade that comprises not only the world market price for the commodity but also the amount of the tariff. Thus the United States domestic term of trade would indicate that a greater quantity of exports is needed to obtain the same quantity of imports. Compared with the free trade terms of trade, therefore, the external terms of trade that the United States faces in world markets have improved, and domestic terms of trade have deteriorated.

The tariff can also be levied in terms of the import commodity, cloth. Under these circumstances the new offer curve for the United States, including the tariff, represents not a horizontal displacement of the free trade offer curve by the amount of the tariff, but a *vertical* displacement, because cloth is measured along the vertical axis. This situation is shown in Figure 9-4,

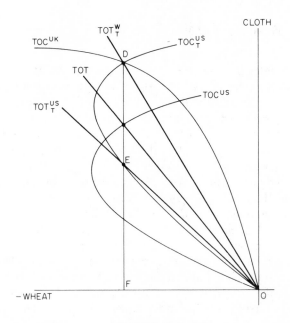

FIGURE 9–4

where the trade offer curve, including the tariff, TOC_T^{US}, is a vertical displacement of the free trade offer curve TOC^{US} by the amount of the tariff. This time the tariff *revenue* DE is collected in terms of cloth, and the tariff *rate* is DE/EF.

An important consideration is the use to which the collected tariff proceeds are put. If the government consumes the tariff proceeds itself, no further problems arise. Both Figures 9–3 and 9–4 were drawn up under this assumption. If, on the other hand, the government wants to consume the other commodity, too, it has to enter the world market to obtain it. By doing this the government will add its own demand to the private demand for this commodity, and new trade offer curves will be generated. The new trade offer curves will lead to different terms of trade thereby inducing the private sector to rearrange its spending patterns to take account of the changing relative prices.

Similar complications will result from government redistribution of the proceeds collected from the tariff if the recipients of these government subsidies do not consume the subsidies directly but intend to consume a different commodity unit. In this case the changing private demand pattern will lead to the formation of new trade offer curves and, in turn, necessitate a readjustment of all equilibria.

It is apparent from the foregoing discussion that tariffs have profound effects on the economic welfare of a country and of different economic groups within a country. A discussion of these welfare repercussions will be postponed until Chapter 11.

THE OPTIMUM TARIFF

A large country in world trade, that is, a country that faces a less than perfectly elastic foreign supply curve, is able to influence the terms of trade to its advantage. If a country wishes to take advantage of this power, it will levy an *optimal tariff*. The optimal tariff is defined as that tariff rate that will permit the country imposing the tariff to reach the highest possible community indifference curve—and by this the highest possible welfare level. The existence of such a tariff is due to two opposing forces that are at work as the height of the tariff is increased: (1) the price paid for imports (exclusive of the tariff) tends to fall, while at the same time (2) the volume of imports tends to be more and more curtailed because of the higher tariff. An optimum position is reached when the gain due to (1) exceeds the loss from (2) by the greatest possible margin.

The country imposing the tariff, here the United States, wishes to reach the highest possible trade indifference curve. She knows that at any given terms of trade the United Kingdom is willing to trade a commodity combination represented by a point on her trade offer curve. The problem is to find the commodity combination that will fulfill both these conditions simultaneously. The desired commodity combination is the one at which one of the United States trade indifference curves is tangent to the U.K. trade offer curve. The tangency position assures that there is no higher United States trade indifference curve than can be reached *given* the U.K. trade offer curve. Such a point is shown by A in Figure 9–5.

Having determined the optimal commodity combination all that is left for the United States to do is to levy a tariff that will bend her own trade offer curve in such a way that it will go through point A. The new United States trade offer curve, after the imposition of the tariff, is labeled TOC_T^{US}.

A further important point requires attention. The position of point A demarks the optimal trade combination for the United States. To offer her residents an inducement to trade precisely this commodity combination, namely, to export AB of wheat in exchange for BO of cloth imports, the price ratio confronting United States residents must be equal to the slope of a line that is tangent to the trade indifference curve TI_0^{US} at point A. This line, labeled TOT_T^{US} shows the domestic price ratio after the imposition of the tariff in the United States.

The world price ratio that will prevail after the United States has imposed the tariff is shown by the terms of trade TOT_T^W in Figure 9–5. Clearly the world price ratio and the United States *domestic* price ratio have to differ by the tariff rate imposed on the commodities entering the United States. The world price ratio is AB/BO, and the domestic price ratio is AB/BC. The nominal tariff rate, t, which will make the two price ratios equal, can be

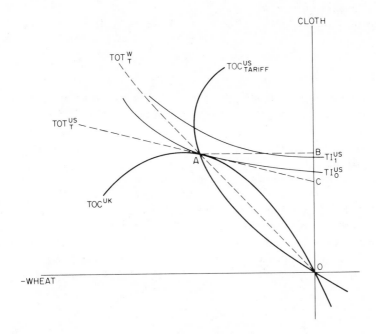

FIGURE 9–5

determined as follows:

$$(1 + t)AB/BO = AB/BC \qquad (9-1)$$

$$1 + t = \frac{AB/BC}{AB/BO} \quad \text{and}$$

$$t = \frac{BO}{BC} - 1 \qquad (9-2)$$

We may rewrite (9–2) as follows:

$$t = \frac{BO}{BC} - 1 = \frac{BC}{BC} + \frac{CO}{BC} - 1 = \frac{CO}{BC} \qquad (9-3)$$

From the elasticity definition of equation (6–4) we obtain

$$\epsilon = \frac{BO}{CO} = \frac{BC}{CO} + \frac{CO}{CO} = \frac{BC}{CO} + 1 \qquad (9-4)$$

or,

$$\frac{BC}{CO} = \epsilon - 1 \qquad (9-5)$$

Inserting the inverse of (9–5) into (9–3) we obtain the final result of

(9–6)
$$t = \frac{1}{\epsilon - 1}$$

which is the desired optimum tariff formula. For instance if the elasticity of the foreign trade offer curve is equal to 3, the optimum tariff formula yields $1/(3 - 1) = 1/2 = .50$. That is, a 50 percent tariff will bring us to the highest trade indifference curve.

A few properties of the optimum tariff formula may be mentioned here. If the elasticity of the foreign trade offer curve is infinity, then the optimum tariff $t = 1/(\epsilon - 1)$ will be equal to zero. A small country facing a *given* set of terms of trade and able to trade any quantity she desires at these terms of trade will find it to her advantage not to levy any tariff at all. On the other hand if a country faces a unit elastic foreign trade offer curve, then she should levy a tariff that approaches infinity. In order to explain this seemingly unusual result let us remind ourselves that a unit elastic foreign trade offer curve means that the other country is willing to accept any quantity of our exports in exchange for a fixed amount of our import commodity. It would be to the advantage of our country to exploit this willingness to the greatest possible extent. The way to do this is to levy an extremely high tariff. Lastly if the foreign trade offer curve has an elasticity smaller than one, the optimum tariff formula will yield a negative value. In this case it will be to the advantage of our country to move all the way to the elastic portion of the foreign trade offer curve, because we will thereby reach a higher trade indifference curve. This follows from the fact that the trade indifference curves in Figure 9–5 slope downward to the right and can therefore be tangent only to a foreign trade offer curve that also slopes downward to the right. An inelastic foreign trade offer curve, however, has a positive slope and therefore cannot be tangent to a downward sloping trade indifference curve.

A country that is able to impose a tariff will always find it to her advantage to trade on a point located on the elastic portion of the other country's trade offer curve. The optimal tariff rate is equal to $1/(\epsilon - 1)$.

Retaliation

Let us suppose that the United States imposes an optimal tariff. She does this by modifying the original trade offer curve TOC_0^{US} shown in Figure 9–6 into TOC_1^{US}. At point B a United States trade indifference curve is tangent to the United Kingdom offer curve TOC_0^{UK}, and B therefore denotes the new point of equilibrium. Faced with the new United States trade offer curve TOC_1^{US}, the United Kingdom might now want to impose an optimal tariff herself. By determining the point of tangency of a British trade

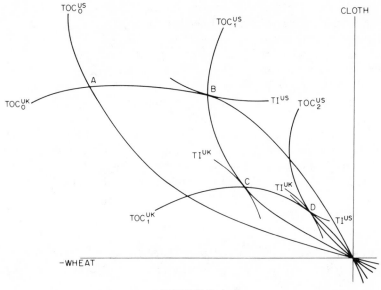

FIGURE 9-6

indifference curve with the new United States trade offer curve, she is able to find the optimal tariff and modifies her trade offer curve to TOC_1^{UK}. The new equilibrium point is marked C. At C the United Kingdom is on a higher trade indifference curve than she was at B.

The procedure of retaliation and counterretaliation can continue for many rounds. After the United States is faced with the new tariff-ridden British trade offer curve TOC_1^{UK} she will want to take another look at her own tariff structure and revise it in the light of the British reaction. Given the shape of the curve as drawn in Figure 9-6, the United States will want to modify her tariff and reshape her trade offer curve into TOC_2^{US}. The new equilibrium is now at D.

We note that the retaliatory tariff increases, and that each countermove to the other country's tariff policy results in a smaller and smaller volume of international trade between the countries. The free trade volume of trade is given by the commodity bundle A. After the imposition of the initial United States tariff the volume of trade is reduced to B, the British retaliation results in C, and the United States counterretaliation pushes the trade volume down to D.

The question arises whether retaliation will continue until finally the volume of trade is reduced to zero. In order to answer this question we recall that the position of one country's trade indifference curve in relation to the other country's trade offer curve is decisive as far as the height of the optimum tariff is concerned. If the first country's trade indifference curve is tangent to the other country's trade offer curve at a point that already lies on the first country's trade offer curve, no further tariff could allow the first country to reach a higher trade indifference curve.

This case is illustrated by point D in Figure 9–6. The United States counterretaliatory move resulted, as we saw, in the trade offer curve TOC_2^{US} and brought the trade volume down to point D. Now we find that a British trade indifference curve, TI^{UK}, is already tangent to the United States trade offer curve at this point. No further tariff imposed by the United Kingdom will allow her to reach a higher trade indifference curve, and the United Kingdom, therefore, has no incentive to modify her trade offer curve TOC_1^{UK} any further. If the United Kingdom does not change her existing tariff structure, the United States has no incentive to modify her tariffs either. Point D will be the final point of equilibrium, and no further retaliatory tariffs are to be expected.

Tariff Cycles

Trade indifference curves and trade offer curves may have a peculiar constellation that will lead to the emergence of tariff cycles. Tariff cycles

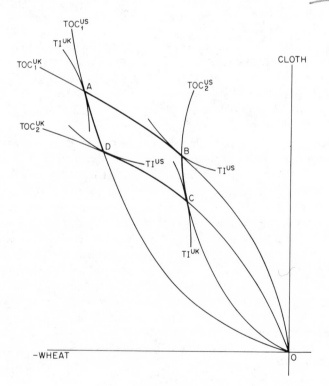

FIGURE 9–7

may be described as situations in which both countries will alternate between high and low tariffs.

Consider Figure 9-7. TOC_1^{US} and TOC_1^{UK} show the initial situation where both the United States and the United Kingdom have a small tariff placed on their imports. The United States will find it to her advantage to move from point A to point B by imposing an optimal tariff, which will change her trade offer curve to TOC_2^{US}. Faced with this new trade offer curve the United Kingdom will want to impose a new tariff herself, changing her trade offer curve to TOC_2^{UK} while reaching the new equilibrium point C. Now the United States will reconsider her previous move, and because one of her own trade indifference curves is tangent to Britain's new trade offer curve TOC_2^{UK} at point D, which lies in the *old* United States trade offer curve TOC_1^{US}, the United States will return to her *old* tariff. Now it is Britain's turn to reconsider the situation, and since one of her trade indifference curves is tangent to the United States TOC_1^{US} trade offer curve at point A, she will also want to return to her old tariff level and trade along offer curve TOC_1^{UK}. This means a return to point A, at which the United States will again find it advantageous to levy a tariff, returning us to point B, and a new round in the tariff cycle will start.

THE EFFECTIVE PROTECTIVE TARIFF RATE

In the previous discussion it was implicitly assumed that we produce the final commodities directly from the original factors of production. Most commodities, however, are *not* produced directly from the original factors of production but utilize intermediate products as inputs. The automotive industry, for instance, uses products manufactured by the tire, paint, steel, glass, and many other industries as inputs for automobile production. Our standard example, the cloth industry, uses yarn as one of the inputs into the production process. We will assume that yarn is also traded internationally but that all other inputs such as land, labor, and the like are primary factors of production. The value added by these primary factors is the value added by the domestic cloth weaving industry.

We will analyze now how much protection is afforded to the U.S. cloth weaving industry as a result of the combined tariffs on cloth and wheat. In other words we will investigate the effects of the whole *tariff structure* on the protection afforded to the cloth industry. The rate of protection to the industry is called the *effective protective rate*. The effective protective rate shows by how much the value added in the industry can exceed the value added in the absence of tariff protection.

The protection afforded to the cloth industry depends on how high a tariff is levied not only on its products but also on its input, yarn. If, for instance, yarn can enter the country at a low duty while cloth is protected by a high duty, the result will be a very high effective protective rate for the cloth weaving industry in the United States. Conversely if inputs can enter the United States only under a very high duty and the final product is not at all or very lightly protected, then the United States weaving industry will be faced with higher than world market prices for their inputs yet must compete in the cloth market against foreign manufacturers. The effective protective rate for the weaving industry in this case is very low and can, indeed, become negative.

We can state formally that the effective protective rate for the cloth industry, epr_c, is equal to the nominal tariff rate on cloth, t_c, minus the weighted tariff rate on the yarn inputs, t_y, divided by the value added in the cloth industry, v_c. The weight, a_{yc}, attached to the input tariff is equal to the share of the yarn input in the value of the cloth output. Obviously $v_c + a_{yc} = 1$.

(9–7)
$$epr_c = \frac{t_c - a_{yc}t_y}{v_c}$$

If we have to deal with more than one input, we simply use a weighted average of the tariff rates imposed on the various inputs, where the weights, a_{ij}, are the share of input i in the cost of j production:

(9–8)
$$epr_j = \frac{t_j - \sum a_{ij}t_i}{v_j} = \frac{t_j - \sum a_{ij}t_i}{1 - \sum a_{ij}}$$

Figure 9–8 reproduces the domestic supply and demand curves for cloth and the world supply curve of cloth introduced in Figure 9–1. In addition we show the U.S. supply curve for yarn, S_{yarn}^{US} and the world supply curve for yarn, S_{yarn}^{W}. We maintain the small country assumption of infinitely elastic foreign supply curves for both cloth and yarn. Also we assume that the U.S. does not specialize completely and that there is a fixed amount of yarn that is used per unit of cloth woven. This latter assumption rules out possible substitution effects among inputs in the U.S. cloth weaving industry. Units in Figure 9–8 are chosen so that one unit of yarn is required for each unit of cloth produced.

Initially, when there are no tariffs at all imposed, the price of cloth is PO, and the U.S. produces OG and consumes OK of cloth. The yarn price is equal to NO and the U.S. produces OZ and uses OG of yarn in the cloth production process. Note that the total yarn input required is determined by the level of U.S. cloth production PC ($= OG$).

The value added in the cloth weaving industry is given by the difference

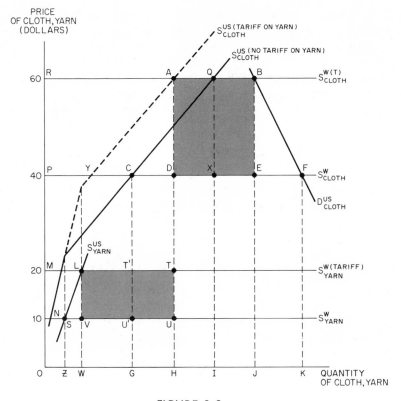

FIGURE 9–8

between the price to be paid for the yarn inputs and the value of the woven cloth, that is, PN.[3] Now let us assume that a nominal tariff rate equal to RP/PO is imposed on cloth imports. We are now in a position to calculate the effective protection afforded to the cloth weaving industry. The value added in the cloth weaving industry rises from PN to RN. That is, the value added changes by RP due to the tariff protection. Thus, the cloth industry enjoys a protective rate equal to RP/PN. We refer to this as the *effective protective rate* (epr) of the tariff.

If instead of levying the tariff on cloth, we would have levied a nominal tariff of MN/NO on yarn imports only, the input prices would have increased to the cloth weaving industry by MN, while the cloth output prices would have stayed at the old level. The tariff on yarn would have resulted in a *negative* effective protective rate of −MN/PN on the value added by the

[3] Let us note that the yarn supply curves show an *input*, and the cloth supply curves show an *output*. The vertical distance between the input and output curves is equal to the value added in the cloth industry.

weaving industry. Rather than being able to compete with foreign producers on even terms, the tariff on the yarn inputs would have raised input prices to U.S. cloth weavers while leaving cloth output prices unchanged.

Finally we may encounter a situation where there are tariffs on *both* cloth and yarn. In that case the cloth tariff increases protection to the cloth industry, but the yarn tariff reduces protection. In terms of Figure 9–8 we can calculate the effective protective rate for the cloth weaving industry by

(9–9)
$$epr_c = \frac{RP - MN}{PN}$$

A numerical example may further clarify the concept. We will use the dollar values of Figure 9–8 to calculate the effective protective rate according to Equations (9–7) and (9–9).

Using Equation (9–9) we obtain:

$$epr_c = \frac{RP - MN}{PN} = \frac{\$20 - \$10}{\$30} = .33$$

Alternatively we could have calculated nominal tariff rates first and then used Equation (9–7):

$$epr_c = \frac{t_c - a_{yc}t_y}{v_c} = \frac{RP/PO - (NO/PO)MN/NO}{PN/PO} = \frac{.50 - (.25)1.00}{.75} = .33$$

The effective protective rate is very important for the assessment of the protection afforded to individual industries of a country. Even without changing the tariff levied on the output of an industry, the effective protection can change if the tariff on the direct inputs changes. Not only is the tariff on the final product decisive, but the whole tariff *structure* plays a role in determining the protection afforded to an industry. It should be noted, however, that only the tariffs levied on the direct inputs to a production process are important. The tariffs levied on inputs used to produce the direct inputs used in the production process are irrelevant for our consideration. Thus the tariff rate on wool that is used to produce the yarn for cloth production is irrelevant for the determination of the effective protective tariff rate of the cloth industry. Only the tariffs on the direct inputs, like yarn, and the product, cloth, are of importance.

Again we are able to identify the familiar production, consumption, revenue, and redistribution effects. Table 9–1 summarizes the various effects as shown in Figure 9–8.

All these effects are obvious. The only complication that occurs is that the U.S. supply curve for cloth shifts from S_{cloth}^{US} to $S_{cloth}^{US(TY)}$ when a tariff

TABLE 9–1

EFFECTS OF TARIFFS ON INPUTS AND OUTPUTS

	Cloth				Yarn			
Tariff on	Production Effect	Consumption Effect	Redistribution Effect	Revenue Effect	Production Effect	Consumption Effect	Redistribution Effect	Revenue Effect
Cloth only	GI	—JK	RPCQ	QXEB	GI	—	—	—
Yarn only	—YC	—	AYCQ	—	—YC	ZW	MNSL	LVU'T'
Cloth and yarn	GH	—JK	RPYA	ADEB	GH	ZW	MNSL	LVUT

is imposed on yarn. This is due to the fact that yarn import prices increase because the tariff and cloth production becomes more expensive—resulting in a higher cloth supply curve.

EMPIRICAL EVIDENCE

Empirical estimates regarding the effects of tariff protection are difficult to come by. In a recent study Giorgio Basevi attempts to estimate the total gains from the existing U.S. tariff structure to the United States.[4] Basevi utilizes effective protective tariff rates and concentrates on the terms of trade effects of U.S. tariffs. Using alternative sets of elasticities for export and import supply and demand curves he estimates the range of possible economic gains for the United States to be between $258 and $558 million. (Annual average for 1958–62.) As Basevi points out, these estimates are surprisingly small, representing at best one-tenth of one percent of the U.S. GNP.

Much more attention has been paid to calculations of the effective protective rate that results from the present tariff structure. Two of the pioneering studies in this area were undertaken by Bela Balassa[5] and Giorgio Basevi[6]. Both these studies point out that the nominal tariff rate is misleading in that it leaves out the effect of tariffs imposed on raw materials

[4] Giorgio Basevi, "The Restrictive Effect of the U.S. Tariff," *American Economic Review*, September 1968.

[5] Bela Balassa, "Tariff Protection in Industrial Countries: An Evaluation," *Journal of Political Economy*, December 1965.

[6] Giorgio Basevi, "The United States Tariff Structure: Estimates of Effective Rates of Protection of U.S. Industries and Industrial Labor," *Review of Economics and Statistics*, May 1966.

TABLE 9–2

NOMINAL AND EFFECTIVE TARIFF RATES, 1962

Commodity	United States		United Kingdom		Common Market		Japan	
	Nominal	Effective	Nominal	Effective	Nominal	Effective	Nominal	Effective
Thread and yarn	11.7	31.8	10.5	27.9	2.9	3.6	2.7	1.4
Textile fabrics	24.1	50.6	20.7	42.2	17.6	44.4	19.7	48.8
Clothing	25.1	35.9	25.5	40.5	18.5	25.1	25.2	42.4
Ingots	10.6	106.7	11.1	98.9	6.4	28.9	13.0	58.9
Rolling mill products	7.1	−2.2	9.5	7.4	7.2	10.5	15.4	29.5
Metal manufactures	14.4	28.5	19.0	35.9	14.0	25.6	18.1	27.7
Ships	5.5	2.1	2.9	−10.2	0.4	−13.2	13.1	12.1
Automobiles	6.8	5.1	23.1	41.4	19.5	36.8	35.9	75.7
Airplanes	9.2	8.8	15.6	16.7	10.5	10.8	15.0	15.9

Source: Bela Balassa, "Tariff Protection in Industrial Countries: An Evaluation," *Journal of Political Economy* (The University of Chicago Press, December 1965), p. 580. Used by permission of the author and publisher.

or intermediate products. It turns out that the effective protective rate is often quite different from the nominal tariff rate, which does not take this into account. Thus traditional nominal tariff rates do not give an accurate picture of the extent of protection afforded any given industry or of the height of the average tariff of a country.

A few selected nominal and effective protective rates for selected industries (1962) and average rates for a group of industrialized countries are given in Tables 9–2 and 9–3.

TABLE 9–3

1962 OVERALL WEIGHTED TARIFF AVERAGES

Country	Nominal	Effective
United States	11.6	20.0
United Kingdom	15.5	27.8
Common Market	11.9	18.6
Sweden	6.8	12.5
Japan	16.2	29.5

Source: B. Ballassa, *op. cit.*, p. 588.

Two observations need to be made. For one the knowledge of nominal tariff rates yields no clue to the height of the effective tariff protection afforded an industry. In the United States we find examples where the effective rate is more than ten times the nominal rate. In other industries the nominal rate and the effective rate are virtually identical. Without doubt the most interesting cases arise when the effective rate is actually negative. We will recall from the previous section that this result occurs if the weighted average of the tariffs on the inputs used in the production process is greater than the tariff on the output. The effective protective rate on the value added by this industry therefore becomes negative.

Secondly the cross-country data indicate that effective tariff rates for the countries studied are almost twice as high as the nominal rates. International comparisons of tariff rates have to be undertaken with care.

However, we should point out that serious problems in effective protective rate calculations arise because inputs may be substituted for each other. For instance a high tariff on yarn made from natural fibers will lead to the substitution of synthetic yarns such as dacron and nylon. Further research into the substitution problem is under way.

SUGGESTED FURTHER READINGS

BALASSA, BELA, "Tariff Protection in Industrial Countries," *Journal of Political Economy* (December 1965). Reprinted in AEA *Readings in International Economics*, eds. Richard Caves and Harry G. Johnson. Homewood, Ill.: Richard D. Irwin, Inc., 1968.

BALDWIN, ROBERT, "The Case Against Infant Industry Protection," *Journal of Political Economy* (May 1969).

BASEVI, GIORGIO, "The United States Tariff Structure: Estimates of Effective Rates of Protection of the United States Industries and Industrial Labor," *Review of Economics and Statistics* (May 1966).

CORDEN, W. M., *The Theory of Protection*. London: Oxford University Press, 1971.

HABERLER, GOTTFRIED, *The Theory of International Trade*, Chaps. XIII–XVI. London: William Hodge & Company, Limited, 1936.

JOHNSON, HARRY G., *International Trade and Economic Growth*, Chap. II. London: George Allen & Unwin, 1958.

LERNER, ABBA, "The Symmetry Between Import and Export Taxes," *Economica* (August 1936). Reprinted in AEA *Readings in International Economics*, eds. Richard Caves and Harry G. Johnson, Chap. XI. Homewood, Ill.: Richard D. Irwin, Inc., 1968.

METZLER, LLOYD, "Tariffs, The Terms of Trade, and The Distribution of National Income," *Journal of Political Economy* (February 1949). Reprinted in AEA *Readings in International Economics*, eds. Richard Caves and Harry G. Johnson. Homewood, Ill.: Richard D. Irwin, Inc., 1968.

STOLPER, WOLFGANG F., and PAUL A. SAMUELSON, "Protection and Real Wages," *Review of Economic Studies* (November 1941). Reprinted in *Readings in the Theory of International Trade*, eds. Howard S. Ellis and Lloyd A. Metzler, Chap. XV. Homewood, Ill.: Richard D. Irwin, Inc., 1950, and in *International Trade*, ed. Jagdish Bhagwati. Baltimore: Penguin Books, Inc., 1969.

10

Economic Unions
and International Trade

The theory of tariffs surveyed in the last chapter constitutes an example of a discriminatory trade policy that is applied uniformly to all countries. But countries will not always want to discriminate equally against all other countries. There are several possible forms of organization that allow countries to discriminate against a select group of countries. Most prominent among these are free trade areas, customs unions, and common markets. The main difference among these three principal ways of organizing a preferential trade area lies in the degree of interdependence achieved by the member countries.

A *free trade area* consists of a group of countries that have abolished all tariff barriers among themselves but maintain their individual tariffs vis-à-vis the outside world. An important problem arises in the implementation of the free trade area concept because commodities imported from the outside world tend to enter the free trade area via the country with the lowest external tariff. Extensive documentation by so-called certificates of origin is required. The policing problem is made somewhat easier if the countries forming the free trade area do not have any joint boundaries, thus making the transfer of commodities inside the area easier to control. A good example that fulfills this condition is the European Free Trade Area (EFTA), which consists of the "Outer Seven": Austria, Denmark, Norway, Portugal, Sweden, Switzerland, and the United Kingdom.

A *customs union* differs from a free trade area in that it has a common external tariff that applies to the imports by any member country from the outside world. Free movement of all products is assured within the union, and thus the problem of intra-union trade of imported commodities no longer exists.

common
market

Finally a *common market* not only allows for the free movement of products, like the free trade area and the customs union, but permits in addition the free movement of all factors of production. Thus the common market represents the most complete concept of economic integration among the three. The European Economic Community, (EEC), composed of Belgium, France, Germany, Italy, Luxembourg, Denmark, Ireland, the United Kingdom, and the Netherlands, now has a complete customs union and is working toward implementation of the common market goal, including monetary union.

In this chapter we will focus attention on the economics of the customs union. The analysis of the customs union can easily be extended to cover the cases of the free trade area and the common market.

EFFECTS OF A CUSTOMS UNION

The formation of a customs union involves the changing of tariff patterns between the countries forming the union as well as between the union members and the outside world. We will analyze the effects of the tariff changes on trade volume and prices and will also try to indicate what changes in economic welfare may be expected in light of the policies pursued.

In our analysis we will assume that there are only three countries: the United Kingdom, France, and Germany. France and Germany will be the two countries that are forming the customs union, and the United Kingdom will represent the "outsider." Let us assume, too, that the German supply and demand curves for cloth, S^G and D^G are as indicated in Figure 10–1, and that cloth can be produced in both France and the United Kingdom under constant cost conditions. The supply curves for these two countries are labeled S^F and S^{UK}. The relevant prices of cloth (in terms of wheat) are also given in Table 10–1. The German tariff vis-à-vis the outside world is assumed to be 50 percent.

TABLE 10–1

	Producer Country	
	France	United Kingdom
Producer's cloth price (in terms of wheat)	100	80
German tariff (50 percent)	50	40
German price including tariff	150	120

Before formation of the customs union between France and Germany we have the following situation: in the absence of any imports the price for cloth in Germany is 180 units of wheat. This price is indicated by the intersection

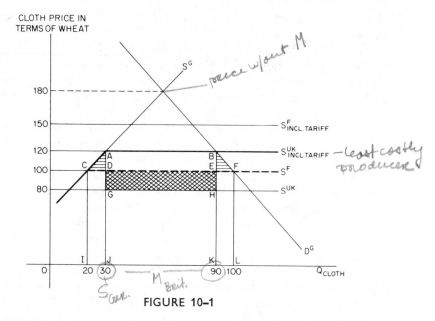

FIGURE 10-1

of the German supply and demand curves for cloth. But the price of cloth will never rise to this level in Germany, because Germans can always buy cloth from the least costly outside producer, here the United Kingdom, and after paying the tariff are able to obtain each piece of cloth for 120 units.

German producers will supply 30 bales of cloth because up to this quantity they are able to supply the markets at a price below 120, and any remaining quantity, here an additional 60 bales, will be imported from the United Kingdom. The effective supply curve before the formation of the customs union is therefore the heavy line in Figure 10–1.

Trade Creation

After Germany and France form the customs union all tariffs between these two countries are abolished, although the tariff toward outsiders remains at, let us say, the customary 50 percent. It is now possible for German residents to buy their cloth in France for 100 units, 20 units cheaper than the British price, which still includes the tariff charge.

As a result of this cheapening of the imported cloth a larger quantity of cloth will be imported. The German cloth industry will cut back production to 20 bales, and German residents will buy an additional 80 bales of cloth from France. Imports increase from 60 to 80 bales.

The increase in imports is the result of a movement to a position of freer trade than prevailed prior to the abolition of the French-German tariff. We refer to this expansion of trade between countries as the *trade-creating effect*.

of the customs union. The total trade-creation effect is due to a production and a consumption effect.

The trade creation due to *production* takes place because before the formation of the union the British price for cloth, including the tariff, was 120, and German manufacturers could produce up to 30 bales (point A on the supply curve) more cheaply than this. After foreign cloth becomes available to the Germans at the price of 100, German manufacturers can produce only 20 bales cheaper than this (point C on the supply curve). Consequently, the quantity CD (equal to 10 bales) will be supplied by foreign sources, leading to greater international trade, hence trade creation.

There is a welfare gain for German residents involved in this process. The resource cost of producing the quantity CD of cloth is equal to the area under the German supply curve,[1] AJIC. When the 10 bales of cloth are imported from France instead of being produced at home, Germans have to pay only 100 units per bale. The total cost to Germany is DJIC. The difference between the costs to German producers and the import cost constitutes a net saving to German residents equal to the shaded triangle ADC. This net saving can be interpreted as an increase in economic welfare due to the trade-creating effects of the customs union.

Similar to the welfare gains resulting from the saving in procurement cost there is a welfare gain on the *consumption* side due to trade creation. Consumption of cloth in Germany expands from 90 to 100 bales with the lowering of the cloth price pursuant to the formation of the customs union. The total utility derived by German residents from the additional cloth can be approximated by the area under the demand curve,[2] BFLK. But the Germans have to pay an amount equal to only FLKE for the additional 10 bales of cloth and experience a welfare gain equal to the shaded triangle BFE.

The total welfare gains from trade creation taking place after the formation of the customs union are the result of production and consumption effects. The magnitude of these welfare effects depends mainly on the following variables: (1) the height of the pre-union tariff, (2) the slope of the supply curve, and (3) the slope of the demand curve. If the pre-union tariff is higher, the welfare gains from the abolition of the tariff tend to be higher. In the figure we can see this as an initially greater spread between the supply price of the United Kingdom, including the tariff, and the supply price of France.

---

[1] To establish this point one has to assume that the German cloth industry is perfectly competitive. For the idea that the area under the supply curve equals the cost of production, see any elementary textbook, e.g., Paul A. Samuelson, *Economics*, 8th ed. (New York: McGraw-Hill Book Company, 1970), Chap. XXIII, or H. Robert Heller, *The Economic System* (New York: The Macmillan Company, 1972), Chap. V.

[2] This holds true if money can serve as an accurate measuring rod of utility derived. C.f. Samuelson, *op. cit.*, p. 418, on this point.

The triangles ADC and BFE showing the welfare gains will also be larger if the German supply and demand curves are flatter. To establish this point we have to remember that the spread between the British and French supply curves is given, thus fixing the distances AD and BE. The flatter the German supply and demand curves, the greater the distances CD and EF, and the greater the area of the triangles.

Trade Diversion

A customs union may succeed in securing the whole union market for the partner country. Quite often, however, it may be true that the partner country is not the world's most efficient producer of the product. This is the case in the example studied here, where the United Kingdom is the lowest cost producer. Only because France is within the union and the products of the United Kingdom are discriminated against by a tariff is it possible for France to secure the union market.

After the formation of the union Germany no longer buys from the most efficient producer in the *world* but merely from the most efficient producer within the union, in this case France. The consequence of this is *trade diversion* from the low cost producer to the high cost producer.

Instead of importing 60 bales of cloth (in Figure 10–1 equal to AB, DE, or GH) from the United Kingdom, Germany will import 80 bales of cloth from France. We saw earlier that the 20 additional bales of cloth imports are due to trade creation, the welfare effects of which were analyzed at that time. Here we will focus attention on the 60 bales that were formerly imported from the United Kingdom and are now imported from France.

When importing the 60 bales of cloth from the United Kingdom, German importers paid a price of 80 units of wheat per bale of cloth to the British exporter. Total payments were equal to the area GHKJ. German consumers had to pay in addition a 50 percent tariff (equal to the area ABHG), which made the total payments equal to the area ABKJ. But note that of these total payments by German consumers, the tariff proceeds went to German customs collectors, thus representing simply an income redistribution within Germany. Crucial for our purposes is that Germans have to pay to the foreign source, the United Kingdom, a total of GHKJ.

After the formation of the customs union German residents have to pay to French exporters an amount equal to DEKJ for the same quantity of cloth. Thus payments for the product have increased by the amount DEHG, which is shown as the crosshatched area in Figure 10–1. Cloth is no longer supplied by the world's most efficient producer but rather by the most efficient producer within the union.

As the formation of the union is responsible for the shifting from the lowest cost producer in the world to the lowest cost producer within the union, we can say that there will be welfare losses due to the trade-diverting effects of the customs union. The magnitude of the losses is shown by the size of the rectangle DEHG.

The net welfare effect of an economic union is the difference between its trade-creating and trade-diverting effects.

The preceding analysis can be extended to the case of foreign supply curves that are less than perfectly elastic. In this more general case the tariff is no longer borne exclusively by the importing country but falls partially on the exporting country. The welfare gains and losses can no longer be assessed by comparing simple triangles and rectangles, and the geometry becomes somewhat involved.[3]

The policy implications of our analysis of customs union formation so far are fairly clear: although it is possible that the welfare gains due to trade creation are larger than the welfare losses due to trade diversion, it is also possible that the reverse holds true. Thus the formation of a customs union will not always lead unambiguously to an improvement in economic welfare. This fact is clearly attested to by the observable behavior of countries. Some countries try to form customs unions because the expected gains are larger than the expected losses, and others refrain from doing so for the opposite reasons.

EQUILIBRIUM PRICES AND QUANTITIES

In most cases we cannot assume that one of the union partners is so small in relation to the other countries that her actions have no influence on the price at which the other countries are willing to buy and sell the commodities under consideration. To analyze the effects of a customs union on prices and quantities in all countries involved is our next task.

In Figure 10–2 we show the supply and demand curves for cloth for each one of the three countries, France, Germany, and the United Kingdom. Again it will be assumed that France and Germany are the two countries forming the union.

The pre-union situation is indicated by the heavy lines. Germany is assumed to impose a 50 percent tariff on cloth, and France imposes a 20 percent tariff. Again, the outsider, the United Kingdom, is assumed to be the low cost producer. The equilibrium prices and quantities exported and imported are given in Table 10–2. Note that the domestic price in the

---

[3] The interested reader is referred to the appendix of Harry G. Johnson's article on "The Economic Theory of Customs Unions," in *Money, Trade, and Economic Growth* (Cambridge: Harvard University Press, 1962).

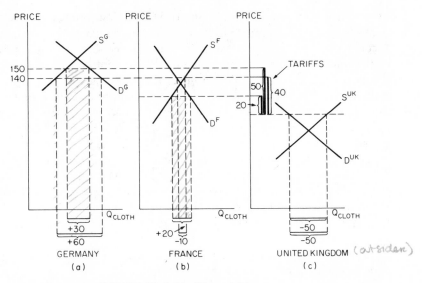

FIGURE 10-2 (a), (b), and (c)

United Kingdom is equal to the price paid by the importers of British cloth. The domestic prices in Germany and France differ from the British price by the amount of the tariff. Germany imports 30 bales of cloth to supplement her domestic production, France imports 20 bales, and, consequently, the United Kingdom exports 50 bales.

When Germany and France form the customs union, they abolish all internal tariffs and adopt a common external tariff that lies, let us say, between the limits set by the pre-union tariffs of 50 and 20 percent. Let us assume that the external tariff fixed by the union members is 40 percent.

We will turn first to the price determination in the union. First we

TABLE 10-2

	Germany	France	United Kingdom
Pre-Union			
Tariff Rate	50%	20%	
Price	150	120	100
Exports (−) or Imports (+)	+30	+20	−50
Post-Union			
Tariff Rate	40%	40%	
Price	140	140	100
Exports (−) or Imports (+)	+60	−10	−50

observe that there is now a common price for cloth in France and Germany, because commodities are free to move from one country to the other without encountering any tariff obstacles. We can now see that the union price for cloth cannot be as high as the pre-union price for cloth in Germany because, if it were actually *equal* to the old price, the following would hold true: (1) Germany would want to import the same quantity as before because the price has not changed; (2) France would want to import less because the price has risen; and (3) the United Kingdom would want to export more given that the price inside the union is equal to the old German price, but the lower tariff that is now in existence means higher receipts for the United Kingdom, thus making exports more profitable. Obviously (1), (2), and (3) cannot all hold true at the same time, because world exports would be greater than world imports. Thus it must be true that the pre-union price for cloth in Germany represents an upper boundary that will prevail inside the union after its formation.

A similar argument can be made to show that in France the union price is no lower than the pre-union price for cloth.

The price for cloth in the United Kingdom may be higher, lower, or equal to the pre-union price. In the numerical and diagrammatical example provided the British price is shown to be the same both before and after the formation of the customs union between France and Germany. In this case we will find that the volume of British trade with the union countries remains unchanged. This is possible because German imports increase in the same amount (30 bales) that French purchases from abroad decrease. (Note that the decrease of French purchases is really made up of a genuine decrease in French imports from 20 to zero and an increase in its exports by 10, providing a net change of 30.)

If German imports had increased *more* than those of France decreased, the net result would have been increased imports by the union countries, meaning a higher price and greater quantity of British exports. Conversely had German imports increased *less* than those of France decreased, the imports of the union countries would have shown a net reduction, resulting in a lower price and export quantity for the United Kingdom.

GENERAL EQUILIBRIUM ANALYSIS

The analysis of the previous section can be extended to the two-commodity case with the help of the general equilibrium model developed in Chapters 2 through 6 of this book. The quantities that the union members are willing to exchange with outsiders, say, the United Kingdom, can be summarized in an *aggregate excess trade offer curve*, which shows the different cloth/wheat combinations that the union is willing to trade with the United Kingdom at different terms of trade. To derive this curve for the union partners we construct first the customary international trade offer curves for the union members: France (TOC^F in Figure 10–3) and Germany (TOC^G). Then we determine the net quantities of the commodities that the partners are willing to trade with the outsider (United Kingdom) at all possible terms of trade. At the terms of trade TOT_0 trade between France and Germany is balanced, and the union will not want to trade with the United Kingdom,

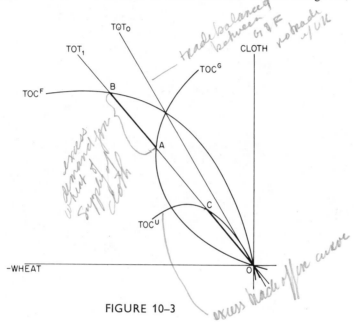

FIGURE 10–3

resulting in a point on the excess trade offer curve that coincides with the origin. At different terms of trade, such as TOT_1, Germany will want to exchange quantities of cloth and wheat shown by OA, although France will want to trade the larger commodity bundle OB. As a result we find that there is an excess demand for wheat and an excess supply of cloth at the going prices. The union partners will wish to import cloth in exchange for wheat, as shown by the distance AB. This is the "excess offer" of wheat for cloth by the union, and it can be shown separately as the distance OC. The collection of all possible excess offers at different terms of trade generates the union's excess trade offer curve TOC^U.

The union's excess trade offer curve TOC^U and the trade offer curve of the outsider, TOC^{UK}, determine the international terms of trade. In Figure 10–4 we show the trade offer curves and the equilibrium international terms of trade TOT_2. At these terms of trade there will be no excess demands or supplies of the two commodities in the world market.

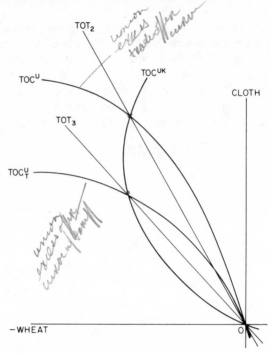

FIGURE 10–4

The union's excess offer curve must now be modified to take account of any tariffs that the union may levy against imports from the outside country. This is shown in Figure 10–4 by the excess trade offer curve TOC_T^U. This curve, including the tariff, is derived by the customary method of displacing the original trade offer curve by the amount of the tariff levied upon the commodities. The external union tariff establishes the new terms of trade TOT_3, which are more favorable to the union. However, all the qualifications discussed in the chapter on the effects of tariffs also apply here. The theory of the optimal tariff can be applied to the customs union tariff, too. The union should levy an external tariff that will allow her to reach the highest possible trade indifference curve, given the position of the outsider's trade offer curve.

The question remains: Are the union partners better or worse off after forming their union and adopting the common external tariff? The answer to this question cannot be given on a priori grounds alone. Not only are the terms of trade important in the determination of welfare gains and losses but other factors enter as well. The final determination concerning the welfare effects of the union depends on which situation will allow the countries to reach the highest possible trade indifference curve. The effects of the formation of a customs union on the member's trade with the outside world cannot be predicted accurately. The theory of customs unions represents a good example of the fact that as soon as we move away from our simple two-country, two-commodity models, there is very little that can be said about possible price and quantity effects due to any change in economic policy.

OTHER GAINS FROM UNION FORMATION

There are other factors that may influence the decision calculus of countries considering forming a customs union. Among the more important economic reasons we find greater efficiency due to greater specialization within the union. The size of the market is enlarged considerably and, with it, the opportunities for large-scale production and distribution methods. At the same time existing monopolies may be faced with more intensive foreign competition by producers located in the partner countries. Also established firms with a secure market will suddenly have to defend their market position against the new competition. Enforced efficiency in the industries concerned can be an important byproduct of the customs union formation.

A final word needs to be said about the *type* of countries most likely to experience large gains from the formation of a customs union. If the countries forming such a union are initially similar, the gains will tend to be larger than if the countries are initially dissimilar. In the latter case countries are already specialized to a large extent in the commodities in which they enjoy a comparative advantage. If, however, the countries are initially similar, then potential gains from specialization pursuant to the formation of the customs union also exist. The total anticipated gains are therefore larger.

Also the greater the *size* of the customs union, the greater the gains are likely to be. We saw in our initial discussion that any customs union combines elements of freer trade within the union and with increased protection of the union market vis-à-vis the outside world. The larger the union, the greater the chance that the world's lowest cost producer is a union member, and that therefore all union members are afforded the advantage of being able to buy from the low cost producer. In other words the chance of trade diversion playing an important role decreases as the size of the union increases. Clearly in the limiting case where the union encompasses the whole world trade diversion is no longer possible, and only gains from trade creation are being reaped—which are now identical with the regular gains from trade due to the introduction of a free trade policy discussed in the first half of this book.

In addition to the economic reasons discussed there may be other reasons, especially of a political nature, that might influence the decision of a country to join or not to join a customs union or, perhaps, to bar certain prospective members from joining an already existing union. To enumerate all possible political implications of a customs union would, however, be considerably beyond the scope of this chapter.

EMPIRICAL EVIDENCE

In this section we will limit ourselves to (1) an assessment of the trade-creating and trade-diverting effects and (2) the probable magnitude of increased efficiency in resource use that can be expected as a result of the abolition of the tariffs among the union partners. By following this procedure we neglect all possible dynamic effects of the union formation. It has been argued that these dynamic effects are very important and of considerable magnitude. But reliable empirical evidence does not exist, and following our usual procedure we will limit ourselves to actual attempts of quantification.

The most comprehensive attempt to measure the trade-creating and trade-diverting effects of the European Economic Community has been undertaken by Bela Balassa.[4] A crucial assumption of Balassa's study is that the income elasticities of demand would have remained unchanged in the absence of the formation of the union. If we should observe, therefore, that the ex-post income elasticity of demand for imports (from partner countries *or* all countries combined) actually increased, we may take this as an indication that trade creation occurred. If, on the other hand, the income elasticity of demand for imports from nonmember countries declines, we can take this as evidence of the trade-diverting effects of the union.

Using aggregate data Balassa finds some evidence of trade creation and no indication of trade-diverting effects. But disaggregation of the data shows that individual commodity classes experience both trade creation and trade diversion. Trade creation is evident in fuels (where we see the effects of the EEC policy of shifting from expensive union sources to cheaper outside energy supplies), chemicals, machinery, and transportation equipment. Trade diversion occurs in the food sector (evidence of the protectionistic agricultural policy of the EEC) as well as in beverages, tobacco, raw materials, semimanufactured commodities, and consumer durables.

In a parallel study of the Central American Common Market (Costa Rica, El Salvador, Guatemala, Honduras, and Nicaragua) W. T. Wilford comes to similar conclusions.[5] His data show that during the first seven years of the CACM aggregate net trade creation occurred. Using disaggregate data he finds net trade creation for most classes of commodities, with the exception of fuels, lubricants, and edible fats and oils. Trade creation was strongest for

[4] Bela Balassa, "Trade Creation and Trade Diversion in the European Common Market," *Economic Journal*, March 1967.

[5] W. T. Wilford, "Trade Creation in the Central American Common Market," *Western Economic Journal*, March 1970.

foods and raw materials. We should note, however, that these results are merely indicative of the short run effects of the common market formation and say little about the long-term repercussions.

Turning to the second problem of the size of the gains from the union we have several pieces of fragmentary evidence.

P. J. Verdoorn has estimated the expected effects of the formation of a European customs union encompassing not only the countries of the present European Economic Community but also the Scandinavian countries and the United Kingdom.[6] Depending on the precise assumption made as far as possible exchange rate adjustment is concerned, he estimates that intra-European trade is likely to increase 15 to 19 percent. Total gains from trade creation are estimated to be $68.8 million, and losses from trade diversion are expected to be $68.0 million, leaving a net gain of less than $1 million as a result of the formation of the union.

Another estimate of the possible welfare effects of freer trade between Britain and the rest of Europe has been made by Harry Johnson.[7] Using trade projections made by the *Economist*'s Intelligence Unit he concludes that the gains to Britain alone are probably in the neighborhood of £225 million in 1970, roughly 1 percent of the Gross National Product.

Even if we allow an error of 100 percent in the estimates cited, we still find that none of the numerical data available suggests sizable gains due to the formation of customs unions. But we should point out again that these estimates of gains refer to static gains only. Dynamic gains may be expected to be higher, but in the absence of at least fragmentary empirical evidence it is difficult to say anything concrete.

SUGGESTED FURTHER READINGS

BALASSA, BELA, *The Theory of Economic Integration*. Homewood, Ill.: Richard D. Irwin, 1961.

————, "Trade Creation and Trade Diversion in the European Common Market," *Economic Journal* (March 1967).

COOPER, C., and B. MASSELL, "A New Look at Customs Union Theory," *Economic Journal* (December 1965).

JOHNSON, HARRY G., "The Gains from Freer Trade with Europe: An Estimate," *Manchester School* (September 1958).

[6] P. J. Verdoorn, "Two Notes on Tariff Reductions," in International Labour Office, *Social Aspects of European Economic Cooperation*, Geneva, 1956.

[7] Harry G. Johnson, "The Gains from Freer Trade with Europe: An Estimate," *Manchester School*, September 1958.

————, *Money, Trade, and Economic Growth*, Chap. III. Cambridge: Harvard University Press, 1962.

LIPSEY, RICHARD G., "The Theory of Customs Unions," *Economic Journal* (September 1960). Reprinted in *International Trade*, ed. Jagdish Bhagwati. Baltimore: Penguin Books, Inc., 1969.

————, *The Theory of Customs Unions*. London: LSE Monograph Series, 1970.

MEADE, JAMES, *The Theory of Customs Unions*. Amsterdam: North-Holland Publications, 1955.

SCITOVSKY, TIBOR, *Economic Theory and Western European Integration*, Chap. I and III. London: George Allen & Unwin, 1962.

VINER, JACOB, *The Customs Union Issue*. New York: Carnegie Endowment for International Peace, 1950.

11

Welfare Aspects
of International Trade

We have thus far been concerned mainly with the reasons for international trade and the consequences of trade intervention. Differences in demand patterns, technology, or factor endowments between countries were cited as some of the factors leading to the emergence of international trade. But, clearly, countries and people would have no incentive to engage in international trade if it were not going to make them better off. Also trade restrictions are often imposed in an attempt to increase economic welfare. Increases in economic welfare make international trade attractive, and it is therefore important to show in greater detail the effects of international trade on economic welfare.

We will start out with an investigation of the effects of trade on world welfare without paying attention to the welfare of individual countries. Then we will proceed to analyze the effects of trade on the welfare of the individual country and we will concern ourselves with the effects of trade on economic groups within a country engaging in international trade. Finally we will address ourselves to the welfare effects of tariffs.

WORLD WELFARE

It can be shown that unrestricted international trade increases welfare for the world as a whole. That is, aggregate world welfare can be increased disregarding for the moment how the possible gains (or losses) from international trade are distributed between different countries.

In Figure 11-1 the production possibility curve of the United States is

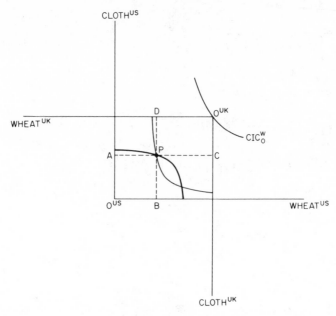

FIGURE 11–1

shown in its customary position. Quantities of cloth and wheat are measured along the two axes. Let us say that taste patterns are such that production and consumption will occur at point P. The United States will be producing and consuming AO^{US} of cloth and BO^{US} of wheat. A similar production possibility curve can be drawn for the United Kingdom and superimposed on the original diagram upside down and with sides reversed. Furthermore the British production and consumption point is placed so that it coincides with the United States production and consumption point P. The United Kingdom produces DO^{UK} of wheat and CO^{UK} of cloth.

Total world production is equal to AO^{US} plus CO^{UK} of cloth and DO^{UK} plus BO^{US} of wheat. With reference to the original (United States) coordinate system, the point O^{UK} shows the total commodity combination that is being produced and consumed in the world as a whole. The two countries together attain a welfare level indicated by the global community indifference curve passing through O^{UK}, that is, the indifference curve CIC_0^W.

It will be noted that at point P the marginal rate of transformation of cloth into wheat in the United States is not equal to that of the United Kingdom. This gives us an indication that resource allocation in the world as a whole cannot be considered optimal.

Total world production can be increased if the two countries rearrange their production patterns in such a way that they will lead to equality of the

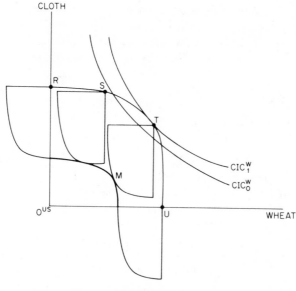

FIGURE 11–2

marginal rates of transformation between the two countries. This condition is fulfilled if the two production possibility curves are tangent to each other. Such a position is shown in Figure 11–2, where the two countries' production possibilities curves are tangent to each other at point M. Naturally there are other production patterns that will lead to the equality of the marginal rates of transformation, too. These different possible product combinations can be derived by sliding the British production possibility curve along the United States production possibility curve in such a way that the coordinate systems of the two countries are always parallel to each other. Measuring with reference to the original (United States) coordinate system we find that the origin of the shifting (British) production possibility curve traces out the *aggregate* commodity combinations that can be produced in the two countries together. The moving origin of the British production possibility curve traces the *world production possibility curve.* This world production possibility curve is labeled RSTU.

The world production possibility curve RSTU will allow the world as a whole to reach the global community indifference curve CIC_1^W that lies above the global community indifference curve CIC_0^W, which could be reached when both countries maintain autarky.

For the world as a whole a free trade situation leads to a higher level of economic welfare than a situation in which there is no international trade.

It may be worth noting that in the very special case in which production and consumption patterns in both countries lead to the same marginal rate of transformation even in the absence of trade, the total amounts produced by the two countries in isolation will define a point on the world production possibility curve. In such a case domestic price ratios are already equal before trade starts, and there is no incentive to engage in international trade. The countries in isolation are as well off as they can be.

THE WELFARE OF A COUNTRY

We have demonstrated that it is advantageous for the world as a whole to engage in international trade, because all countries together are able to achieve a higher aggregate utility level as indicated by the higher global community indifference curve that can be reached. Yet this does not permit us to draw any conclusions about the welfare of the individual countries concerned. It might be that the gain is distributed in some inequitable fashion between the two countries; it might be that one country reaps all the benefits, leaving the other country just as well off as it was without trade; or one country might even experience a gain in welfare larger than the aggregate increase in welfare for the world as a whole. In the latter case the other country would actually experience a decrease in utility because of the opening up of trade relations.

The Welfare of a Small Country

Let us suppose initially that the country under consideration is relatively small. As before the actions of this country are not likely to influence the international terms of trade, which she considers as given because she acts like a perfect competitor.

Figure 11–3 shows the production possibility curve of such a small country. Under conditions of autarky the commodity bundles that the country can attain are limited to those commodity combinations on or below the production possibility curve. The highest possible community indifference curve that the country can reach is curve CIC_0, which is tangent to the country's production possibility curve at point P.

Being able to trade at the fixed terms of trade TOT, the small country can reach any commodity combination that lies on or below the international terms of trade line that is tangent to the production possibility curve at R. Thus she is able to attain commodity combinations that contain more of *both* commodities than can be produced under autarky. It is clear that given the possibility of obtaining larger commodity combinations via trade, she is also able to reach a higher community indifference curve, such as CIC_2.

The ability to attain a higher community indifference curve indicates that

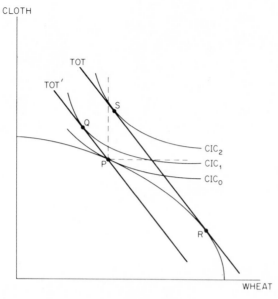

FIGURE 11-3

free trade has made the country as a whole better off and constitutes, therefore, an improvement in economic welfare for this country. It is immaterial
whether the terms of trade line is steeper or flatter than the price line showing
the pretrade domestic exchange ratio. In either case the country will find
that the attainable commodity combinations with international trade are
greater than the commodity combinations that can be produced at home in
isolation.

The total gain from trade that the country derives can be subdivided
into the gains from exchange and the gains from specialization. The *gains
from exchange* accrue to the country because she is able to trade internationally and to modify the commodity bundle that she produces under autarky.
To isolate these gains from exchange we assume that the production pattern
of the country remains the same as under autarky. Thus the country continues
to produce at point P. However, she can now modify this commodity
bundle by trading at the terms of trade that prevail in the world market.
(Note that TOT′ is parallel to TOT.) Thus she is able to reach the higher
community indifference curve CIC_1. This movement represents the welfare
gain from exchange.

The country also reaps *gains from specialization* in production. At the
new terms of trade the marginal rate of transformation is no longer equal to
the price ratio of the two commodities. It is advantageous for the country to
rearrange her production pattern in such a way that the marginal rate of
transformation is equal to the new international price ratio. In Figure 11-3

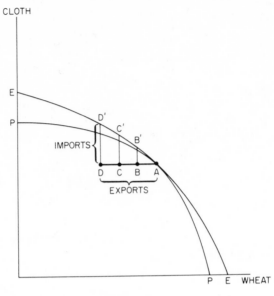

FIGURE 11-4

this is true at point R, where the terms of trade line TOT is tangent to the production possibility curve. The country is now able to reach an even higher community indifference curve, CIC_2, and the resulting welfare increase can be attributed to gains from specialization.

The total welfare gain realized by the movement from indifference curve CIC_0 to CIC_2 made possible by international trade can thus be decomposed into the gains from exchange (CIC_0 to CIC_1) and the gains from specialization (CIC_1 to CIC_2).

The Welfare of a Large Country

If the country under consideration is relatively large, the assumption that the international terms of trade at which the country can trade will remain constant is no longer valid. As soon as the large country enters the international market her trading activities will tend to drive up the price of her imports and lower the price of her exports. For this reason the trading opportunities of the large country can no longer be represented by a straight line showing the terms of trade prevailing in the world market. Figure 11-4 shows the production possibility curve PP for a large country. Let us assume that her own community indifference curve is tangent at point A, which represents the no-trade autarky position. If the country exports wheat and imports cloth, she may be able to reach points A, B', C', D', and E. The more trade the country wishes to engage in, the worse the terms of trade will be. Exporting AB in exchange for B′B, the terms of trade are B′B/AB. As the country attempts to export more, prices of the export good wheat will be depressed in world markets. At the same time the greater demand for imports will drive up prices of the import commodity cloth.

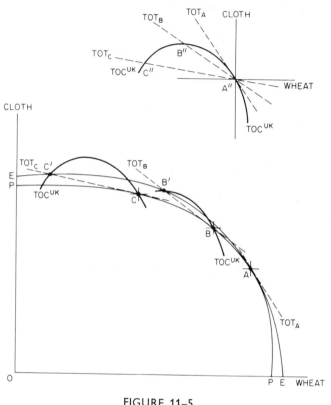

FIGURE 11–5

The terms of trade will change to C′C/AC and D′D/AD as the trade volume increases. From Figure 11–4 it is evident that B′B/AB > C′C/AC > D′D/AD. That is, the terms of trade turn against the country, and the country's *consumption possibility curve*, showing all commodity combinations attainable by free trade, is shown by the curve EAB′C′D′E.

We have to show now the precise way in which the large country's consumption possibility curve is determined. In Figure 11–5 we show the production possibility curve PABCP for the United States, the large country of our example. The insert shows the foreign trade offer curve for the United Kingdom, including several different possible terms of trade. The first step in the construction of the trade possibilities curve for the United States is to assume any arbitrary terms of trade, say, TOT_C, and to place the origin of the British coordinate system in such a position that the terms of trade line TOT_C is tangent to the United States production possibility curve. For the terms of trade TOT_C this is true at point C. The British offer curve shows the willingness of the United Kingdom to trade and, given the terms of trade TOT_C, indicates that she will want to move to point C′.

The process has to be repeated now for every conceivable terms of trade ratio, such as TOT_B. Again the British origin is placed on the United States production possibility curve so that the terms of trade line TOT_B is tangent to the production possibility curve. At the new terms of trade the United Kingdom will want to move to point B′. It is possible to generate a whole set of points showing the United Kingdom's willingness to trade with the United States, and the line connecting all such points, EC′B′AE, shows the commodity combinations that are attainable for the United States by trading with the United Kingdom. EC′B′AE delineates, therefore, the United States consumption possibility curve. Because this curve lies above the production possibility curve at all points (except for point A, at which they coincide), we can conclude that free trade will permit the large country to attain greater commodity combinations that she could attain without trade. For any given commodity bundle that can be produced in isolation, a commodity bundle containing more of *both* commodities can be found with the introduction of free trade. Because a commodity bundle containing more of both commodities will enable us to reach a higher community indifference curve than a bundle containing less of both commodities, it is possible to state unambiguously that free trade will always lead to an improvement in economic welfare for a country.

Free international trade will make it possible for the country as a whole to achieve a higher level of welfare than can be achieved under autarky. The welfare gains for a large country are smaller than the gains that may be realized by a small country.

Welfare Effects of a Tariff

Next we will consider the welfare implications of a tariff imposed by a large country. It is clear that a country will impose a tariff only if it will make her in some sense better off. In discussing the free trade opportunities of a large country, we introduced the *consumption possibilities curve* to show the commodity combinations attainable by a country engaging in international trade. The same tool may be utilized to show the trade possibilities open to a large country imposing a tariff. The case of a small country facing a given set of terms of trade becomes redundant in connection with the imposition of tariffs, because the optimal tariff a small country should levy is zero, as was shown in Chapter 9. Thus we will deal only with the large country case in the subsequent discussion of the effects of a tariff.

The consumption possibilities curve is derived in a similar fashion as in the free trade case. That is, the origin of the foreign (United Kingdom) country's coordinate system is moved along the production possibility curve PP of the large country (United States). This is done in Figure 11–6. If the

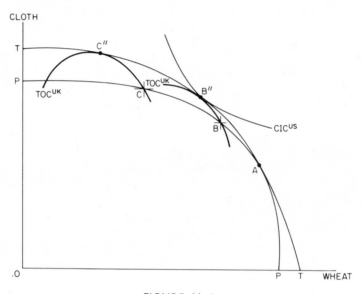

FIGURE 11–6

United States is able to impose a tariff, she can trade *any* commodity combination she desires, provided she chooses a point located on the United Kingdom's trade offer curve. By slowly shifting the origin of the United Kingdom's trade offer curve along the production possibility curve of the United States, we can trace the collection of *maximum* commodity combinations that the United Kingdom is willing to trade. Points A, B″, and C″ in Figure 11–6 are points that can be reached in the manner described. The collection of these points may be described as an "envelope" of all possible British trade offer curves. The envelope describing the United States consumption possibility curve, allowing for the imposition of a tariff, is labeled TT.

By comparing Figure 11–6 to Figure 11–5, which depicted the trade possibility curve in the free trade (no-tariff) situation, we can immediately see that the trade possibility curve for the tariff case (TT) will always be located outside the trade possibility curve for the free trade case (EE in Figure 11–5). The actual commodity combination the United States chooses to trade with the United Kingdom is determined by the point at which the highest possible United States community indifference curve is tangent to the envelope trade possibility curve. This point is labeled B″ in Figure 11–5. Evidently point B″ lies on a higher trade possibility curve than the points on the trade possibilities curve for the free trade case, allowing the country to attain a superior commodity combination.

By imposing an optimal tariff it is always possible for a country to reach a commodity combination that is superior to the free trade situation.

Two *caveats* are in order. First there is the possibility that the commodity bundle that is attained by restricted trade contains less of one commodity than the free trade bundle. The index number problem then looms over our heads. It is sufficient to point out here that there is always a commodity combination that can be reached by subsequent trade that will be superior in the sense that it actually contains more of both commodities than the free trade situation. Thus there is always the *potential* for an unambiguous welfare increase. Second it is clear that the other country will experience a decrease in her welfare due to the fact that she will wind up on a lower trade indifference curve. There is the possibility that retaliatory actions taken by the other country will lead to an ultimate decrease in the welfare of one or both countries involved, despite the fact that at each successive step in the retaliatory process the country imposing the tariff will gain slightly compared to the step before (see Chapter 9).

The final welfare gains and losses will depend on the position of the final equilibrium that obtains. Let us say that the initial no-tariff situation is represented by point A in Figure 11–7. If the final equilibrium point is a point such as E, located in the region bordered by the United Kingdom's trade offer curve and the United States' trade indifference curve through A, the United States will gain. This follows from the fact that any point that is located on a trade indifference curve higher than TI^{US} represents a potentially superior welfare position for the United States. Plainly the United Kingdom is worse off as a result, since any final equilibrium point to the right of her trade indifference curve TI^{UK} represents a lower level of welfare. Similarly a final equilibrium point in the region bounded by the United States trade offer curve and the British trade indifference curve will denote a higher level of welfare for the United Kingdom and a lower one for the United States. It is also possible that both countries wind up on a trade indifference curve that is lower than the free trade indifference curve through point A and, as a consequence, both countries will lose due to the tariff measures taken. A joint effort to remove the tariffs will then lead to an increase in welfare for both countries.

The dilemma facing countries contemplating the imposition of tariffs is that quite often the incentive system is such that for one country alone it will be beneficial to impose a tariff, but for both countries together it will be better

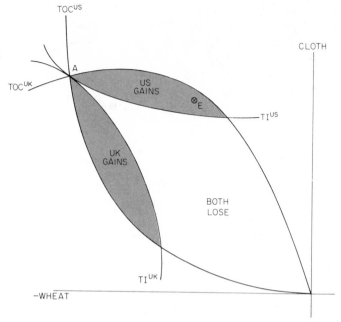

FIGURE 11-7

to refrain from the imposition of a tariff. The problem appears to be one of setting up appropriate machinery that will either remove the incentive for a single country to impose a tariff and/or distribute the gains to be derived from mutual tariff reduction in an appropriate fashion.

THE WELFARE OF AN ECONOMIC GROUP

Although we previously analyzed the gains that accrue to the world as a whole and to individual countries engaging in free international trade, we will now address ourselves to the changes in economic welfare that may be experienced by one economic group within a country.

Specialized Factors of Production

It is easily seen that a factor that is completely specialized in the production of the commodity in which the country has a comparative *dis*advantage will suffer if the country engages in free international trade. This is because after the opening of trade the country will specialize in, and therefore expand the production of, the product in which it has a comparative advantage. Simultaneously the country will reduce production of the product in which it has a comparative disadvantage. If there is a factor of production that is specialized in the production of this latter commodity, it will be impossible for this factor to find employment in the expanding industries. In such a case the specialized factor will experience a reduction in its economic welfare.

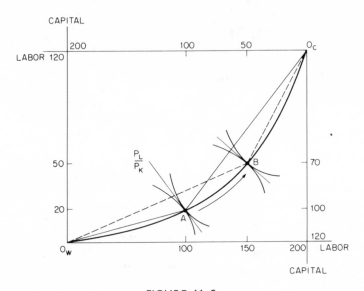

FIGURE 11–8

Mobile Factors of Production
(The Stolper-Samuelson Theorem)[1]

More interesting than the case of a completely specialized factor of production is the case of a broad group of *un*specialized factors. We may think in this context of aggregate factor groups such as land, labor, and capital, and we will assume that these factors of production are free to move between different employments.

In Figure 11–8 we show the Edgeworth Box diagram for the country. Inputs of labor and capital are measured along the axes. Isoquants are assumed to be linear homogeneous. Before trade starts the country produces at point A on her contract curve; after trade opens up she rearranges her factors of production so that she will be able to produce at point B, also

[1] See Wolfgang F. Stolper and Paul A. Samuelson, "Protection and Real Wages," *Review of Economic Studies*, November 1941.

located on the contract curve. Wheat production, which is labor intensive in our example, expands, while the capital-intensive cloth production contracts.

The contracting cloth industry will release relatively more capital than will be absorbed at the going wage rate in the expanding wheat industry. In order to find employment, the capital wage will have to fall. At the same time the expanding wheat industry will want to employ more workers than can be hired at the going wage. Consequently the wage of labor will be driven up. The *relative* wage of the factor used intensively in the contracting industry will fall, while the relative wage of the factor used intensively in the expanding industry will rise.

Owing to the relative factor price changes, making capital cheaper, *both* industries will tend to employ more capital. Because the total amount of labor is fixed in our model, each unit of capital will have a smaller quantity of labor to work with. Under conditions of perfect competition each factor is paid the value of its marginal product. But the marginal productivity of a factor is absolutely lower if the quantity of other factors in conjunction with which it works is lowered. As the marginal productivity of capital decreases absolutely, capital will be paid an *absolutely* lower wage. This is true in both industries and must therefore be true for all units of capital within the country.

The reverse argument applies to the factor that is used intensively in the expanding industry: labor. Each worker will have a larger quantity of capital to work with, increasing labor's productivity and increasing its absolute wage in both industries.

It may seem paradoxical at first that the capital/labor ratio in both industries can increase while the overall capital/labor ratio for the country as a whole stays constant. The solution to this apparent inconsistency is found in the fact that the overall capital/labor ratio is a weighted average of the two industries. As the relative size of the industries changes, the weights change, too. If the weight assigned to the industry with the higher capital/labor ratio decreases, while the weight of the industry with the lower capital/labor ratio

TABLE 11–1

		Wheat		Cloth		Overall
Capital	Before	20	.2	100	1	120
Labor	trade	100	1	100	1	200
Capital	After	50	.33	70	1.4	120
Labor	trade	150	1	50	1	200

increases, it is possible for the overall ratio to stay constant. This can easily be seen from Table 11–1, where the numerical values of the capital/labor ratios corresponding to Figure 11–8 are shown.

It is evident that the capital/labor ratio in both the wheat and the cloth industry increases after international trade is introduced, while the aggregate quantities stay constant.

Finally we may observe that as the total quantity of capital and labor remains unchanged, an increase in the absolute wage received by each worker will lead to an absolutely larger wage bill for all workers together. At the same time the lower absolute wage of capital means that the absolute amount received by owners of the factor of production capital will decrease. A larger absolute wage bill received by a factor will allow the owners of this factor to achieve a higher level of welfare, because the larger wage bill permits the purchase of an absolutely larger commodity bundle.

International trade will increase the level of welfare of the owners of the factor of production that is used intensively in the expanding industry; the owners of the factor used intensively in the contracting industry will be worse off.

Tariff Protection of a Factor

This analysis can be applied conveniently to the changes that are brought about by the introduction of a tariff. Imposition of a tariff will tend to increase the domestic production of the protected commodity, while the production of the unprotected commodity will decrease. Consequently the factor of production that is used intensively in the contracting industry will have to accept a lower wage if it is to find employment in the expanding industry. Only if the factor is willing to accept a lower wage will factor intensities in production be changed so that more of this factor will be used in the expanding (tariff-protected) industry.

The imposition of a tariff will improve the welfare of the factor used intensively in the protected industry while lowering the welfare of the other factor.

Compensation

The argument of this section shows that the opposition of individual economic groups within a country to a change in trade policy may well be justified, if these economic groups are the ones that are actually going to be hurt. Yet it should be noted that our conclusion that the country as a whole will be better off still holds. Consequently we find that the gains realized by one economic group consist essentially of two parts: (1) the gains that accrue to the country as a whole and that are reaped by the gainers, and (2) the losses that are experienced by the other economic group and that must (in our two-factor model) be reaped by the gainers, too. If the owners of the gaining factor of production are able to compensate the owners of the losing factor for the losses suffered, there must still be some additional gains left for the owners of the gaining factor.

Here we will show that we can devise a scheme that will allow everybody to purchase the commodity bundle he actually did purchase before the introduction of trade *and* leave some additional gains for the community.

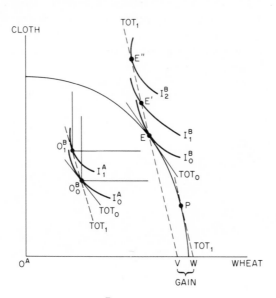

FIGURE 11–9

We will deal only with the two-person case, but the extension to many individuals is obvious. In Figure 11–9 we show the indifference curve attained by individual Alpha in the no-trade situation as I_0^A. The coordinate system for individual Beta is placed on the equilibrium point attained by Alpha. Mr. Beta reaches his equilibrium at E and attains indifference curve I_0^B.

With the introduction of international trade at the terms of trade TOT_1 Alpha is able to reach the higher indifference curve I_1^A with the same budget that allowed him to reach point O_0^B before. Now the origin of Beta's coordinate system moves to O_1^B, and the consumption and production point to E'. With optimization under trade, a further movement of the consumption point to E'' occurs, permitting Beta to reach I_2^B.

There are gains due to the attainment of higher indifference curves for both individuals: Alpha moves from I_0^A to I_1^A, and Beta moves from I_1^B to I_2^B. In addition there is a gain equal to VW (in terms of wheat) that represents a surplus available for distribution between Alpha and Beta.

All persons can be made better off with trade, if appropriate compensations are arranged for.

THE UTILITY POSSIBILITY CURVE

Modern welfare theory has developed a useful geometric technique that allows us to make welfare comparisons between alternative economic policies. As we know, most of the problems of welfare economics are due to the reluctance of economists to engage in interpersonal welfare comparisons. If there were a reliable way of making interpersonal utility com-

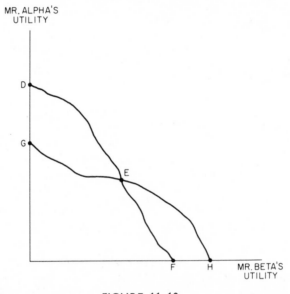

FIGURE 11–10

parisons we would be on much firmer ground regarding the normative implications of our economic policies.

The *utility possibility curve* is a tool that allows us to make welfare judgments not about the *actual* welfare levels attained but about the welfare levels which are *possible*. In Figure 11–10 we measure the utility of Mr. Alpha along the vertical axis and the utility of Mr. Beta along the horizontal axis. Utility is measured in an ordinal sense. Hence as we move away from the origin we know only that utility increases but not by how much. We may now derive a utility possibility curve that shows the alternate utility combinations that may be achieved by Mr. Alpha and Mr. Beta, *given* a fixed commodity bundle. If all commodities are given to Alpha, only he derives utility, and

Beta's utility is zero. Such a situation is shown by point D in Figure 11–10. On the other hand if Beta has all commodities, we obtain point F. Intermediate positions such as E are possible. The line connecting all conceivable distributions of the fixed commodity bundle between the two persons is the *point utility possibility curve* DEF. The point utility possibility curve denotes

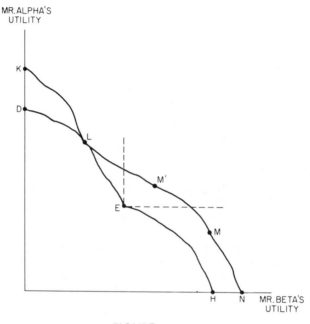

FIGURE 11–11

all utility combinations that may result from the distribution of one fixed commodity bundle, which may be represented by a single point on the production possibility curve.

We proceed by plotting the point utility possibility curves corresponding to each and every point of the production possibility curve. Only one such additional point utility possibility curve is shown by the line GEH in Figure 11–10. The *envelope* formed by the furthest outlying segments of the point utility possibility curves, shown as DEH, is defined as the *situation utility possibility curve*. That is, the situation utility possibility curve shows the maximum utility combinations that are attainable by Alpha and Beta if we consider all possible production patterns.

Now we will consider the various situation utility possibility curves that result under conditions of autarky, free trade, and tariffs. In Figure 11–11 we again show the situation utility possibility curve DEH that is attainable under conditions of autarky (when we are restricted to points on the production possibility curve). In addition we show the situation utility possibility curve that results from all commodity combinations attainable under conditions of free trade, such as shown by the line EE in Figure 11–4. This free trade situation utility possibility curve is labelled KLMN.¹ Note that the free trade curve KLMN lies above the autarky curve DLEH. At one point, L, the two curves touch each other. This point L corresponds to point A in Figure 11–4, which denotes the one price ratio at which the country will not engage in international trade. Here the autarky and free trade commodity combinations are identical.

We may now compare the utility combinations that can be attained by Alpha and Beta under autarky (DLEH) and free trade (KLMN). There will always be a point on the free trade situation utility possibility curve that is superior to points attainable under autarky—except point L. Hence, we may conclude that free trade is *potentially* superior to no trade. We must say "potentially," because a comparison between two points, such as no-trade point E and free-trade point M, yields inconclusive results. But we always have the possibility to redistribute the commodities in such a way along KLMN that we reach a point, such as M', at which both Alpha and Beta are better off than in the no-trade situation at E.

We may conclude that free trade is potentially superior to no trade (autarky).

In a similar fashion we can derive the situation utility possibility curve that corresponds to the consumption possibilities attainable under tariff-restricted trade, as shown by the curve TT in Figure 11–6. We will also find that the situation utility possibility curve for the tariff case lies above the situation utility possibility curve for autarky.

Tariff restricted trade is potentially superior to no trade.

Unfortunately it is not possible to make a general statement about the relative merits of the free trade versus the restricted trade cases. As was shown in Figure 11–7 much depends on the final equilibrium situation that develops. Also the relative size of the country in world markets (small versus large country) plays an important role. Each case will have to be considered on its own merits.

A final word of caution: although we are able to make welfare comparisons on the basis of potential superiority (as opposed to actual superiority) of different situations, we are not able to say which point on the situation utility possibility curve is optimal. To make a choice between points K, L, M', M, and N we need a *social welfare function* that helps us to determine the optimal income distribution between Alpha and Beta. Nobody has as yet been able to define such a social welfare function. A dictator may impose his social welfare function and thereby select a specific point on the situation utility possibility curve as optimal. Once we have this point on the situation utility possibility curve we may determine the optimal commodity combination to be consumed by each member of the community, the optimal commodity combination to be produced, the optimal amount of trade, relative prices of commodities, prices of factors of production, optimal production techniques, and the like.

Unfortunately the chances are slim that such a social welfare function will ever be derived. As a matter of fact Arrow has shown in his famous "Impossibility Theorem"[2] that such a social welfare function does not exist—unless it is imposed or dictated.

SUGGESTED FURTHER READINGS

BALDWIN, ROBERT, "The New Welfare Economics and Gains in International Trade," *Quarterly Journal of Economics* (February 1952). Reprinted in AEA *Readings in International Economics*, eds. Richard Caves and Harry G. Johnson. Homewood, Ill.: Richard D. Irwin, Inc., 1968.

BHAGWATI, JAGDISH, "The Gains from Trade Once Again," *Oxford Economic Papers* (July 1968).

CAVES, RICHARD, *Trade and Economic Structure*, Chap. VIII. Cambridge: Harvard University Press, 1960.

CORDEN, W. M., "Recent Developments in the Theory of International Trade," *Special Papers in International Economics*, No. 7, Chap. IV, International Finance Section, Princeton University (1965).

ROTHENBERG, JEROME, *The Measurement of Social Welfare*. Englewood Cliffs, N.J.: Prentice-Hall, Inc., 1961.

SAMUELSON, PAUL A., "The Gains from International Trade," *Canadian Journal of Economics and Political Science* (May 1939). Reprinted in *Readings in the Theory of International Trade*, eds. Howard S. Ellis and Lloyd A. Metzler, Chap. XI. Homewood, Ill.: Richard D. Irwin, Inc., 1950.

———, "The Gains from International Trade Once Again," *Economic Journal* (December 1962). Reprinted in *International Trade*, ed. Jagdish Bhagwati. Baltimore: Penguin Books, Inc., 1969.

———, "Welfare Economics and International Trade," *American Economic Review* (June 1938).

SOHMEN, EGON, *Flexible Exchange Rates*, rev. ed., Appendix on Welfare Aspects of International Trade. Chicago: University of Chicago Press, 1969.

[2] Kenneth Arrow, *Social Choice and Individual Values* (New York: John Wiley & Sons, Inc., 1951).

STOLPER, WOLFGANG F. and PAUL A. SAMUELSON, "Protection and Real Wages," *Review of Economic Studies* (November 1941). Reprinted in *Readings in the Theory of International Trade*, eds. Howard S. Ellis and Lloyd A. Metzler, Chap. XV. Homewood, Ill.: Richard D. Irwin, Inc., 1950, and in *International Trade*, ed. Jagdish Bhagwati. Baltimore: Penguin Books, Inc., 1969.

The Closed Economy:
A Review
of Some Basic Concepts

A self-sufficient country produces all the goods that its inhabitants consume. The analysis of a self-sufficient country, often referred to as a *closed economy*, will serve as a review of some of the basic economic concepts to be employed in our analysis of an *open economy*, that is, a country that engages in international trade. Naturally it is impossible to give a complete review of all the relevant economic theory in this appendix, and the reader is referred to any of the many excellent textbooks available on the subject.

PRODUCTION

The Production Possibility Curve

The total volume of productive resources available to any country is generally fixed at any given point in time. There is only so much land available, the population and therefore the size of the labor force is given, and the quantity of man-made resources (capital equipment) is fixed.[1]

The productive resources, or *factors of production*, can be used to produce commodities desired by the inhabitants of the country. Because the amount of factors of production is limited, we will be able to produce only

[1] This assumption holds true, of course, only within limits. If prices paid for land increase, more "marginal" land might be pressed into use: deserts might be irrigated, swamps be drained, lakes or ocean bays be filled in. Similarly if wages increase, the size of the labor force might increase because people would be willing to perform overtime work for the higher wages, housewives might take on a job, and people might postpone retirement. Yet, as a first approximation, it is useful to assume that the quantities of factors of production available are fixed.

a limited amount of commodities. As long as their desires are not completely satiated consumers will want to have more of the commodities than can be produced with the available resources. This makes it necessary to choose between different products the country can produce with its limited factors of production.

To simplify matters we will assume that there are only two commodities that our country (or, if you prefer, our Robinson Crusoe on his island) produces: cloth and wheat. If we devote all our resources to the production

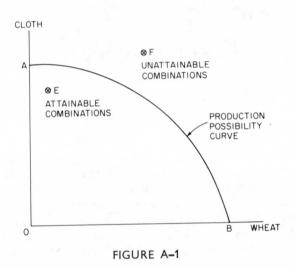

FIGURE A–1

of cloth, there will be a maximum amount of cloth that we can produce, *given* the technologically most efficient way to produce cloth and, of course, our fixed amount of resources. Also there is a maximum amount of wheat that can be produced if we devote all our resources to wheat production.

Naturally it is also possible to produce various combinations of cloth and wheat. For each additional unit of wheat that we want to produce we must reduce cloth production to free the additional resources needed for wheat production.

The maximum wheat/cloth combinations that can be produced delineate our production possibilities. These possibilities can be depicted graphically. In Figure A–1 we show the quantity of wheat along the horizontal axis and the quantity of cloth along the vertical axis. The maximum cloth/wheat combinations that can be produced are plotted on the graph. The collection of all these points depicts the *production possibility curve* AB for the country.

Technological Efficiency

All the points on the production possibility curve are *efficient* in a technological sense: given our resources and production techniques, it is not possible to produce more of one commodity without reducing the output of the other commodity. From this definition of technological efficiency it follows that all points that lie below and to the left of the production possibility curve AB are technologically inefficient points of production.

Product combinations that can be attained with our resources and production techniques are often referred to as the *attainable set* or the attainable combination of commodities. The attainable set includes all technologically efficient (the points on the curve) as well as all technologically inefficient (the points below the curve) product combinations. Naturally we are most interested in the maximum attainable product combinations that are represented by the borderline of the attainable set, that is, the production possibility curve.

There are two major reasons for the nonattainment of a technologically efficient output combination. First, some of our resources may be *unemployed* or underemployed: factories may be working below capacity, workers may be out of work, and natural resources may lie idle. But it is also possible that even with all resources fully employed we are still not producing at a point located on the production possibility curve. This will be true if there are *inefficiencies* in how we use our productive resources: some of the factors of production are not used in the place where their return is the highest, resulting in output that falls below its maximum level. We might think of highly trained engineers driving trucks, while truckdrivers are trying to design complex technical equipment. Obviously aggregate output could be increased if the truckdrivers were to drive the trucks and leave the design work to the engineers.

Output combinations that are located above and to the right of the production possibility curve are termed *unattainable* or infeasible. Given the amount of resources available and the state of the technology, it will not be possible to produce output combinations that fall in this unattainable region.

Opportunity Costs and the Marginal Rate of Transformation

We have already stated that it is possible to expand the production of one commodity, provided we are willing to cut down on the production of the other commodity. The amount of wheat that must be sacrificed to obtain an additional unit of cloth is referred to as the *opportunity cost* of producing a unit of cloth. The term opportunity cost calls our attention to the fact that in order to produce one commodity we have to forego the opportunity of producing other commodities. The opportunity cost of production may vary (see below) as we move along the production possibility curve.

The rate at which we have to sacrifice one commodity in order to obtain one additional unit of the other commodity is referred to as the *marginal rate of transformation* in production (MRT). Graphically the MRT is shown

by the (negative) slope of the production possibility curve. Consider Figure
A–2. At point A the country is producing 4 units of cloth and 10 units of
wheat. In order to expand the production of wheat by one unit the country
will have to sacrifice two units of cloth. In other words: the opportunity cost
of the eleventh wheat unit is 2 cloth units; or, to use our present terminology,
the rate at which cloth production can be transformed into wheat production

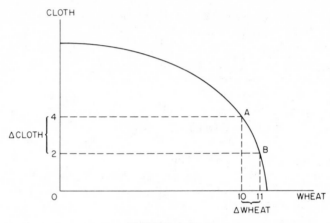

FIGURE A–2

is two to one at the margin, that is, the MRT is equal to 2. This, however,
is also the (negative) slope of the production possibility curve between the
points A and B.[2]

We can write:

(A–1)
$$MRT_{WC} = -\frac{\Delta\,Cloth}{\Delta\,Wheat}$$

Increasing, Decreasing, and Constant Opportunity Costs

The various factors influencing the shape of the production possibility
curve are discussed in greater detail in Chapter 4. Here, however, we have to
pay attention briefly to the implications that arise out of the different possible
shapes of the production possibility curves. Viewed from the origin the

[2] Actually the slope of the production possibility curve changes slightly
between points A and B. What we are measuring here is the slope of a straight line
through A and B. As we make the distance between A and B smaller and smaller
and finally infinitesimally small this line will become the tangent to the production
possibility curve.

production possibility curve may appear as concave (Figure A–3), convex (Figure A–4), or as a straight line (Figure A–5).

If the production possibility curve is concave as viewed from the origin, it indicates the existence of increasing opportunity costs for the two commodities. As the output of one commodity is expanded we will have to give up successively larger quantities of the other commodity in order to obtain equal increases in the output of the first commodity. Successive units of wheat become more and more expensive in terms of cloth, indicating that the opportunity cost of obtaining additional units of cloth increases. It is also

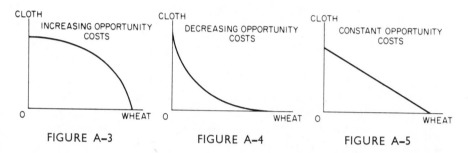

FIGURE A-3   FIGURE A-4   FIGURE A-5

possible to show the process in reverse: if we want to obtain more and more units of cloth, we have to sacrifice ever larger amounts of wheat.

The case of decreasing opportunity costs is shown in Figure A–4. Here the production of additional units of wheat requires the sacrifice of successively smaller amounts of cloth.

The constant opportunity cost case is illustrated in Figure A–5. For each additional unit of wheat we have to give up equal amounts of cloth. The opportunity cost of wheat production in terms of cloth is the same throughout the range of production possibilities, resulting in a straight line production possibility curve.

Two Factors of Production

1. *Isoquants.* The basic geometric tool used to analyze the two-factor case is the *isoquant*, also referred to as an *equal product contour*. An isoquant is defined as the locus of all efficient input or factor of production combinations that will yield the same quantity of output. The quantities of the two inputs that are employed in the production of the output are measured along the two axes. In Figure A–6 inputs of labor (L) are measured along the horizontal axis, and inputs of capital (K) are measured along the vertical axis.

From the technological information given to us we are able to derive a whole map of isoquants for different levels of output. The isoquant map fills the input space shown in Figure A–6.

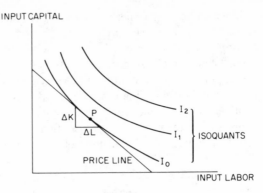

FIGURE A–6

The slope of an isoquant is referred to as the *marginal rate of technical substitution* (MRTS). The marginal rate of technical substitution gives the quantity by which one factor has to be increased if the other factor is decreased by one unit, while the total quantity of output stays constant. The loss in output from the reduction of one factor must be made up by the increase in output resulting from the increase of the other factor. The slope of the isoquant shows the quantity of K that must be added (or subtracted) divided by the quantity of L that must be subtracted (or added) in order to maintain a constant level of output. The negative slope $(-\Delta K/\Delta L)$ is defined as the marginal rate of technical substitution.

$$(A\text{--}2) \qquad\qquad MRTS_{LK} = -\frac{\Delta K}{\Delta L}$$

If we are interested in finding out which is actually the most efficient combination of inputs to be used in the production of a given quantity of output, we have to introduce *relative factor prices* into our analysis. The slope of the price line for the two factors of production $(-\Delta K/\Delta L$ in Figure A–6) shows the relative factor prices. The optimal combination of inputs is found at the point where the price line is tangent to the isoquant representing the desired output level. Such a point is given by P in Figure A–6. At point P the following conditions are fulfilled:

$$(A\text{--}3) \qquad\qquad MRTS_{LK} = -\frac{\Delta K}{\Delta L} = \frac{P_L}{P_K}$$

The marginal rate of technical substitution is equal to the relative price ratio.

There are four characteristics of isoquants that are worth bearing in mind: (1) Isoquants slope downward to the right. If the output level is to remain constant, a decrease of one input will have to be compensated for by an increase of another input. (2) Isoquants are convex to the origin. This is because successive reductions by equally large amounts of one factor have to be compensated for by larger and larger additions of the substitute factor. Another way of expressing the same idea is to say that the rate at which two factors of production can be substituted for each other diminishes. (3) Isoquants cannot intersect. This is easily shown with the help of Figure A–7. Input combinations A and C are on the same isoquant I_0, yielding an equal quantity of output. The same is true about A and B, both of which are located on isoquant I_1. But if A yields the same output as B, and it is also

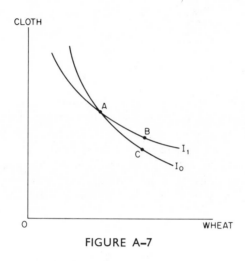

FIGURE A–7

true that A yields the same output as C, then B and C must yield the same output, too. As all input combinations yielding the same quantity of output constitute an isoquant, B and C should also be located on the same isoquant—which they are not, according to Figure A–7. Also input combination B contains more of both inputs and should therefore yield a higher output than C. Clearly we have a contradiction that can be eliminated only by postulating that isoquants cannot intersect. (4) Isoquants that are located farther away from the origin denote higher levels of output than isoquants closer to the origin. There will be an isoquant through every point of our input space.

In general we are interested not only in the determination of one specific efficient factor combination, but in the locus of the efficient factor combinations for all levels of output. In other words we want to derive the point of tangency of the factor price ratio with *all* isoquants. The locus of all these tangency positions is called an *expansion path* and shows the efficient factor combinations for all output levels, given the relative factor price ratio. An expansion path is shown in Figure A–8.

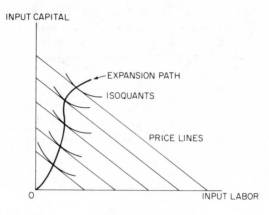

FIGURE A–8

2. *Homogeneous and Homothetic Functions.* Among all the various shapes that can be assumed by isoquants, two sets have attracted the particular attention of economomists: homothetic and homogeneous isoquants.

Homothetic isoquants are characterized by the fact that the MRTS is the same along any ray from the origin. That is, all isoquants will have the same slope at the point at which they are cut by the ray from the origin as shown in Figure A–9. Homothetic isoquants satisfy the relationship

$$(A\text{–}4) \qquad\qquad F(bx) = \psi(b) \cdot F(x),$$

for all numbers b > 0 and all vectors x for which the function F(x) is defined.

Homogeneous isoquants are a subset of all homothetic isoquants in that

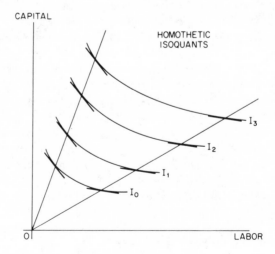

FIGURE A–9

the relationship $\psi(b)$ is defined to be of the form b^r. That is, for all homogeneous isoquants

$$F(bx) = b^r F(x) \tag{A-5}$$

is satisfied. The exponent r denotes the degree of homogeneity. Functions for which $r = 1$ are said to be homogeneous of degree one or *linear homogeneous*.

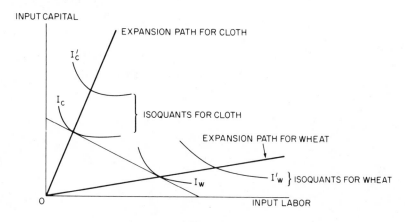

FIGURE A–10

In such a set of isoquants a doubling of *all* inputs leads to a doubling of the level of output—that is, the additions to output produced by a given addition to all inputs are the same, no matter what the level of output—and we have constant returns to scale. Any isoquant showing twice the amount of output as another isoquant will be exactly twice as far removed from the origin as the other isoquant.

3. *Factor Intensity.* Often we are interested in the production of not only one commodity but of two (or more) commodities. In Figure A–10 we show sets of homothetic isoquants of two commodities, cloth and wheat. It is now possible to say something about the *relative intensity* with which the two factors are used in the production of the two commodities. With the price ratio indicated in Figure A–10 cloth production uses relatively (to wheat production) more capital and less labor at all output levels. On the other hand wheat production uses relatively (to cloth production) more labor than capital. One can, then, refer to cloth production as being relatively capital intensive and to wheat production as being relatively labor intensive. Note that the absolute amounts of the two factors used in production do not have to be specified. It is not *absolute* factor intensities that count here but merely *relative* factor intensities. This enables us to avoid the thorny problem

of having to decide on the appropriate unit of measurement for the two dissimilar factors of production.

4. *The Edgeworth Box Diagram.* In order to show the efficient combinations of inputs to be used in the production of the two outputs we utilize an *Edgeworth Box diagram.* In Figure A–11 we show the set of isoquants for wheat production drawn in its usual position and the set of isoquants for cloth production upside down and with sides reversed. Thus the origin of the coordinate system for cloth production lies in the upper righthand corner

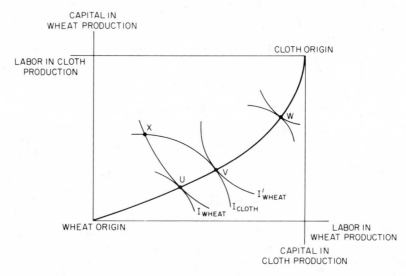

FIGURE A–11

of the box. The size of the box shows the total factor endowments (factor supplies) available to the country. The vertical size shows the total quantity of capital available, and the horizontal size shows the total quantity of labor available.

We are now interested in establishing which input combinations will be efficient in the sense that no reallocation of inputs would lead to an increase in the level of output of one commodity *without* decreasing the level of output for the other commodity. All points of tangency of two isoquants represent such *technologically efficient input combinations.*

The curve connecting all technologically efficient input combinations such as U, V, and W in Figure A–11 is called the *contract curve.* At the points of tangency it will be true that the marginal rate of technical substitution is the same for both commodities. In equation form:

(A–6) $(MRTS_{LK})_C = (MRTS_{LK})_W$

If this condition is not fulfilled, it will always be possible to reallocate some factors of production in such a way that the output of one commodity will be increased (a higher isoquant can be reached), while the output of the other commodity will stay constant. Such a situation is shown by point X, which is not located on the contract curve. Moving from point X to point V does not change the output level of cloth production since we stay on the same isoquant. However, the output of wheat will increase from the output level associated with the isoquant through X (and U) to the higher output level indicated by the isoquant through point V. Thus we are able to increase the total output by reallocating our resources in the fashion indicated. Once a point on the contract curve itself is attained no reshuffling of resources will help to achieve a higher output level of one commodity without reducing the output level of the other commodity simultaneously: a technologically efficient production pattern has been achieved.

CONSUMPTION

Production takes place not for its own sake but only in order to satisfy some further objective: consumption of the goods and services produced. The act of consumption yields utility to the consumer, and the consumer is assumed to maximize the utility obtained from his total consumption. To achieve this goal he should act in a rational manner, which implies—among other things—that his choices should be *transitive*. Transitivity of choices refers to the notion that a consumer who prefers X to Y and also prefers Y to Z will, when confronted with a choice between X and Z, always choose X. A consumer who acts in such a rational way should be able to rank all commodities or commodity bundles in order of preference. In this ordering or ranking the consumer is not assumed to be able to say by how much he prefers one commodity to another commodity; a mere ordinal ranking of different commodities will suffice. There also exists the possibility that a consumer is indifferent between two commodity bundles if they yield the same level of utility.

Indifference Curves

The possibility that a given level of utility can be derived from many different commodity combinations will occupy our attention somewhat more. If consumption of one commodity is reduced, it will in general be possible to compensate the consumer for this loss in utility by enabling him to increase his consumption of another commodity. If the decrease in utility experienced due to the reduced consumption of one commodity is merely offset as the increase in utility due to the increased consumption of another commodity, we may expect that the consumer is indifferent between these two situations because his aggregate or total utility level has remained unchanged.

If we plot all points showing different commodity combinations yielding the same level of utility, we derive a so-called indifference curve or equal utility contour. The term *indifference curve* stems from the notion that a consumer is indifferent between all commodity combinations yielding the same amount of utility to him. Such an indifference curve is shown in Figure A–12.

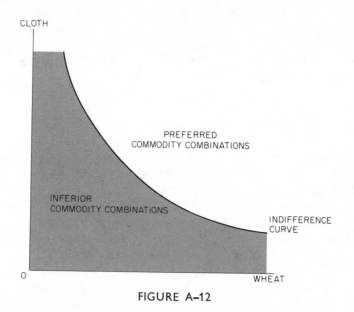

FIGURE A–12

Indifference curves have properties very similar to those of isoquants: (1) they slope downward to the right, (2) they are convex to the origin, (3) they cannot intersect, and (4) a higher indifference curve denotes a higher level of utility. Indifference curves are distinguished from isoquants in that we make no attempt to attach numerical values to the level of utility achieved by the consumer, but restrict ourselves to a *ranking* of all commodity bundles in order of preference without stating by how much one bundle is preferred to the other. This type of "better-or-worse" relationship is referred to as an *ordinal* relation; the term *cardinal* relation is applied to a situation in which we are able to specify quantitatively (as in the case of isoquants) how much more we are able to produce. Indifference curves that have the same slope along any ray from the origin are called *homothetic* indifference curves, a usage similar to that for homothetic isoquants.

The Marginal Rate of Substitution

A word has to be said about the slope of the indifference curves. We said above that an indifference curve is the combination of all cloth/wheat collections yielding a constant amount of utility to the consumer. In other words as we move along one indifference curve, the consumer gives up some units of wheat in order to obtain some units of cloth (or vice versa). The rate at which these two commodities can ge substituted for each other without changing the level of utility is called the *marginal rate of substitution* (MRS). Graphically the slope of the indifference curve is given by the change in the quantity of cloth divided by the change in the quantity of wheat, and the negative of this slope $(-\Delta C/\Delta W)$ is defined as the marginal rate of substitution of wheat for cloth. We can write:

$$\text{MRS}_{WC} = -\frac{\Delta C}{\Delta W} \tag{A-7}$$

EQUILIBRIUM

We are now in a position to combine our tools of analysis to derive the country's optimal production and consumption pattern. Let us start with a given production possibility curve reflecting the country's production opportunities and a set of indifference curves depicting the taste patterns of the residents of the country. (See Figure A-13.) Initially the country in question produces a combination of cloth and wheat shown by point P on the production possibility curve. If the country does not engage in international trade, point P will also show the amounts of cloth and wheat that are available for consumption. This bundle of goods will allow the residents of the country to achieve the utility level indicated by the indifference curve through P, namely, I_1. If we change the production pattern such that more wheat and less cloth is produced, the residents of the country will be able to reach successively higher indifference curves. At point P' the highest attainable indifference curve is reached, showing that the residents have achieved the highest possible utility level consistent with the country's production possibilities. At point P' the slope of the production possibility curve is equal to the slope of the indifference curve as the two curves are tangent to each other. We will recall that the slope of the production possibility curve shows the marginal rate of transformation, and the slope of the indifference curve shows the marginal rate of substitution.

The point on the production possibility curve at which the indifference curve is tangent is also referred to as an *economically efficient* point. We recall that technological efficiency refers to *all* the points on the production possibility curve. Among the maximum output combinations that can be

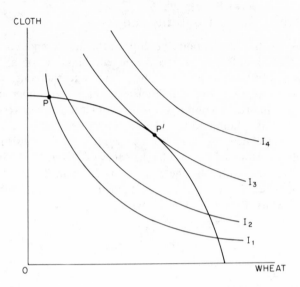

FIGURE A-13

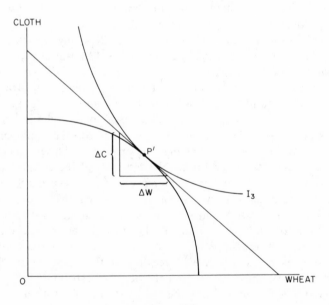

FIGURE A-14

produced, given our technology and resources, there will be *one* point describing the commodity combination that is economically most desirable in that it allows the country to attain the highest utility level.

THE TERMS OF TRADE

If production and consumption takes place at point P' (Figure A–14), the two commodities will exchange for each other in the proportion $\Delta C/\Delta W$. This *physical exchange* ratio is often referred to as the *terms of trade*. Once we know in what quantities the two goods exchange for each other it is only a small step to the determination of the relative prices of the two commodities. It is clear that the relative prices of the two commodities are inversely related to the quantities of the two goods that can be exchanged for each other. If the price of one of the two commodities rises relatively to the other one, this means that we obtain a smaller quantity of the commodity in exchange for the other commodity than previously.

The terms of trade at which the two commodities will be traded in the market is given by the slope of the tangent to both the production possibility curve and the indifference curve. Point P' in Figure A–14 shows the overall equilibrium condition for a closed economy. At point P' the marginal rates of substitution and transformation are equal to each other and they are equal to the price ratio and the negative inverse of the quantities of the two commodities that exchange for each other.

$$\text{MRS}_{\text{WC}} = \frac{P_W}{P_C} = -\frac{\Delta C}{\Delta W} = \text{MRT}_{\text{WC}} \qquad \text{(A–8)}$$

Thus the quantities of both commodities produced and consumed, their relative prices, and their physical exchange ratio (terms of trade) are determined.

For a country that does not engage in international trade the optimal consumption and production pattern is reached when the marginal rate of transformation between any two commodities is equal to the marginal rate of substitution between the same two commodities.

Index

A–B

Ad valorem tariff, 165
Aggregation, 23
Analysis, 2
Arrow, K., 67n., 138n., 215n.
Assumptions, 2, 5
Attainable set, 219
Autarky, 204
Balassa, B., 46n., 179n., 194n.
Barter, 5
Basevi, G., 179n.
Bhagwati, J., 159n.
Bharadwaj, 69n.

C

Capital/labor ratios, 69, 123
Central American Common Market, 194
Chenery, H., 67n., 138n., 161
Closed economy, 217
Community indifference curve, 72
  income distribution, 76
  justification, 76
  problem, 75
  slope, 74
Common market, 184
Comparative advantage, 34
Comparative cost, 34, 46
Compensation payments, 210
Complete specialization, 41, 129
Concentration of trade, 10
Consumption, 72–88, 227
Consumption and growth, 141
Consumption possibility curve, 203
Constant cost, 32, 108, 220
Constant returns, 51
Contract curve, 51, 226
Cost, 30
  decreasing, 44
  increasing, 42
Country size, 19, 40, 110
Crusoe, R., 76
Customs union, 183
  general equilibrium, 190

D–E

Decreasing cost, 44, 220
Decreasing returns, 53

Demand, 16
Demand reversal, 82, 101, 127
Deutsch, K., 160n.
Direction of trade, 34, 79, 83
    demand reversal, 101
Eckstein, A., 160n.
Economic efficiency, 229
Economies of scale, 44
Edgeworth Box, 226
Effective protective rate, 175, 179
Efficiency, 218, 229
Elasticity, 24
    trade offer curve, 96
Empirical problems, 21
Empirical verification, 2
Endowment ratio, 123
Equilibrium, 14, 89–118, 229
    multiple, 103
    stability, 103
Estimation problems, 21
European Economic Community, 161,
    184, 194, 195
European Free Trade Area, 183
Excess demand, 18
Excess supply, 18
Excess trade offer curve, 190
Exchange gains, 201
Exchange ratio, 36, 231
Expansion path, 223
Expenditure curve, 96
Export market share, 47
Export supply, 21

F

Factor abundance, 119
Factor demand reversal, 127
Factor endowment, 63, 64, 68
Factor intensity, 64, 68, 225
Factor intensity reversals, 131, 139
Factor prices, 120, 222
Factor price equalization, 125
    obstacles, 128
Factor price line, 122
Factor of production, 119–40, 217
    and tariffs, 210
Factor quantity changes, 133, 146
Factor scarcity, 119

Factory supply and production, 136
Feasible region, 124
Foreign trade sector, size, 161
Free trade area, 183

G–H

General Agreements of Tariffs and
    Trade, 161
General equilibrium, 14, 89–118
Gains from exchange, 201
Gains from specialization, 201
Growth, biased, 142, 149
    and consumption, 141
    neutral, 142, 149
    and production, 143
    and technological progress, 153
Haberler, G., 39n.
Heckscher, E., 64n.
Heckscher-Ohlin Theory, 64, 68, 116
Heller, H. R., 186n.
Homogeneous, 224
Homothetic, 224, 228
Houthakker, H., 24n., 86, 87n.
Hypothesis, 2

I–L

Ichimura, S., 70n.
Immizerizing growth, 159
Import demand, 21
Impossibility theorem, 215
Income elasticity, 24
Increasing cost, 30, 42, 53, 220
Indifference curve, 72, 227
Indifference curve, trade, 91
Infant industry, 164
Input-output table, 68
Intensity reversal of factor, 60
Isoquant, 221
Johnson, H. G., 195, 188n.
Labor theory of value, 34
Latin American Free Trade Area, 162
Leontief, W., 68n.
Linear homogeneous, 225

M–O

MacDougall, G. D. A., 46n.
Magee, S., 24n.
Marginal rate of substitution, 229
Marginal rate of technical substitution, 222
Marginal rate of transformation, 53, 218
Market demand, 16
Market supply, 15
Measurement errors, 23
Methodology, 1
Microeconomics, 15
Mill, J. S., 29
Minhas, B., 67n., 138n., 139n.
Models, 2
Multi-commodity cases, 116
Multi-country cases, 112
Neutrality of money, 5
Nominal tariff, 165
Normative economics, 3
Offer curve, 83
   constant cost, 108
   trade, 90
Ohlin, B., 64n.
Open economy, 217
Opportunity cost, 39, 51, 55, 218
Optimal tariff, 170, 206

P

Partial equilibrium, 14
Point utility possibility curve, 213
Positive economics, 1
Potential welfare, 206
Prais, S., 87
Prediction, 2
Preference patterns, 72
Price determination, 80
Price elasticity, 24
Price of factor, 120
Price taker, 42
Production, 50–71, 217
   and growth, 143
Production factor, 119–40, 207
Production function, 67, 138

Production, optimal, 80
Production possibility curve, 29, 217
   and factor supplies, 136
Production price line, 122
Protection, 163

R–S

Ratio of exchange, 231
Real cost, 34
Reciprocal demand, 96
Resource allocation, 231
Retaliation and tariff, 172
Returns to scale, 51, 67, 138
Ricardo, D., 29, 34, 39
Roskamp, K., 70n.
Samuelson, P., 78n., 186n., 208n.
Scale economies, 44
Self-sufficiency, 163
Situation utility possibility curve, 213
Size of country, 19, 40, 110
Smith, A., 29
Social welfare function, 214
Solow, R., 67n., 138n.
Specialization, 29, 111, 129
   of production factor, 207
Stability conditions, 103
Stern, R., 46n.
Stolper, W., 70n., 208n.
Stolper-Samuelson Theorem, 208
Supply, 15

T

Tariff, 163–82
   cycles, 174
   effects, 164
   effective protective rate, 175
   and factors, 210
   retaliation, 172
   revenue, 168
   structure, 175
Taussig, F., 29, 39
Tatemoto, M., 70n.
Technological efficiency, 51, 218, 226

Technological progress, 153
  biased, 155
  neutral, 154
Terms of trade, 80, 85, 231
  and country size, 111
  equilibrium, 38, 100
  indeterminacy, 106
  limits, 37
  tariffs, 167
Theory, 3
Thompson, E., 67n.
Time, 21
Time path of adjustment, 23
Time series, 22
Trade creation, 185
  direction, 79
  diversion, 187
  indifference curve, 91
  indifference curve, slope, 93
  matrix, 11
  offer curve, 90, 95

  offer curve, elasticity, 96
  volume, 7, 9
Transitivity, 227

U–W

Union gains, 193
Unions, 183–96
Utility possibility curve, 212
Verdoorn, P. J., 195
Wahl, D., 70n.
Walters, A., 67n.
Welfare of country, 200
  of economic group, 207
  of world, 197
Wilford, W. T., 194n.
World production possibility curve, 199
World welfare, 198

There will be a meeting for all those interested
in entering Reform school in WLH 425 on
Sat January 23(:) at 8:30. Please bring resume
("Rap" sheets only accepted if properly notarized)
and 12 recommendations for each activity.
Applicants must display a varied record
and at least one conviction in 3 areas
of specialization.